# MODERNISM AND TIME

In *Modernism and Time*, Ronald Schleifer analyzes the transition from the Enlightenment to post-Enlightenment ways of understanding in Western thought. Schleifer argues that this transition in the late nineteenth century and early twentieth expresses itself centrally in an altered conception of temporality. He examines this period's remarkable breaks with the past in literature, music, and the arts more generally. Whereas Enlightenment thought sees time as a homogeneous, neutral medium, in which events and actions take place, post-Enlightenment thought sees time as discontinuous and inexorably bound up with both the subjects and events that seem to inhabit it. This fundamental change of perception, Schleifer argues, takes place across disciplines as different as physics, economics and philosophy. Schleifer's study engages with the work of writers and thinkers as varied as George Eliot, Walter Benjamin, Einstein, and Russell, and offers a powerful reassessment of the politics and culture of modernism.

RONALD SCHLEIFER is Professor of English at the University of Oklahoma. He is editor of the journal *Genre* and has published several books, most recently as co-author of *Culture and Criticism: The Role of Critique in Modern Literary Theory* (1991) and *Culture and Cognition: The Boundaries of Literary and Scientific Inquiry* (1992); *Rhetoric and Death: The Language of Modernism and Postmodern Discourse Theory* (1990) is closely related to *Modernism and Time*.

# MODERNISM AND TIME

*The Logic of Abundance in Literature, Science, and Culture, 1880–1930*

RONALD SCHLEIFER

PUBLISHED BY THE PRESS SYNDICATE OF THE UNIVERSITY OF CAMBRIDGE
The Pitt Building, Trumpington Street, Cambridge, United Kingdom

CAMBRIDGE UNIVERSITY PRESS
The Edinburgh Building, Cambridge, CB2 2RU, UK
http://www.cup.cam.ac.uk
40 West 20th Street, New York, NY 10011–4211, USA
http://www.cup.org
10 Stamford Road, Oakleigh, Melbourne 3166, Australia

First published 2000

Printed in the United Kingdom at the University Press, Cambridge

Typeset in Baskerville 11/12.5pt [CE]

*A catalogue record for this book is available from the British Library*

*Library of Congress Cataloguing in Publication data*
Schleifer, Ronald.
Modernism and time: the logic of abundance in literature, science, and culture, 1880–1930 /
Ronald Schleifer.
p. cm.
Includes bibliographical references and index.
ISBN 0 521 66124 2 (hardback)
1. Modernism (Literature)
2. Literature, Modern – 20th century – History and criticism.
3. Literature, Modern – 19th century – History and criticism.
4. Consumption (Economics) – History – 20th century.
5. Consumption (Economics) – History – 19th century.
6. Civilization, Modern – 20th century.   7. Civilization, Modern – 19th century.
8. Literature and history.   9. Literature and science.
10. Time in literature.   I. Title.
PN56.M54S35   2000
809′.9112 – dc21     99–29139   CIP

ISBN 0 521 66124 2 hardback

*for my father,*
*Cy Schleifer*

# Contents

# Preface

Several years ago, Stephen Toulmin wrote *Cosmopolis: The Hidden Agenda of Modernity* in which he argued that the origins of Enlightenment modernity in the seventeenth century, based upon the work of Descartes, Leibniz, and Newton, is best understood in the context of the great tumultuous epoch of the Thirty Years' War. Toulmin dates "the starting date for Modernity... somewhere in the period from 1600 to 1650" (1992: 7), dates which almost precisely correspond to the lifetime of Descartes. "Far from the years 1605–1650 being prosperous or comfortable," he argues, "they are now seen as having been among the most uncomfortable, and even frantic, years in all European history. Instead of regarding Modern Science and Philosophy as the products of leisure, therefore, we will do better to turn the received view upside down, and treat them as responses to a contemporary crisis" (1992: 16). Thus, he argues, "the 17th-century philosophers' 'Quest for Certainty' was no mere proposal to construct abstract and timeless intellectual schemas, dreamed up as objects of pure, detached intellectual study. Instead, it was a timely response to a specific historical challenge – the political, social, and theological chaos embodied in the Thirty Years' War" (1992: 70).

In *Modernism and Time*, I am confronting the similar problem of understanding that was occasioned by the remarkable transformations of intellectual life, social life, and private experience in the years preceding the great thirty years of European warfare in our century, the period of the second Industrial Revolution roughly spanning the late nineteenth century through the first decades of the twentieth century. This is the period of twentieth-century cultural "Modernism" that witnessed remarkable breaks with the past in literature, music, and the arts more generally, reorientations of the sciences in post-Newtonian physics and powerful reconceptions of mathematics, and almost overwhelming transformations in the experience of everyday life driven by powerful new technologies, abundances of consumer goods, and the emergence of new social formations – particularly finance capital, a new "lower middle class" of information workers, and the reconfiguration of the nation-state in relation to late nineteenth-century imperialism. All of these things – and the crisis of the long-standing assumptions of secular Enlightenment culture that literally exploded in the great European wars of our century – created the powerful revolution in culture, experience, and social organization that has gone under the name of twentieth-century Modernism. Walter Benjamin, who figures promi-nently in this book, confronted the crises in politics, culture, and representation in the early twentieth century with great passion and anguish; it is no accident that his longest published work, the *Origin of German Tragic Drama*, is a study of the transformation of modes of representation in German literature during the Thirty Years' War.

*Modernism and Time* explores the intellectual, personal, and cultural phenomena of the early twentieth century by examining the trans-formations in the modes of representation in the arts and sciences of this period. Its basic argument is that the "crisis" of European culture before the Great War – a crisis that extends itself forward in our century to encompass the politics of imperialism that was a central issue of the First World War (at least in part) and the politics of social organization that was an issue of the Second World War – is not the crisis of political and social "chaos" that manifested itself, as Toulmin argues, in conflicts over aspects of theological "certainty" in the early modern period. Rather, in this book I argue that the crisis of European culture before and after the Great War is that of the fulfillment and exhaustion of the liberal-secular Enlightenment project begun in the seventeenth century – which Bruno Latour describes as "the double task of domination and emancipation" (1993: 10) and which I characterize here as the combination of subjective idealism and general semiotics governing Enlightenment understanding and behavior. This crisis expresses itself in conflicts over *whose* legacy, exactly, is the Enlightenment project, who was left out and, in terms of the more or less secularization of educated opinion, *what* was left out – conflicts, that is, arising out of the abundances produced by the fulfillment and the mixed successes of the Enlightenment project politically, economically, and in defining the very horizon of experience of its subjects.

It may well be that the crisis of Renaissance humanism, as

Toulmin describes it, manifests itself *both* in the detachment and decontextualization of philosophy and natural philosophy in Descartes and Leibniz from particular kinds of worldliness and moral inquiry *and* in the ferocity of the Thirty Years' War. But it seems clear to me, as I argue here, that the crisis of Euro-American culture at the turn of the twentieth century – the crisis of the secular humanism of our Enlightenment inheritance – is a function, to a large degree, of its success in creating enormous abundances of wealth and knowledge, in dominating both nature and non-Western societies, in promoting as well as denying canons of equality and abstract conceptions of humanity, and in desacralizing quotidian and social experience. These achievements of the Enlightenment project are both powerful and awful, giving rise to enormous hopefulness and enormous dread, emancipating vast numbers of people (including most of my forebears) and dominating vast numbers of people, and encompassing the horrifying ferocity of our own thirty years' war of the first half of the century. That is, the crisis of twentieth-century Modernism manifested itself not in the detachment of the subject of knowledge from the vagaries of time – even if one powerful response to the tumult of our century, like that to the tumult of the seventeenth century, which I scarcely touch upon here, took the form of a retreat from time in the arts, in politics, and in the sciences – but in the impossibility of maintaining this detachment in the light of its *timely* successes.

This crisis of Enlightenment humanism in the early twentieth century, as Stephen Kern describes it in his social history of this period, is a "crisis of abundance" (1983: 9) insofar as it confronts the problem of too much in addition to the problem of not enough. Along with the simple answers to problems of dearth – the necessary and sufficient truths of Leibniz in philosophy, mathematics, and theology; the self-evident distinction between use-value and exchange-value in Marx; and the organization of experience around the possibility of discovering a "disinterested" vantage point such as Kant's transcendental subject or the novel's omniscient narrator – Euro-American culture at the beginning of the twentieth century confronted problems of abundance that called for the complexities of possible and overdetermined truths, confusions of products and consumption, and experience which, at its best, was alternatively unprovincial and interested.

The adverb "alternatively" is important here – as I note in the

Introduction and in chapter 5, it is a term I have learned from Werner Heisenberg's representation of post-Newtonian physics – because it suggests that the experience of time in this period is one way of gathering together and configuring the crises of understanding and representation that confronted received Enlightenment values in the new century. Time is closely tied to the problem of representation – which, as Michel Foucault says, possesses "the obscure power of making a past impression present once more" so that an impression can "appear as either similar to or dissimilar from a previous one" (1976: 69) – and if we can comprehend the various presentations and articulations of seemingly novel conceptions and experiences of time in this period we can comprehend what we can keep, what we must discard, and what we must transform from the past – the very time – of our Enlightenment inheritance. This, at least, is my hope. What I am sure of is that the looming figures of our cultural life from the period of twentieth-century Modernism I examine in *Modernism and Time* – Benjamin, Joyce, Woolf, Lawrence, Nietzsche, Heidegger, Einstein, Russell, Heisenberg, Jakobson, Bakhtin – as well as the neoclassical economists from the late nineteenth century and many of my contemporaries and friends who have helped me understand reading and representation in relation to cultural and social history and whom I cite throughout this book, all struggled and continue to struggle to find significant relationships between historical experience and significance, understanding and representation.

That struggle – the problem of representation – is closely tied to the exploding abundances of knowledge, experience, and social formations associated with the second Industrial Revolution of the turn of the twentieth century that transformed and continues to transform our world. The exploration of this problem as it was confronted in the early decades of the century – "apprehensions" of logics of abundance as I describe it in this book – is one way (among many) of configuring what is at stake in our intellectual work, in imagining possible worlds for ourselves and our children, and comprehending the variousness of our private and common experiences. It is my hope that this book might contribute to this exploration and comprehension of our world, our past, and our inheritances. Doing this, as Benjamin generously imagined, we might "redeem" the past and transform to some degree the empty fullness – what Kafka describes as the meaningless abundances – of knowledge, wealth, and our time itself into a legacy for those who come after us and a fulfilment for those who preceded us. This, in any case, is my fondest hope for the intellectual energies of our time.

THE STRUCTURE OF THE BOOK

In the Introduction I discuss some of the themes of *Modernism and Time* presented in and informing its various chapters, but here I want to address one particular issue which is central to the book as a whole. Its global aim is to create a kind of phenomenology of the early decades of our century – of what has been called twentieth-century Modernism – and to this end it attempts to create what I like to imagine is a sense of wholeness without simplicity. (In the final chapter I describe Roman Jakobson's goal in scientific linguistics to achieve "simplicity without wholeness.") A central concern of this task is to articulate the relationships between cultural formations – what one reader of this book in manuscript called the "political/economic/technological culture" of these decades – and the personal and intellectual experience of those who lived through this period. All of the chapters touch upon historical-cultural phenomena, but chapter 3, "The second Industrial Revolution: history, knowledge, and subjectivity," focuses upon it in the most thoroughgoing manner. The title of this chapter gathers together the three largest themes of the book, repeated in each of the three chapters of part I and part II, of social life, intellectual life, and private experience.

I had considered, even in late stages of its composition, beginning *Modernism and Time* with this chapter. After considerable thought, however, I decided to place the discussion focusing on technological and cultural history last rather than first in part I of the book because I did not want to suggest (even implicitly in the structure of chapters) that quotidian and intellectual experience is simply reducible to historical "causes"; I did not want to suggest that, in the language of the reader I have cited, art and understanding each is simply "a reflex of political/economic/technological culture." In the vocabulary the book takes up from Benjamin, I am hoping that the three chapters of part I present a "constellation" of phenomena without the simplifying reductiveness of cause and effect. To this end, Benjamin's conception of "redeeming" the past, discussed in both chapter 1 and chapter 2, can help us comprehend the social and historical phenomena of this period by tutoring our understanding, arranging, deepening, and enchanting it. The operational definitions of Einstein and Russell (chapter 4), Heisenberg's "alternating" explanations (chapter 5), and Bakhtin's "answerability" (chapter 6) all attempt to examine possible alternatives to the parsimonious simplicities of cause and effect that we have inherited from the Enlightenment, not to supersede them, as I argue throughout, but to supplement them with complex along with simple explanations. Thus I hope to show not that the principle of parsimony somehow became invalid at this time in some kind of historical "paradigmatic" shift, but precisely that on the different levels of private experience, thought, and historical experience the principle of parsimony was being challenged in alternating contexts by complex and varying experiences of time.

The relationships among these "levels" – and thus among the parts of my book – are themselves complex but, I hope, offer a kind of phenomenological "wholeness." Throughout the book I describe these relationships as forming "analogies" with one another, what I described several years ago in *Rhetoric and Death* – a book closely related to this one – as the "resonations" of modes of understanding, objects of understanding, and experiences with and upon one another. To this end throughout this book – but especially in the Introduction and in chapter 5 – I have pursued the development of analogies between and among these levels as an alternative to the hierarchic parsimonious thinking of causal explanation. (I also do so in another book that will appear about the time *Modernism and Time* does entitled *Analogical Thinking*.) Igor Stravinsky describes such resonating analogies in the possibilities of a "reflective system between the language structure of the music and the structure of the phenomenal world" (1982: 147) in exploring the relationship between art and history; Werner Heisenberg describes them in the grasping of "a distant formal similarity" between mathematical understanding and physical phenomena (1952: 62); and Wolfgang Schivelbusch describes them in the "infiltration" of old technologies by new technologies (1988: 50) in his history of the industrialization of light in the nineteenth century. In these cases – and in the kind of "post-Enlightenment" understanding I am pursuing more generally – I hope to achieve what the second reader of the manuscript described as a "a resonant, compelling analogy" between "economic abundance and the world of thought" that might help us to grasp and comprehend experience in the time of the early twentieth century.

One danger of the kind of global argument I pursue in *Modernism and Time* is the tendency it creates to see manifestations of abundance everywhere. The reason for this, I believe, is that its aim is to articulate a manner of understanding, a mode of apprehension, that allows things to be grasped together, what I describe in chapter 4, following Paul Ricoeur, as a kind of "configurational" understanding. Yeats made a similar point at the beginning of *A Vision* when he addresses the question of whether he believes "in the actual existence of my circuits of sun and moon." "To such a question I can but answer," he responds, "that if sometimes, overwhelmed by miracle as all men must be when in the midst of it, I have taken such periods literally, my reason has soon recovered; and now that the system stands out clearly in my imagination I regard them as stylistic arrangements of experience comparable to the cubes in the drawing of Wyndham Lewis and to the ovoids in the sculpture of Brancusi. They have helped me to hold in a single thought reality and justice" (1965: 24–25). Yeats's figure of "arrangement" is repeated throughout this study, and – in the cultural analysis of Benjamin, the scientific exposition of Russell, as well as the aesthetics of Yeats – it takes its place as a global comprehension of the abundant wealth of history, thought, and experience in the early twentieth century. Yet even Yeats suggests that, if such a mode of argument seems totalizing, it is neither exclusive nor achieved once and for all. Rather, it is timely in its understanding in that it exists among alternative understandings against which it defines itself; and it is timely in that its understanding is only attained in time, over and over again. Finally, like the analogical thinking I examine throughout this book, the global argument I pursue aspires to illuminate without coerciveness and to achieve the kind of local generosities towards both the past and future that Benjamin teaches.

ACKNOWLEDGMENTS

As my quotations from the anonymous readers suggest, I have greatly benefited from the careful and sympathetic readings *Modernism and Time* has received from Cambridge University Press. Such anonymous professionalism forms the backbone of our intellectual lives, and if I have taken the unusual step of quoting from these reports, both here in the Preface and below in the Introduction, I have done so both to acknowledge the ways in which these readers have helped me to clarify my argument and also to temporalize that argument in relation to ongoing questions and issues that we are collectively facing in the humanities now in the late twentieth century. My editor at Cambridge, Ray Ryan, has, in the choice of readers as in many other things, brought remarkable sympathy and encouragement to this project with great timeliness: our transatlantic work has repeated the three categories of this study in its intellectual strength, fruitfulness, and personal friendliness.

In addition to the editor and these readers, my old friend Robert Markley has read through the manuscript in ways that have benefited every page and the project as a whole. As in many other things, Bob has helped me to see things clearly. Readings of smaller portions and extensive discussions with my colleagues in the English Department of the University of Oklahoma – Eve Tavor Bannet, Hunter Cadzow, Daniel Cottom, Robert Con Davis, Lawrence Frank, David Gross, Catherine Hobbs, Susan Kates, Vincent Leitch, Janet McAdams, Henry McDonald, and Alan Velie – have consistently helped me. More generally, my participation in the Bible and Culture Collective has made this a clearer and more thoughtful book. Nancy West helped me to clarify my thinking about the relation among the Enlightenment, abundance, and the forms of wisdom, especially in the first and last chapters; Shawn Paul, James Hawthorne, and Peter Barker helped me understand Einsteinian mathematics; Ken Kenospel and Kate Hales helped my comprehension of Heisenberg's uncertainty; and Igor Shaitanov, Daphna Erdinast-Vulcan, and Marshall Brown helped me to describe Bakhtinian aesthetics. Russ Reising and Laurie Finke, each in their way – as my boys, Cyrus and Benjamin have, each in *their* ways – helped tutor what I like to think of as this book's cheerfulness. Moreover, I have had the opportunity of sharing much of this book with colleagues and students at the University of Haifa, Texas Tech University, Kansas State University, Witchita State University, the History of Science Colloquium at the University of Oklahoma, Georgia Institute of Technology, Wayne State University, Kenyon College, and Moscow Pedagogical University. In an important way, this book got started with the invitation by Janie Hinds to participate in the Neal Cross Lecture Series at the University of Northern Colorado. Mitchell Lewis compiled the index with great care.

An early version of part of chapter 2 appeared in *Death and Representation*, ed. Sara Goodwin and Elisabeth Bronfen (Baltimore: Johns Hopkins University Press, 1993); much of chapter 5 appeared in *Criticism*, 33 (1991); and a very different version of chapter 6 appeared as "Обобщающая Эстетика Жанра: Бахтин, Якобсон, Беньямин" ["The Global Aesthetics of Genre: Bakhtin, Jakobson, Benjamin"], trans. Igor Shaitanov, in *Вопросы Литературы* [*Problems of Literature*], 40 (1997), 76–100. I am grateful to all these publications for the opportunity to rework and reproduce this material.

Finally, I would like to thank my family, my wife Nancy Mergler, and our boys Cyrus and Benjamin, for helping to create the cheerful seriousness in which I have been able to pursue this project. Our lives together have helped me experience in my time the erasure of the line between work and life that makes both work and life fulfilling. My larger dedication of this book is to my father, that other Cy Schleifer, who has bequeathed to me our great inheritance of Enlightenment optimism and has given to me, as he has to many others, abundances of kindness and intelligence.

# Introduction: Post-Enlightenment Modernism and the experience of time

## ENLIGHTENMENT TEMPORALITY

Jürgen Habermas begins *The Philosophical Discourse of Modernity* with a chapter entitled "Modernity's Consciousness of Time and Its Need for Self-Reassurance," and in that chapter he focuses on Walter Benjamin as a chief example of a person burdened by an extreme consciousness of time that helps to define, by contrast, the secular values of Enlightenment modernity. The reason and humanism of the Enlightenment, Habermas argues, are characterized among other things by a sense of the temporality of existence that is promising rather than overwhelming. "Because ... the modern world," he writes, "is distinguished from the old by the fact that it opens itself to the future, the epochal new beginning is rendered constant with each moment that gives birth to the new" (1987: 6). Hegel, he goes on, identifies the beginning of the modern with the break that the Enlightenment and the French Revolution signified for the more thoughtful spectators at the close of the eighteenth and the start of the nineteenth century. With this "glorious sunrise" we come, as the old Hegel still thought, "to the last stage in History, our world, our own time" (1987: 6–7). In this analysis Habermas is describing (and repeating) the Enlightenment combination of a conception of time as comprised of interchangeable parts which, taken together, accomplish universal progress. This combination of the democratic individualism and the almost mystical hopefulness of classical liberalism – the combination of what I call the subjective idealism and general semiotics of the Enlightenment in chapter 1 – strikingly manifests itself throughout Habermas himself and makes him a powerful advocate of the reason, consciousness, and humanism of Enlightenment values.

As such, he would, I think, dispute what I am calling the "logic"of

I

abundance in this book. In fact, he does dispute it in his representation of Benjamin and Benjamin's comprehension of temporality in the early twentieth century that is so different from the comprehensions of temporality articulated in Newtonian science, Hegelian philosophy, and the literary realism that arose with the novel in the eighteenth and nineteenth centuries. Benjamin, he argues, with his "singular mixture of surrealist experiences and motifs from Jewish mysticism [that] enter unmistakably into his notion of 'now-time'" (1987: 11), is struggling with "two conceptions" implicit in the homogeneous time of Newton, namely the metaphysical progressivism of Hegel and the transcendental subjectivity of realism's narrative. The first of these received Enlightenment conceptions, Habermas argues, is "the idea of a homogeneous and empty time that is filled in by 'the stubborn belief in progress' of evolutionism and the philosophy of history"; the second is "the neutralization of all standards fostered by historicism when it imprisons history in the museum and 'tell[s] the sequence of events like the beads of a rosary'" (1987: 11; Habermas is citing Benjamin 1969: 263). The two frameworks Habermas is describing in which time is comprehended – the belief in evolutionary "progress" born in the Enlightenment and almost universally subscribed to by educated opinion in the nineteenth century; and the seemingly contradictory belief in a "subjective" historical relativism that became the prevailing intellectual ideology in the last decades of the nineteenth century – came to crisis by the time Benjamin was writing after World War I. (See Bambach 1995 for a detailed explanation of the "crisis of historicism" in German philosophy.)

Implicit in these classical conceptions of time are the central assumptions of Enlightenment "modernity" that are called into question in the work of Benjamin, Virginia Woolf, and indeed almost all of the writers engaged with in this book, ranging from Bertrand Russell's cheerful science to Heidegger's sense of the need for the "*destruktion*" of the Western tradition. These assumptions include the self-evident truths that time is always and everywhere the same, succession without content; that time does not affect the events taking place "within" time; and that the individual subject of knowledge and experience is atemporal. These assumptions were most clearly articulated in what was understood to be the tradition of Newtonian "mechanical" time in the eighteenth century (but see Markley 1993 for a discussion of the relationship between Newton and the Newtonian tradition); in the conception of "progress" that endless time gives rise to in the classical economics of Adam Smith (as opposed to apocalyptic, momentary time Benjamin attempts to describe); and the idea of the secular *atemporality* (as opposed to the religious *eternity*) of both the subjectivity of the individual and the objectivity of "facts" and "events" in the world (which Habermas figures as "history in the museum"). Such subjective and objective atemporality – and the conception of a neutral, objective observer, a view from nowhere – follows from the formally "contentless" and historically progressive nature of Newtonian time. Moreover, these qualities of Enlightenment temporality – the interchangeability of its formal parts, its progressiveness, and the possibility that subjects and objects can be "abstracted" from it – give rise to the absolute distinction between present and past and modes of representation that possess what Michel Foucault calls "the obscure power of making a past impression present once more" (1970: 69).

POST-ENLIGHTENMENT TEMPORALITY

The experience of time in the early twentieth century that Habermas and I are, in our very different ways, representing in the work of Benjamin called the self-evidence and universality of these assumptions into question. That is, for Benjamin – and for many living within the enormous changes in wealth, knowledge, and experience at the turn of the twentieth century – time is inhabited by "constellations" of historical events, meaning, and consciousness, "collisions" of the Then and the Now (Benjamin's lightning flash of messianic time), and the possibility of a "post-Enlightenment" subjectivity that Benjamin describes as possessing a "chaste compactness which precludes psychological analysis" (1969: 91). Such constellations, collisions, and subjectivity suggest a different arrangement of the relationship between past and present and different modes of representation from the hierarchical reductions of Enlightenment science, the progressive continuities of political economy, and the enlightened consciousness of Hegelian metaphysics. In *Modernism and Time* I trace these changes in the experience and understanding of time in the history, science, and aesthetics of the early twentieth century.

One difference between the classical Hegelian "modernity" with which Habermas begins – that is, the responses to experience Hegel shares with the Enlightenment thinkers of the eighteenth century and humanists, such as George Eliot, of the nineteenth century – and that of the post-Enlightenment Modernism of the early twentieth century I am figuring here in Benjamin is that Hegel is responding to the historical event of the first Industrial Revolution while twentieth-century Modernism responds to the second Industrial Revolution. In the first Industrial Revolution of the late eighteenth century – most fully characterized by Adam Smith – future-oriented "productive labor" offered the possibility of an open-ended future of ever-increasing wealth and progress. In the second Industrial Revolution of the late nineteenth century, Smith's opposition between productive and non-productive labor, between wealth and consumption, and the "classical" Marxian opposition between use-value and exchange-value, lose their clear self-evidence in the enormous multiplication of commodities available for consumption in a world seemingly filled with abundances of *things*. The huge multiplication of consumer wealth (as opposed to the consolidation of capital wealth) made the categories of "production," "wealth," and "use" problematic at the turn of the twentieth century. If it is true, as Richard Terdiman (among others) contends, that the very "mystical character" of the commodity which Marx describes is closely tied to the erasure and transformation of time – "the process," Terdiman argues, following Benjamin and Theodor Adorno, "of reification [that] cut entities off from their own history" (1993: 12) – then the overwhelming multiplication of commodities in the second Industrial Revolution transformed the experience of time for people living through it. Concomitant with the vast multiplication of commodities in the last decades of the nineteenth century were vast multiplications of knowledge – enormous increases in data within the remarkable creation and professionalization of intellectual disciplines in the emerging system of research universities in the West – and the vast multiplication of populations in Europe and North America in both the relative peacefulness of Europe since the Napoleonic wars and the remarkably temperate weather patterns of the eighteenth and nineteenth centuries.

In the late twentieth century the problematic and critical nature of these abundances are less pressing. In our time, the creation of capital means of production by labor, the accumulation of wealth, and the positivist measure of value in "use" are more difficult to distinguish from the dissipations of labor that does not result in capital production, from wealth that is consumed, and from value that is relationally measured in exchange. In our time, the failures of the sense and sense-making capacity of "progress" as a framework in which to comprehend temporality and the concomitant phenomenon of the multiplication of isolated moments of historicism seem less an earthshaking crisis than they did at the beginning of the century when, as Benjamin says, "a generation that had gone to school on a horse-drawn streetcar" now found itself within "a field of force of destructive torrents and explosions" in terms of warfare, economic life, bodily life, and moral experience (1969: 83–84). I am not claiming that these classical categories – the oppositions between base and superstructure, use and exchange, meaning and intention – no longer exist or no longer have force but, rather, that the clear and "positive" nature of these distinctions loses its distinct and unproblematic efficacy – its *atemporal* force – in the face of abundances of consumable wealth, of systems of (disciplinary) knowledge, and of sheer numbers of people. In other words, these distinctions still function, at least at times, but they do not count once and for all. The difference between abundance and scarcity makes a difference for value and understanding precisely in this *temporal* mode of qualifying assertions of *once and for all*. "Abundance" is not an absolute or monumental category. Rather, it is relative and, above all, relative to time: abundance is always momentary, even if such "moments" – like the "garden party" of Edwardian England both Barbara Tuchman and Samuel Hynes describe, or the post-war boom of the 1950s and 1960s in the United States – stretch on to become particular historical "periods." Thus, with the surfeit of consumable wealth of the second Industrial Revolution, the category of "scarcity," paradoxically, arose along with the sense that the present moment had become paramount, rather than a conduit to the unending future of ongoing Newtonian time (see Birken 1988: 27–28; Blaug 1985: 294–95; and Sassover 1990 and Xenos 1989 for histories of "scarcity"). It is of this historical moment, rather than that of Hegel, that Paul de Man has written in observing that "modernity invests its trust in the power of the present moment as an origin, but discovers that, in severing itself from the past, it has at the same time severed itself from the present" (1971: 149). Another way to say this is to note that a significant difference between Hegel and Benjamin is the remarkable sense of dislocations in time and space occasioned by the second Industrial Revolution that cultural historians as different as Stephen Kern and Wolfgang Schivelbusch chronicle.

Implicit in the difference between what has come to be called the "early modernism" of Enlightenment thinking and twentieth-century Modernism is the very conception of time. Hegel, like Enlightenment modernity more generally, participates in "classical" models of temporality (see Plotnitsky 1993: 114). Such models are Newtonian: time is "objective," self-same, and simply a surrounding "ether" to events. In twentieth-century Modernism, however, unlike the positivism of classical temporality, the sense of time often assumes the fully historical nature of particular moments – what D. H. Lawrence calls "the quick moment of time" (1966: 109) and Heidegger, following Nietzsche, describes as simply the "Moment" where the past and the present "collide" (1984: 57). Such a collision is marked in the apologetics for imperialism in this period, which repeatedly uses temporal contrasts to justify Western colonization (see Said and Spurr). But it is also present, less glaringly marked, in the displacement of such apologies into the metaphysics of the "apocalyptic" nature of twentieth-century Modernism, its crisis consciousness, and, in Yeats's cyclical vision of history, his sense that the collision of past and present create feelings that seem to be "unnatural." And it is present, also, in the displacements of history into the various "formalisms" – linguistic, mathematical, and aesthetic – of the early twentieth century. As Raymond Williams notes, in the metropolitan unrootedness of this period, where "many of the major innovators [of cultural Modernism] were, in this precise sense, immigrants," language and representation were "no longer, in the old sense, customary and naturalized, but in many ways arbitrary and conventional" (1989: 45–46).

Benjamin describes – or at least circumscribes – the "unnaturalness" of experience and discourse in what he describes as the "image" and as "dialectics at a standstill" (discussed in chapter 2) and Heidegger describes it in his sense of European "crisis" (discussed in chapter 3), just as Yeats attempts to articulate the "antithetical" nature of meaning – its connection with a sense of temporal instability, cultural collapse, and apocalyptic change – in a poetry that, as he says of Maud Gonne, is "not natural in an age like this" (1969: 89). In Conrad as well as Yeats, in Joyce as well as T. S. Eliot, there is a sense of arrested time – aesthetic time – captured in discourse reduced to image. In the 1920s Mikhail Bakhtin described such a discourse in the aesthetics of temporality (discussed in chapter 6), that goes beyond the communicative function of language assumed by the secular Enlightenment. Daniel Albright describes "the unnaturalness of nature" in relation to the music of Stravinsky as "the deep equivalence of the natural and the artificial" (1989: 4) in order to explore the complicated relationship between natural presentation (and "presentness") and cultural representations in terms of what Stravinsky called the "'reflective system' between music and the world of experience" (1989: 3). Throughout this book I continually figure such "reflection" under the rhetorical figure of analogy in an attempt to avoid both the impression of a historical base governing an intellectual superstructure and the impression of an intellectual framework conditioning the apprehension of phenomena. The first impression might well be produced by the syntax of my argument, which begins chapter 1 by discussing the second Industrial Revolution and then discusses the representations of the arts and sciences; the second might well be produced by the order of chapters in part I, which presents a basic intellectual framework (somewhat akin to Thomas Kuhn's "paradigms") and the subsequent apprehension of experimental and historical "facts."

A third difference between Enlightenment modernity and twentieth-century Modernism can be discerned in the assumption of the full and present consciousness that is the dream of "enlightenment" altogether. Thus Arkady Plotnitsky asserts that Hegel is "a great philosopher of classical temporality," which makes him "a great master of the narrative, particularly narratives about time, history, and consciousness" (1993: 115). Because it is everywhere the same and because its parts are fully interchangeable, Newtonian time, like the so-called ether of Newtonian mechanics, can be unapprehended without unconsciousness. That is to say, the *subject* of experience – including temporal experience – in the idealizations of the early-modern Enlightenment is fully conscious and that consciousness itself, like the narrator in *The Mill on the Floss* examined in chapter 2, is in no way affected by the accidents of time. For twentieth-century Modernism, the unconscious becomes a crucial category precisely because the subject of experience is *temporalized*: the temporal situation of the subject of experience – situated within the contours of his or her own life and within the "events" of history more generally conceived – is a constituent element in the nature of that experience. This is why Benjamin takes such pains to imagine experience beyond the individual subject. And it is why, I believe, that Habermas defines modernity in terms of time and begins with Benjamin as a chief example. Experience and understanding in the early twentieth century involved an *awareness* of time, as Benjamin describes it in his extraordinary conception of allegory, that hovers on the side of experience, pressuring the present moment, doubling and complexifying experience, in a way that is not quite conscious, yet which flashes forth. Habermas describes this as "mystical" but without "any return to forms of religious thought, whether dogmatic or heretical" (1987: 336). He calls this "the radical critique of reason" (1987: 336), but in his description of reason he denies any place for temporality, Heidegger's "temporalized *Ursprungsphiloso-phie*" whose truths, Habermas argues, "are in each case provincial and yet total; they are more like the commanding expressions of some sacral force fitted out with the aura of truth" (1987: 154). The combination of "provincial yet total," which expresses Habermas's disdain of any kind of post-Enlightenment (or "postmodern") revision of the received truths of Enlightenment reason, is precisely what I explore and attempt to valorize in this study. Habermas's expression is a version of what Edward Said calls, with a positive valence, an understanding of knowledge that is "unprovincial yet interested" (1994: 151). In chapter 5, I examine a version of this attitude toward experience when I look at the ways in which Werner Heisenberg's meditations on post-Newtonian science suggest a return to the pre-Enlightenment "ontological argument" refuted by Hume and especially by Kant, just as in chapter 2 I examine Benjamin's articulations of experience as distinct from those of George Eliot.

In other words, Habermas – and the secular humanist tradition of Enlightenment values he defends – denies to the experience of time any constituent agency in truth. Yet it is precisely the *experience* of time that Benjamin, Heidegger, and the early twentieth-century writers and scientists I treat in this book cannot simply avoid, domesticate, or transcend. The lack of this avoidance informs the experience of consciousness, the historical events, and the nature of meaning of early twentieth-century Modernism. In chapter 1, I describe modes of understanding and explanation as they are affected by temporal abundance. In the following chapter, I present the experience and representation of time in contrasting the assumptions concerning time in the continuous narrative of *The Mill on the Floss* and the discontinuous discourse of Benjamin. In chapter 3, I make explicit three "marks" – in the sense of "markedness" that was developed in Prague linguistics at this time and that I discuss in chapter 5 – of the changing experience and conception of time as it emerged in twentieth-century Modernism. These marks are implicit in Benjamin, but they can be best understood in three terms that delimit cultural experience at the turn of the twentieth century: the "collision" of past and present in the second Industrial Revolution; the sense of a temporally bound crisis consciousness closely connected to the exhaustion of bourgeois and Enlightenment values and the rise of a lower middle class that was both continuous with and separate from the petty bourgeoisie of industrial capitalism; and a conception, or at least an apprehension, of "temporal subjectivity" that includes but is not limited to Enlightenment individuality.

The concept of "emergence" itself doesn't deny the idea of the universal validity of truth that is important to Habermas and whose abandonment, in my judgment, would be – and, in the light of the irrationalities of twentieth-century politics, has been – dangerous indeed. It is for this reason that in part I of *Modernism and Time* I examine the felt responses, often inarticulate and unconscious, to the transformations of the second Industrial Revolution in terms of panic, free-floating anxiety, bewilderment, and a pervading sense of crisis – responses gathered up in the overdetermined meanings of "post-Enlightenment apprehensions." Still, in the concept of *emergent* significance and meaning I am attempting to describe valid truths that can be understood in terms of their historicity and temporality in such a way that their validity does not transcend their origin or emergence even if, once established, they are, in fact, valid. (See Schleifer et al. 1992: ch. 1 for a discussion of "emergent understanding.") Such truths are not "relative" or "subjective," even if the *temporalized* subject of their apprehension, like the subject of the experimental data of post-Newtonian mechanics or the subject of systems of order in post-Cantorian mathematics, participates, *momentarily*, in truth itself. Such a sense of temporalized "truth," I believe, governs Benjamin's idea of redemption of history that I trace in chapter 2, Said's "worldliness" I touch upon in chapter 1, and the aesthetics of Woolf, Joyce, and Lawrence variously examined in part I. Such an idea – constellated, arrested, and both terrifying and hopeful – captures, to some degree, the experience of modern time expressed in Benjamin and, often less articulately, in his contemporaries.

## HISTORY, EXPERIENCE, UNDERSTANDING

In examining the idea and experience of temporality at the turn of the twentieth century I hope to delineate a mode of comprehending experience that arose with cultural Modernism. This mode of comprehension, like narrative, attempts to discover meaning in action, to relate the semantic void of ongoing time to the meaningful temporality of narrative discourse and logical argument. This "marking" of time is part and parcel of narrative discourse, and throughout this book, but especially in chapter 5 in relation to Heisenberg's attempt to articulate a language for the anti-intuitive data of post-Newtonian science, I examine this general phenomenon. But at the time of Modernism – that is, in the midst of the enormous transformations in social organization, thought, and daily life that took place in Western life during the second Industrial Revolution at the turn of the twentieth century – the marks of time took on three particular forms. One of these marks was a transformation in the canons of understanding, a transformation of exactly what constituted a satisfying explanation of experience and value. A second mark of time at the turn of the twentieth century is the ubiquitous and often unnoticed transformation in the *experience* of time that conditioned the apocalyptic sense of the "new" – a "crisis consciousness" – articulated throughout literary Modernism in America and England. A third was a transformation in the understanding of history as continuous into what Heidegger describes as a sense of history as the "collision" between the past and the present in his study of Nietzsche's conception of the eternal recurrence of the same (1984: 56). These things taken together – the transformations of understanding, experience, and apprehensions of history itself – helped condition an often unnerving sense of discontinuous subjective experience in the late nineteenth century, what William Everdell calls "the collapse of ontological continuity" (1997: 11; see also 1988). They called for the rethinking of Enlightenment assumptions about the constitution of truth, the delineations of the subject of knowledge, and the nature of the world. Charles Bambach describes this rethinking of Enlightenment assumptions in terms of "the crisis of historicism" in continental philosophy at the turn of the twentieth century. "The 'crisis' of historicism," he writes, "... is really nothing other than the coming to self-consciousness of the temporal, historical, cultural, and institutional character of scientific

inquiry itself – a topic that we now conveniently label 'postmodern'"
(1995: 124). Bambach describes Enlightenment assumptions – which,
for my purposes, entail the *idealization* of understanding, experience,
and history at a limit of "purity" (to use a term of Kant's which
Bruno Latour takes up [1993]) rather than the often contentious and
time-laden anxieties that accompanied their articulation in the
eighteenth and nineteenth centuries – in terms of a "logico-mathe-
matical model of time," "abstract epistemology," and "an aggregation of [historical] facts" (1995: 169). It is my argument here that
such rethinking – including such descriptions of understanding,
experience, and history – respond and contribute to what Kern has
called the "crisis of abundance" of the years between 1880 and 1918
(1983: 9) with what might best be called "post-Enlightenment"
thinking, values, and temporality.

Such thinking is characterized by a plethora of terms, not exactly
"key words," in Raymond Williams's sense, but repeated *analogical*
terms that proliferate in the discourses of people struggling to
describe phenomena for which received vocabularies do not work.
These "analogical" discourses offer a supplement to received
"logical" discourses in their seriality without paradigm (in Jacques
Derrida's phrase, 1979: 130). Thus, Eve Tavor Bannett has argued in
an essay examining Wittgenstein's philosophical revolution in the
early twentieth century that "for Wittgenstein, and indeed for
traditional rhetoricians, an analogy is not an identity; it is a figure
which marks both the likeness and the difference in our application
of words from case to case. The gaps, the discontinuities, and the
differences are as important as the likeness because, Wittgenstein
insists, we are always moving meaning from one situation to another
which might not be quite the same" (1997: 656). The "always" of
this argument underlines the temporality of analogical thinking, the
fact that analogy, as distinct from logical thinking, traffics in
temporally specific relationships. Thus, chapter 1, "The Enlightenment, Abundance, and Postmodernity," traces the "modes of understanding" as they were transformed from Enlightenment self-evident
truth – the accuracy, simplicity, and generalizability (or "wholeness")
governing secular-scientific understanding in the Enlightenment – to
more capacious modes of understanding of the twentieth century,
what Gaston Bachelard calls "the *complexification* of what appeared to
be simple" (1984: 45). In chapter 2, I describe the experience of
Modernist temporality by contrasting George Eliot's Enlightenment

"realism" and the assumptions about the nature of temporality implicit in her narrative style with Benjamin's sense of the crisis of representation and the burden of time in the twentieth century. This chapter focuses on an apocalyptic sense of experience – the "crisis consciousness" I discuss later – by focusing on Benjamin's complex definition of "idea" as a *constellation* that does "not make the similar identical" (1977: 41). Later, in chapter 3, this "crisis consciousness" is revisited in terms of historical change and new discursive formations that are described in terms of *retrospection* and historical *infiltration*. The whole of chapter 3 – the final chapter of part I – moves to a wider historical and cultural examination of the three categories of the comprehension and representation of post-Enlightenment understanding, the experience of crisis, and the elaboration of subjectivity, in D. H. Lawrence. The three chapters of part I – examining temporal discontinuity and the modes of understanding created by the great success of the second Industrial Revolution, the experience and representation of temporality, and the historical moment of Modernism in terms of the "collision" of past and present in the decades before World War I – retraverse these categories more globally.

In Roman Jakobson, the intellectual transformations of this period can be discerned in ways that take in history and consciousness as well, the three categories that govern my exposition. Just as Newton and Leibniz grounded their work in pre-Enlightenment religiosity but paved the way for thoroughly *secular* conceptions of knowledge and experience (see Markley 1993 for a detailed discussion of the transformation from mystical to secular science by means of the displacement and repression of the religious metaphysics of Newton and Leibniz), so Jakobson developed possibilities of post-Enlightenment understanding by pursuing as singlemindedly as he could the scientific project of the atemporal reason of the Enlightenment into the social realm of discourse. Thus, when Jakobson developed and pursued the project of "structuralism" – which Claude Lévi-Strauss, citing Paul Ricoeur, later described as "Kantism without the transcendental subject" (1975: 11) – he marks precisely the crisis of subjectivity and knowledge in the new century by removing the linchpin that held together the subjective idealism and general semiotics of Enlightenment understanding, classic liberalism, and Cartesian subjectivity. Henceforth, the simplifying assumptions of the Enlightenment, held together by a transcendental subject that allowed the coexistence of semiotics and subjectivity within a simple temporality – and the simple possibility of "atemporality" – could no longer fully, once and for all, accommodate experience and understanding that had been overdetermined, socialized, pluralized by time. At the turn of the twentieth century these three categories – knowledge, history, and subjectivity – were sensed, often unconsciously, to be inhabited, by the great anxiety of insistent temporality.

### ANALOGIES OF COMPREHENSION

It is legitimate to ask, as I ask throughout this study, why it is that such general and universal "truths," such as those of Jakobson, Einstein, and even the unlikely pair of Heidegger and Russell, emerge at one historical moment rather than another and what are the relationships among historical moments, personal experience, and the impersonal experience we have called, since the Enlightenment, "science." The relations among experience, history, and understanding at the particular time of the turn of the twentieth century are best understood, I believe, in terms of analogical figures I elaborate in the chapters of *Modernism and Time*. Such figures replace cause with configuration as a mode of explanation; they replace continuous development with confrontation as a description of history; and they replace the secular linear ongoingness of time with crisis-ridden moments as the very experience of human and social life. Thus David Wood, in his discussion of Husserl, emphasizes the relationship between phenomenology and the simultaneously "very obvious and also very strange ... discussion of absolute flux" (1991: 108). Wood's observation, I think, links the experience of temporality to the emerging understanding of time and temporality at the turn of the twentieth century and to other historical phenomena – technological, economic, intellectual, sensible, and other transformations in experience comprehended under the heading of "abundance" – not in any causal way, but as one element in a constellation of factors.

In short, Benjamin's term *constellation* – analogous to Russell's description of mathematics at the turn of the century as the science of *arrangement* examined in chapter 4, to Werner Heisenberg's description of post-Newtonian physics as a science of temporally governed *alternations* examined in chapter 5, and to Mikhail Bakhtin's description of a post-Kantian aesthetics of temporality in terms of

*borders* examined in chapter 6 (as well as *answerability* examined later
in this introduction) – might do well to articulate what I am calling
the logic of abundance. Heidegger's figure of *collision* also presents an
analogy to Benjamin's figure, but it lacks, I believe, any possibility of
redeeming and preserving the great and valuable contributions of
the bourgeois/Enlightenment civilization of the West that emerged
in the early modernism of the seventeenth and eighteenth centuries.
Bruno Latour describes the great achievement of Enlightenment
modernity as the "double task of domination and emancipation"
(1993: 10), and it is precisely the emancipatory aspect of Enlightenment secularization that Heidegger – unlike Benjamin, Russell,
Einstein, Bakhtin, or even Joyce and Woolf discussed in chapter 1 –
fails to grasp. "Heidegger's understanding of modernity," Bambach
writes, "situates the heritage of Cartesian and Enlightenment thinking within a narrative of technological domination and will to
power" (1995: 267) without any glance toward the liberty, equality,
and solidarity that, along with will to power, also characterize
Enlightenment values.

All of these terms – *constellation, collision, arrangement, alternation,*
Einstein's *operational definition,* and even Bakhtin's remarkable assertion that "a cultural domain has no inner territory ... [but it] is
located entirely upon boundaries, boundaries intersect it everywhere, passing through each of its constituent features" (1990: 274),
or my own discussion of *analogical thinking* in chapter 5 – all of these
terms participate in the enactment of a powerful new sense and
relationship to time. Time and space within the contexts of early
modern Enlightenment thinking and the "classical" science of
Newton and Kant, above all, call for measurement and quantification: thus Kant writes that "in any particular doctrine of nature only
so much *genuine* science can be found as there is mathematics to be
found in it" (cited in Heidegger 1967: 68). Thus "classical" science,
Heidegger writes, "is a factual, experimental, measuring science"
(1967: 68; see also Toulmin 1992: 104); it traffics, as he says in a
powerful metaphor, in "stretches of the measurable" (1967: 87). The
figures I appropriate from Benjamin, Heidegger, Russell, Woolf, and
others throughout this book – and which proliferate, abundantly, in
the early twentieth century – are different: their focus is arrangement
and order, not measurement. "In former days," Russell writes in
*Mysticism and Logic* (1917), "it was supposed (and philosophers are still
apt to suppose) that quantity was the fundamental notion of mathe-

matics. But nowadays, quantity is banished altogether, except from one little corner of Geometry, while order more and more reigns supreme" (1917: 87). The supplementation (not the replacement) of precisions of measured quantities by arrangements of order (or "constellations," "operational definitions," "alternations," interfacings of "borders," "collisions," and multiplications of analogical thinking) both results in and results from conceptions and experience of time as no longer *simply* "stretches of the measurable." Moreover, they arise in the context of a world where abundance along with dearth is a problem. It is no accident that, as Russell asserts, "the solution of the difficulties which formerly surrounded the mathematical infinite is probably the greatest achievement of which our own age has to boast" ([1917]: 61). Russell's assertion is both "Enlightenment" and "post-Enlightenment" insofar as it sums up the decoupling of the infinite from the theological – or at least overtly theocentric – debates of Newton and Leibniz, which helped initiate Enlightenment humanism. Such secular humanism, as I note in chapter 1, also decoupled "eternity" and timeless "atemporality."

## TIME AND ETHER

One of the great intellectual events of the late nineteenth century was the Michelson-Morley experiment in 1897 that failed to detect the motion of the light through "luminiferous ether." The existence of ether was necessitated by the need to maintain continuous time and linear causation as conditions of explanation. "One thus felt compelled," Albert Einstein wrote in *Relativity*, "even in the space which had hitherto been regarded as empty, to assume everywhere the existence of a form of matter, which was called 'aether'" (1961: 146). Such compulsion to posit the existence of ether, despite its unavailability to measurement, is related to Newton's Enlightenment conception of an "absolute, true, and mathematical time, [that] of itself, and from its own nature flows equably without relation to anything external" (Newton 1964: 17). Like Newtonian time, ether is a featureless "substance" that is necessary to make sense of the positive mechanics of Newtonian physics but, as Russell says in the *ABC of Atoms*, "does not really add anything to our knowledge" (1925: 49). It was precisely Einstein's reimagining of the nature of light that transformed the physical conceptions of time and space assumed in secular Enlightenment understanding at the beginning of the twentieth century.

In Newtonian mechanics, both ether and time are without any attributes; they both embody the self-contradiction of an "unmarked" substance that is discussed in chapter 5. Ether is the medium through which light waves were thought to be propagated; time is the medium in which the quasi-theological "force" of Newton's science and the quasi-secular "cause and effect" of scientific positivism take place. Newtonian time governed the literary discourse of bourgeois humanism in the eighteenth and nineteenth centuries; and the transformed sense of time I examine in terms of the discourse, history, and understanding of twentieth-century Modernism in part I is most explicitly undertaken in chapter 2 through a comparison of the unspoken assumptions about time in the fiction of George Eliot and the explicit contemplations of time in the writings of Benjamin and in chapter 3 through a rhetorical analysis of Lawrence's novel, *The Rainbow*. The cross-generic comparison I pursue in chapter 2 – and, indeed, throughout part I – marks the problematization of time within the Modernist period, the crisis of twentieth-century Modernism, in terms of the ways that time is represented in discourse and how the very categories governing discourse called for new understandings.

In part II I explore the "logics" of those understandings that do away with the simplifying effects of the mechanics of an ether-like time in the mathematics of Einstein and Russell, the post-Newtonian physics of Heisenberg, and the aesthetics of Bakhtin. Moreover, just as chapter 3 retraverses the concerns of part I, so chapter 6 gathers together and "constellates" the logics of abundance described in part II by examining aesthetics in relation to received ideas of scientific cognition and historical ethics in configuring Bakhtin in relation to Jakobson and Benjamin. Moreover, this chapter enacts the "collision" of Enlightenment and post-Enlightenment apprehensions examined explicitly in part I by demonstrating, in the Modernist figures of Bakhtin, Jakobson, and Benjamin, the *temporalization* of the atemporal ruling criteria of Enlightenment knowledge – the simplicity, generalizability, and accuracy governing Enlightenment science. Another way to say this is to note that the three chapters of part II rethink and elaborate – they "complexify" – Leibniz's principle of sufficient reason in the discussions of operational definitions and narrative understanding in chapter 4, his principle of contradiction in the discussion of negation in chapter 5, and the "given moment" of Enlightenment aesthetics in the discussion of Bakhtin's momentary aesthetics in chapter 6. They do so by reimagining time itself as something other than a featureless "ether" of experience, a constituent element of explanation and experience.

MULTIPLYING REASON: THE LOGIC OF ABUNDANCE

Towards the end of the *ABC of Atoms* Russell returns to ether in his discussion of sub-atomic physics. In doing so, he historicizes understanding under the category of "orders" of understanding, alternative modes of comprehension, to imagine the ways in which understanding emerges within time and, at the same time, he multiplies reason itself. "It is necessary," he writes,

to utter a word of warning, in case readers should accept as dogmatic ultimate truth the atomic structure of the world which we have been describing, and which seems at present probable. It should not be forgotten that there is another order of ideas, temporarily out of fashion, which may at any moment come back into favour if it is found to afford the best explanation of the phenomena. The charge on an electron, the equal and opposite charge on a hydrogen atom, the mass of an electron, the mass of a hydrogen nucleus, and Planck's quantum, all appear in modern physics as absolute constants, which are just brute facts for which no reason can be imagined. The aether, which used to play a great part of physics, has sunk into the background, and has become as shadowy as Mrs. Harris. It may be found, however, as a result of further research, that the aether is after all what is really fundamental, and that electrons and hydrogen nuclei are merely states of strain in the aether, or something of the sort ... This suggestion is purely speculative; there is nothing in the existing state of physics to justify it. But ... [i]f the possibility should be realized, it would not mean that the present theory is false; it would merely mean that a new interpretation had been found for its results. (1925: 152–53)

I have quoted Russell at length because in these speculations of possibilities and, indeed, "possible worlds," he is pursuing a logic of abundance that is fully marked by time and narrative. Moreover, he is presenting the logic of "post": "postmodern" or, as I call it here, "post-Enlightenment," or even the term "post-structuralism" I touch upon in chapter 5. The "coming after" of post-Enlightenment Modernism does not require the "falsification," as Russell says, of what came before – as Heidegger seemed to think in his apocalyptic forgetting and "*destruktion*" of the most enlightened aspects of our

Western tradition in his philosophy, which he enacted in his political life. Such falsification does away with time as a category of understanding, experience, and of history itself. Rather, the "coming after" of the post-Enlightenment apprehensions of the early twentieth century is a way of comprehending abundance as well as parsimony and the very temporality of both the past and the present as richnesses to be gathered up and handed down within the temporalities of our different and common experiences. It is my hope, as it was Benjamin's and Woolf's – and even Russell's and Bakhtin's – to gather up and pass along a sense of our cultural inheritance inhabited and modified by our experiences of time, abundance, and understanding.

MULTIPLYING VALUE: THE TEMPORAL ECONOMY OF CHOICE

Werner Heisenberg describes such temporal modifications when he argues that certain kinds of statements about the world are "not decided." "The term 'not decided,'" he writes, "is by no means equivalent to the term not known. Not known would mean that the atom is really left or right, only we do not know where it is. But not decided indicates a different situation, expressible only by a complementary statement" (1958: 184). This situation, he makes clear at the beginning of his discussion, has to do with time and the temporality of choice: "the concept of complementarity introduced by Bohr into the interpretation of quantum theory has encouraged physicists ... to apply alternatively different classical concepts which would lead to contradictions if used simultaneously" (1958: 179). These alternative and alternating applications cannot simply bracket time and purport to make their choices atemporal, once and for all.

That is, Heisenberg's "undecidability" underlines the constituent element of time within understanding and evaluation just as – *analogically* – the neoclassical economists of the late nineteenth century do in their analysis of value. Nicholas Xenos describes this as the "restless quality" of the "particular experience of need" at the turn of the twentieth century and quotes the economist Alfred Marshall explaining marginal utility as an example of this restlessness. "With every increase in the amount of a thing which a man has," Marshall wrote in 1890, "the eagerness of his desire to obtain more of it diminishes; until it yields place to the desire for some other thing, of which perhaps he had hardly thought, so long as his more urgent wants were still unsatisfied. There is an endless variety of wants" but there is a limit to each separate want (cited in Xenos 1989: 69). The sense of limit is the measure of choice and value in the economies of understanding and value. Moreover, such economies are, above all, conditioned by time: the "limit" is a temporal limit of alternating wants. "A moral choice between two objects," Xenos argues,

may very well decide the matter once and for all, and so the choice is absolute. An economizing choice [based upon marginal utility] only entails a particular choice at a particular time, since, having decided that one object will give greater satisfaction to desire than another or others, a person may find that the spurned choice, or one of them, now presents itself as a newly powerful want, and so it becomes the preferred object of acquisition ... (1989: 78)

Such a mode of defining value shows at least a distant formal similarity to what Benjamin calls "dialectics at a standstill," a momentary "answer" to a particular situation such as the one Russell describes in what I have termed a "coming after."

## MULTIPLYING EXPERIENCE: THE ANSWERABILITY OF ART

My choice to end *Modernism and Time* – which, given the "logic" of its exposition, might go endlessly on, like a patch-work quilt, reconfiguring itself over and over again – with a discussion of the aesthetics of Mikhail Bakhtin participates in the kind of economizing choice the neoclassical economists defined at the turn of the century. At the heart of the aesthetics Bakhtin developed in the 1920s is his conception of "answerability" – another "coming after" – to describe the ways that art responds to and participates in the culture it seems to "reflect" by pursuing an aesthetics governed by its own material, content, and purposes. I have already touched upon the ways that Stravinsky asserts that it is "possible to discover a reflective system between the language structure of the music [of Beethoven] and the structure of the phenomenal world" (1982: 147; cited in Albright 1989: 3), and in a moment I will examine Stravinsky more closely in relation to the dialectic of abundance and poverty. But the larger question here concerns the relationship between the *structures* of experience, which are organized – and, if I can say so, both "finalized" (to use a term of Bakhtin's) and multiplied – within the

arts and sciences, and the political/economic/technological culture
in which they emerge.

   In other words, throughout this book I am not arguing that art
*simply* reflects the culture in which it arises. Neither am I arguing
that the arts – and, for that matter, the sciences in their open-
endedness – *simply* delimit the possibilities of cultural formations. In
important ways, cultures are not governed by intellectual paradigms
in the manner that Thomas Kuhn describes them, which simply
provide its subjects with horizons of understanding and experience.
Rather, an art, as Stravinsky suggests, follows the logic of its
particular "language," the logic implicit in the media with which it
"structures" experience. In such an artistic "logic" the multiplication of voices implicit in the "scrupulous meanness" of Joyce's style
in *Dubliners* or the multiplication of rhythms explicit in Stravinsky's
mechanical dance or even the multiplication of planes of visual
experience represented in Picasso's portraits can all be seen, *simply*,
as the developments of Flaubert's aestheticism, Beethoven's late
chamber music, or Cézanne's landscapes.

   Yet such "developments" are not, in fact, simple. At the same
time that they present simple systems of development they also
present – *alternatively* – a "reflective system" between the language
structure of the art and the structure of the phenomenal world.
Above all, such "reflection" is *analogical*: as Stravinsky's term "structure" suggests in both the case of art and of experience, art does
more than simply reveal the "structures" implicit in experience; it
also organizes that experience as well – momentarily configures and
answers it – so that, as Wallace Stevens says at Key West *after* the
singing he had heard had ended, the remaining light at end of day
"Mastered the night and portioned out the sea, / Fixing emblazoned
zones and fiery poles, / Arranging, deepening, enchanting night"
(1972: 98). That the experiential and aesthetic "mastery" Stevens
describes – its "ghostlier demarcations, keener sounds" (1972: 99) –
come in the silence after the singing ended repeats my focus on the
temporality inhabiting even the illusion of atemporality and "finalization" that might well be the experiential goal of the "language
structures" of art. (The retrospective nature of this experience offers
a fine analogy to the retrospective understanding of Heisenberg's
physics I examine in chapter 5.) In any case, Stevens describes the
reflective system between the language structure of the unheard
music and the structure of the phenomenal world, "the glassy lights,

/ The lights in the fishing boats at anchor there" (1972: 98). Moreover, Stravinsky continues his remarks about Beethoven by asserting that "the quartets are a charter of human rights, a perpetually seditious one" (1982: 147) that may not bring much balm to the dispossessed or to activists, but may yet – in what Heisenberg calls the "distant formal similarity" (1952: 62) I am identifying with analogical thinking – *answer* the world with "a high concept of freedom" and a "guarantee" (1982: 147). The momentary analogies of this mode of apprehension – momentary analogies between aesthetic experience and ordinary experience, between new understanding and familiar understanding, between the present and the past – enact what Benjamin calls the "redemption" of time.

The aesthetic "mastery" Stevens and Stravinsky describe and enact can help us to understand Bakhtin's nuanced understanding of the relationship between art and the culture that produces it. The nature of aesthetic mastery is responsibility, what Bakhtin calls its "answerability." "Answerability" is a translation of the Russian word *otvetstvennost'* which, as Gary Saul Morson and Caryl Emerson note, can be rendered as *responsibility* or as *answerability*. By Bakhtin's work of the mid-1920s, they argue,

a case could be made for either translation, ethical responsibility or addressive answerability (that is, the presence of response). There is an ethical component in answerability as well, of course, but it is more abstract and less tied to a specific act. One's obligation in answerability is to rescue the other from pure potential; reaching out to another consciousness makes the other coalesce, and turns the other's "mere potential" into space that is open to the living event. (1990: 76)

In chapters 4 and 5 I examine the abstraction of answerability – and of analogical thinking more generally – in terms of what I call its "semantic formalism." But here this description of "answerability" offers an important gloss on Stravinsky's description of the "reflective system" between the formal, aesthetic "language structure" of a particular art-form and the "structure" of experience. That is, if we ignore Bakhtin's psychological vocabulary of interpersonal relationships – which is precisely what Benjamin does in his description of the ways in which storytelling "answers" the needs of a community within its "chaste compactness which precludes psychological analysis" (1969: 91) – "answerability" describes the ways in which aesthetic phenomena such as the novels, essays and even the "pure" mathematics I examine in this book allow the political/economic/

technological culture in which they emerge to "coalesce" as living events which themselves call for a response, an answer, over and over and over again. Answerability is predicated on the (aesthetic) possibility of grasping phenomena whole, momentarily, in order to render a judgment and, as Benjamin says, by means of their temporally enlarged wholeness to "redeem" them. As such, art is not simply a reflex of techno-political culture; it momentarily and repeatedly coalesces such culture into something to be comprehended, evaluated and valued, marked by poverty and wealth.

## THE DIALECTIC OF ABUNDANCE AND POVERTY

Morson and Emerson, following Bakhtin, use the term "coalesce," but the term I follow throughout *Modernism and Time* is Benjamin's concept of "constellate," which precludes a too-quickly apprehended sense of wholeness and allows for a more fully achieved sense of a temporal (rather than a logical) dialectic, what he calls "dialectics at a standstill." Thus Benjamin writes that "it isn't that the past casts its light on the present or the present casts its light on the past: rather, an image is that in which the Then [*das Gewesene*] and the Now [*das Jetzt*] come into a constellation like a flash of lightning. In other words: image is dialectics at a standstill. For while the relation of the present to the past is a purely temporal, continuous one, the relation of the Then to the Now is dialectical – not development but image leaping forth" (1989: 49). Such an image is aesthetic in its momentariness, but it also embodies – and, as Stravinsky might say, systematically and analogically reflects – the values a culture holds and the values which govern, more or less unconsciously (but not on the level of "psychology"), experience and understanding within that culture in terms of the continuous/discontinuous constellation of Then and Now.

One of the readers for this book described both it and myself as "reasonably optimistic": "*Modernism and Time*," he wrote, "is sufficiently celebratory that no one will want to throw away his or her eighth pair of shoes." Yet beyond its optimism and, indeed, beyond the optimism seemingly inherent in "abundance" altogether lies a certain kind of poverty, a certain kind of despair. If the simplicities of Descartes and Leibniz erase contingency from experience – or at least transmute it into order and meaning – then the abundances I describe throughout this book present themselves as apotheoses of contingency, meaningless repetitions. Even the "redemption" of such contingency – the momentary aesthetics I describe in the final chapter and outline throughout under the figure of *constellation* – is not unmixed in its motive and result. This mixture of celebration and despair was aptly articulated in Paul de Man's famous statement about Nietzsche's aesthetic "redemption" in *The Birth of Tragedy*: "'Only as an *aesthetic phenomenon* is existence and the world forever *justified*': the famous quotation, twice repeated in *The Birth of Tragedy*, should not be taken too serenely, for it is an indictment of existence rather than a panegyric of art" (1979: 93).

Much of the art of early twentieth-century Modernism that I do not consider in this book – that of Yeats, for instance, who wrote in his diary that "history is necessity until it takes fire in someone's head and becomes freedom or virtue" (1962: 336), or that of Beckett or Mondrian or, as I will discuss in a moment, Messiaen – offers an image and practice of art that are the opposite of the celebration of the logic of abundance. Rather, their art pursues the articulation or gesture towards transcendental simplicity, the opposite of abundance, taking the forms of Yeats's atemporal vision, Beckett's pursuit of articulate inexpressiveness, the seeming colorlessness of Mondrian's flat colors and lines, or Messiaen's spare apocalypse. The abundances I describe in this book, then, are only half the story of Modernism and the experience of time, many of whose most articulate spokes-people strive to articulations of non-contingent simplicities, atemporal value, aesthetics of transcendental and time-less detachment. Thus Daniel Albright focuses upon the self-contained simplicity of much Modernist art. "What Beckett likes," he argues, "is a language that refers to nothing beyond itself, a language that is not contingent, is not a system of arrows and index fingers pointing to things in the world of experience, but a language that has attained the dignity of *being*" (1981: 168), and more generally Albright pursues analyses of artists (and he could have added scientists and ethicists) "searching for the magical seizure of reality, the collapse of the analogy that representation offers into identity" (1981: 13–14). Even Benjamin himself, as I note in chapter 2, figures allegory as a kind of minimalist skeletal rictus. Thus, as well as articulations of abundance, the arts in the early twentieth century offer the opposite of abundance, spare apocalyse, universal poverty, sustained silence.

Yet even this bifurcation – the comprehension of Modernism in terms of two experiences and comprehensions of time – is itself a realization of a species of abundance, the overdetermination of a non-logical – an *ana-logical* – complexity. It is for this reason that I begin the first chapter with Jean-François Lyotard's dark observation that in our time the "claim for simplicity" is barbarous precisely because mankind seems divided into two parts, one "confronted with the challenge of complexity; the other with the terrible ancient task of survival" (1993: 173). This bifurcation between what I am calling abundance and dearth, he says, is a major aspect of the failure of the project of Enlightenment modernity. That project, as Latour argues most cogently, was to comprehend abundances as "pure" simplicities, to imagine the possibility of the erasure of contingency, to apprehend, beyond the increasingly noisy busy-ness of the temporal world, atemporal essences.

An examination of Olivier Messiaen's *Quatuor pour la Fin du Temps* (Quartet for the End of Time), written in a Nazi prison camp during World War II, might well help articulate or at least gesture towards the terrible dialectic between abundance and dearth that governs so much of the sense of value that developed in the twentieth century. As Paul Griffiths has noted, "the first performance of this work at the Stalag in January 1941 has, together with the première of *The Rite of Spring*, become one of the great stories of twentieth-century music" (1985: 90). The contrast of the exuberance of Stravinsky with the austerity of Messiaen might help me to sketch out the dialectic of abundance and dearth underlying this book and to note, at least in passing, the poverty of abundance and a minimalist Modernism not examined here. *The Rite of Spring* – with multiplications of rhythms, its genesis in Stravinsky's vision of a young girl dancing herself to death, and what Albright describes as "the obliterating music of [its] score" (1989: 15) stands in striking counterpoint to Messiaen's quartet. This contrast is underlined in Albright's suggestion to use T. S. Eliot's observation "that the music seemed to 'transform the rhythm of the steppes into the scream of the motor-horn, the rattle of machinery, the grind of wheels, the beating of iron and steel, the roar of the underground railway, and the other barbaric noises of modern life'" as directions for what could be a powerful staging of the ballet (1989: 17).

In any case, in its first performance *The Rite of Spring* was a scandal, first of all to music, in which, as Modris Eksteins argues, its lack of ornamentation, melody, and even "moral intimation" all contributed to violations of "the laws of harmony and rhythm"

(1989: 50). In contrast to the *Quatuor*, with its stark instrumentation of piano, clarinet, violin, and cello, and with only four of its eight parts scored for all four instruments (and three of the eight scored for two or less instruments), *The Rite of Spring* was organized on a very different scale. "Instruments," Eksteins writes,

that have no vibrato were intentionally chosen in order to eliminate any trace of sentimentality. New sounds were created by the use of extreme registers for woodwinds and strings. The orchestra called for was immense, 120 instruments, with a high percentage of percussion, which could produce a formidable eruption of sound. With its violence, dissonance, and apparent cacophony, the music was as energetic and primitive as the theme. (1989: 50)

Moreover, the choreography compounded the scandal of the music, eliminating "every virtuosity" and stylizing movement to the point that "the dancers were no longer individuals but parts of the composition" (1989: 51).

Even more to the point, *The Rite of Spring* was a scandal to art and culture themselves. If traditional Western music from that of Mozart, written during the Enlightenment, was "put together with relatively large building blocks: scales, arpeggios, long cadences," then by the end of the nineteenth century "music had been reduced to individual notes or, at most, short motifs. As in architecture, the arts and crafts movement, and painting, there was a new emphasis on basic materials, primary colors, and elemental substance" (Eksteins 1989: 29). At the turn of the century, art participated in the logic of abundance I describe in this book in its multiplication of parts, its confusions of elements – including the confusion of the natural and the artificial, as in Albright's argument concerning Stravinsky – whose clear delineations have been the very definition of Enlightenment aesthetics, its new experiences and comprehensions of time. (Latour underlines this definition in his description of the absolute separation in early-modern Enlightenment ideology and practice between "purity" and "hybridity." The work of hybridization, which he calls "translation" [1993: 10], might well be understood as apprehended analogies.) Even the stark opposition between audience and artist was confused at the premiere of *The Rite of Spring* so that "the brouhaha surrounding *Le Sacre*," Eksteins argues, "was to be as much in the reactions of the members of the audience to their fellows as in the work itself. The Dancers on stage must have wondered at times who was performing and who was the audience" (1989: 11).

The contrast to the *Quatuor* is remarkable. Messiaen and his fellow prisoners performed the piece before an audience of 5,000 prisoners who were workers, peasants, priests, doctors, intellectuals, "people from every station in life" (Bell 1984: 70). Later, Messiaen himself wrote that "never have I been heard with as much attention and understanding" (cited in Griffiths 1985: 90). The very quiet of the *Quatuor*, against the noisiness of Stravinsky's ballet, offers a different response to the experience, understanding, and wealth of the new century, a logic, so to speak, of austerity. (For a fine technical description – on the level of the language structure of the music – of what Messiaen described as his "wish to articulate my desire for the dissolution of time," see Iain Matheson in which this quote from Messiaen's is cited [1995: 236].) That is, the *Quatuor* marks an aspect of our century and of "abundance" that, like the apocalyptics of Yeats, Rilke, or Schoenberg, is little addressed in what follows. If abundance, as I argue throughout this book, characterizes the problem of the new century in the arts and sciences, then one response to that problem is the rigorous pursuit of the austerity and scarcity of artistic and spiritual value: the pursuit of abstract formalism in art, transcendental meaning in the convergence of religion and politics, unified theory in the sciences. Much of the burden of my earlier book, *Rhetoric and Death* – which the present book focusing on time in many ways continues – is the articulation of the hauntings of death within everyday experience in the early twentieth century. In a similar fashion, the poverty of austerity – nicely imaged in Messiaen and his fellow prisoners, performing on makeshift instruments in an imprisoned winter – "haunts" abundance. Thus I note in chapter 1 – as I noted in *Rhetoric and Death* (1990: 81) – Kafka's observation in *The Castle* that, in the midst of a plethora of choices, K. found that "there was nothing more senseless, nothing more hopeless, than this freedom, this waiting, this inviolability" (1974: 139). Albright makes a homologous argument in discussing Schoenberg when he describes what I am calling the dialectic of abundance and poverty: "side by side with the impatient elaboration of images, there arose an art that is skeptical of mimesis, that insists on the gulf between representation and the thing represented, that denies the referentiality of image and symbol" (1981: 11).

The denial of reference is the burden of Messiaen's music of the "end" of time even if the multiplication and bewilderment of reference in *The Rite of Spring*, where music becomes "all-expressive" and objects become "super-saturated" (Albright 1989: 14, 16), is the burden of Stravinsky's music of the "beginning" of time. Like Theodor Adorno's description of Benjamin's philosophy I quote in chapter 2 – "just as in its most uncompromising representatives modern music no longer tolerates any elaboration, any distinction between theme and development, but instead every musical idea, even every note, stands equally near the center, so too Benjamin's philosophy is 'athematic'" (1992: 229) – Messiaen offers a quartet whose aim, embodied in the sustained and almost silent note with which it ends, is a kind of erasure – a "dissolution" – rather than elaboration of time. "Instead of a metre," Griffiths writes,

which gives each moment in the bar a different significance and hence fosters a sense of orderly progression, Messiaen's music is most frequently tied to a pulse, which insists that all moments are the same, that the past, the present and the future are identifiable. Sometimes the pulse is so slow that causal links are sufficiently distended not to be felt: in these extreme adagios the possibility of eternity becomes actually present in the music. (1985: 15)

Such an "eternity" is, in an important way, the opposite of the abundances described in this book, just as "identity" is the opposite of its multiplied analogies. Such eternity is based upon a strict opposition between the immanent and the transcendental, between the noisy clamor of our world and what Messiaen calls in his Preface to the *Quatuor* "the harmonious silence of heaven" (cited in Griffiths 1985: 94). This opposition also implies the absolute separation of aesthetics and experience, meaning and events, law and phenomena, and the very progressive notions of time that governed Western understandings since the Enlightenment.

This separation is, for Messiaen, very different from the humanist aesthetic of the Enlightenment. "It is a truism," Griffiths writes, "that Western music since the Renaissance has been about man, about beings whose existence in time is short, directed and hopefully progressive. The capacity to speak of God comes only when the march of time is forgotten" (1985: 17). Stravinsky, Griffiths argues, never could forget time – he "never missed keeping his eye on his watch" (1985: 17) – while Messiaen aims at such forgetfulness. Both composers enact in the different language structures of their music what Griffiths calls the "dislocation between music and time" (1985: 106) – both respond to and participate in what I am calling the disruptive abundances of the early twentieth century – but Messiaen's dislocation articulates this response by means of austerity, reduction, and poverty. That is, as I have already said, abundance is only half the story of twentieth-century culture, and many – Yeats and Eliot, and even important moments in Lawrence and Woolf (whom I treat in part I) – like Messiaen, pursue the simplicities of the abstractions that Yeats describes at the beginning of *A Vision* in relation to Brancusi and Russell discovered in the elegance of the identification of mathematics and logic.

Beckett is another, whose art, as he says, attempts to circumscribe or gesture towards (but not "express") what he calls "the ultimate penury" of the world and a "fidelity to failure" of expression (1984: 143, 145). Hugh Kenner nicely describes Beckett's aesthetics of poverty, the erasure of worldly abundance found in his work – as it is in that of Messiaen or even the severe simplicities of Russell's mathematical logic. Kenner quotes Beckett's Malone who begins again "no longer in order to succeed but in order to fail," and goes on to say:

*In order to fail*: in order to accept the inexpressible, which will seep through any membrane art's alchemy can contrive … So like some Henry Moore sculpture, shaping the empty spaces which perforate it, a Beckett play or novel locates and shapes unreason, some unsubduable stuff which permeates the universe and is not to be abolished by refusal to think about it.
… The mysteriousness around the Beckett cosmos is unsubdued, neither equipped with identity papers nor toyed with as Franklin's kite toyed with the lightning. We defer to its circumambiant presence, even while we cherish the rituals round which it seeps; the symmetries of syntax and order, the luminous precisions of phrase. (1973: 188–89)

The severity of this aesthetic, the felt simplicity of its etherous mystery, longs for the end, not the multiplication, of time, timeless moments that in Messiaen are religious and Beckett aesthetic. In this urge Beckett remains a high "Enlightenment" figure, a hero of simplifying spirit against the contaminations of time, just as – in his plainchant as well as his religiosity – Messiaen remains a "pre-Enlightenment" figure.

I am measuring both gestures towards simplicity – aesthetic and scientific-theological – against what I call the "post-Enlightenment" world of abundance. In fact, the very multiplication of responses – this "dialectic" of abundance and poverty where synthesis is impossible – is a form of abundance, in the same way, as I note in chapter 1 and emphasize with its epigraph, that a focus on abundance in the early twentieth century should not "forget" the poverty that exists side by side with abundance and be taken with Whiggish satisfactions. In this book I have little to say about the masters of austerity in the arts and sciences of the early century – of Einstein's anxieties over post-Newtonian science, of Adorno's despair over fascism and its origins in the Enlightenment, of Yeats's horror at the "filthy modern tide," of the powerful transcendentalism of Messiaen's Catholicism and the equally powerful transcendentalism of Beckett's aesthetics of despair. Yet the figure of Benjamin is a thread that holds much together in *Modernism and Time* – even if the ideal of "holding things together" is one of our inheritances that came into question at the turn of the twentieth century – insofar as he brings together in his work both the exuberance and the hopelessness of abundance. It might well be he does so, as I am trying to do, by attempting to hold in a single thought the values of our Enlightenment inheritance – its humanism, its harmonies, its sense of the goodness of worldly wealth – and their concomitant costs. All these things, including the "dialectic" of abundance and poverty, can, I believe, be apprehended in the textures of experience and understanding haunted by time.

### THE TIME OF MODERNISM

For finally, the values of the early twentieth century – like its reason and its aesthetics – provoke, so to speak, a kind of phenomenal temporality (which Habermas apprehends as destructive) that haunts the comprehensions of reason, the experience of art, and the substantiality of those values themselves. In the last essay in *Essays in Persuasion*, entitled "Economic Possibilities for our Grandchildren" (1930), John Maynard Keynes argues that the period of the "modern age" – which he dates from Drake's victory over Spain in 1580 – witnessed the greatest transformation of "the standard of life of the average man living in the civilised centres of the earth" (1931: 360). "From the sixteenth century," he writes,

with a cumulative crescendo after the eighteenth, the great age of science

and technical inventions began, which since the beginning of the nineteenth century has been in full flood – coal, steam, electricity, petrol, steel,
rubber, cotton, the chemical industries, automatic machinery and the
methods of mass production, wireless, printing, Newton, Darwin, and
Einstein, and thousands of other things and men too famous and familiar
to catalogue. (1931: 363)

He goes on to argue that the rate of technical improvements in the
decade since the end of World War I has been so enormous that he
can reasonably imagine that the material needs of human beings –
that had seemed to be "the primary, most pressing problem of the
human race" (1931: 366) – will no longer be the overriding problem
of human life, and that "man will be faced with his real, his
permanent problem" of discovering value in freedom and leisure
without the absolutizing measure of material need (1931: 367).

   Keynes is describing the remarkable *rate* of change at the turn of
the twentieth century – the transformation of industrial capital to
finance capital – and the concomitant re-evaluation of the nature of
need, understanding, and (aesthetic) experience. This transformation
entailed a sea-change in the order of understanding and experience:
to the more or less explicit positivism of "realist" comprehensions of
understanding, value, and experience were added more or less
semiotic comprehensions, which didn't quite supersede received
ideas and experience, but complicated them with the reconceptuali-
zation of need as desire, the raised status of money over "real"
estate, and the recognition of complexities of overdeterminations as
phenomena not easily reduced to atemporal formulas, among other
things. In this book I am arguing that a focus on the experience of
time can help us to gather together and comprehend the understanding and experience of people living through these changes –
that which has come to be called the cultural Modernism of the
early twentieth century. Time is not the only way to arrange and
comprehend Modernism – literary critics such as Donald Davie,
Hugh Kenner, Sheri Benstrock have attempted to capture its sense
by focusing on the intellectual and experiential lives of particular
literary figures living through this period; historians like Stephen
Kern, Eric Hobsbawm, and David Harvey have attempted to
capture its sense by focusing on the economic and technological
innovations of this period; intellectual historians such as Jackson
Lears, Carolyn Marvin, and Bruno Latour have attempted to
capture its sense by focusing on the transformation of ideas of this

period. But a focus on the experience of time allows me to present an understanding of the wealth, experience, and intellectual assumptions of this era without positing the economic as the "cause" of the seeming "superstructure" of experience, value, and ideology. Instead, the experience of time "answers," in Bakhtin's sense, other departments of life, informing them, shaping their assumptions, and responding to their forces. It is some soundings of such answers that I hope to describe in what follows.

# PART I

*Post-Enlightenment apprehensions*

CHAPTER I

# The Enlightenment, abundance, and postmodernity

We are in this techno-scientific world like Gulliver: sometimes too big, sometimes too small, never at the right scale. Consequently, the claim for simplicity, in general, appears today that of a barbarian.

From this point, it would be necessary to consider the division of mankind into two parts: one part confronted with the challenge of complexity; the other with the terrible ancient task of survival. This is a major aspect of the failure of the modern project (which was, in principle, valid for mankind as a whole).

Jean-François Lyotard, "Defining the Postmodern" (1993: 173)

Many scholars have argued that great intellectual and social shifts of the seventeenth and eighteenth centuries – what has recently come to be called the early modern period of Western culture, but what has been called the Enlightenment – culminated in the triumph of the scientific-secular middle-class culture of the late nineteenth and early twentieth century.[1] Such a triumph manifested itself in what Fredric Jameson describes as

one of the most active periods in human history, with all the smoke and conveyance inherent in new living conditions and in the rapid development of business and industry, with the experimental triumphs of positivistic science and its conquest of the university system, with all the bustling parliamentary and bureaucratic activity of the new middle-class regimes, the spread of the press, the diffusion of literacy and the rise of mass culture ... [in] an increasingly consumer-oriented civilization. (1981: 251)

In this chapter, I argue that the very success of the Enlightenment, its creation of vast wealth in terms of material goods, of intellectual accomplishments and, indeed, of human populations led to a "crisis of abundance" in the twenty years leading up to the First World War (Kern 1983: 9). Such a crisis, I hope to demonstrate throughout

35

*Modernism and Time*, conditioned remarkable transformations in the arts and sciences and in the experience of everyday life for people living through it. It demanded new ways of making sense out of experience, whose confusions weren't the result of need and dearth, as they were for such great Enlightenment figures as Isaac Newton, Adam Smith, and George Eliot, but whose confusions stemmed from difficulties that arise from abundance and plenty.

This is not to say that the achievements of the Enlightenment – the great "second Industrial Revolution" of the late nineteenth century and the coincident rise of literary and cultural Modernism, post-Newtonian science, and the creation of social sciences such as psychology, anthropology, and systematic semiotics – did away with need and scarcity. Rather, the material, intellectual, and human abundance of this period, recorded in cultural Modernism and Modernist science, created a world in which abundance and scarcity existed side by side so that the modes of understanding conditioned by need – that is, Enlightenment modes of understanding – existed alongside modes of understanding conditioned by abundance. Such a multiplication of ways of making sense of experience is, in fact, itself a kind of abundance, and it raises important questions about the basic assumptions of Enlightenment knowledge, its reason, its criteria for judging truth, and its humanist understandings of who, precisely, is the "subject" of reason, knowledge, and experience itself.

In the course of pursuing this argument I will present some representative figures from our cultural history. Specifically, in this chapter I discuss briefly Adam Smith, along with his heir in classical economics, Karl Marx, in relation to political economy and the underlying values of Enlightenment understanding; I discuss Werner Heisenberg, along with his contemporary in post-Newtonian science, Norbert Wiener, in relation to the transformation from a mechanical world-view to an informational world-view in the context of post-Enlightenment value; and I frame these discussions of wealth and understanding by examining literary works of twentieth-century Modernism – Virginia Woolf's critique of Enlightenment aesthetics (from the vantage of the upper middle class) in *Mrs. Dalloway* and James Joyce's critique of Enlightenment modernity more generally (from the vantage of the lower middle class) in *Dubliners* – in the context of Jonathan Swift's "pre-Enlightenment" critique of the new world of Enlightenment modernity (from the

vantage of the aristocracy) in *Gulliver's Travels.* I will also glance at
one of the great Enlightenment humanists, George Eliot, whom I
treat at greater length in chapter 2: in my mind George Eliot joins
Thomas Jefferson as the embodiment of the highest values of the
Enlightenment.

Let me make clear what is at stake in my discussion of the relationship between Enlightenment understanding and post-Enlightenment
apprehensions of knowledge, wealth, and meaning. To define ourselves in relation to the Enlightenment, now in the late twentieth
century, is to engage ourselves with our cultural past. For Enlightenment modernity, time is simply and absolutely succession: in Isaac
Newton's famous description, it exists as an "absolute, true, and
mathematical time, [that] of itself, and from its own nature flows
equably without relation to anything external" (Newton 1964: 17). In
this definition, time is always and everywhere the same; it is the
container of events that in no way affects or is affected by the events
that make up its "content": as I mentioned in the Introduction, it is
a mystical, non-material ether that makes experience comprehensible. Religion and God served this function, less neutrally and less
"simply," for pre-Enlightenment experience. In our time we have
returned to kinds of baroque and piecemeal comprehensions, what
Jean-François Lyotard calls the confrontation of different modes of
necessity in the epigraph to this chapter, and what I am calling the
particular problems – the logic – of abundance.

In the pre-Enlightenment understanding of medieval historiography and narrative, as Elizabeth Ermarth has argued, the meaningful distinctions in comprehending time "depend upon the
contrast between time and eternity" (1983: 25). Enlightenment
definitions, such as Newton's, homogenize time so that the opposite
of time is not another species of time, "eternity," but the (logical)
absence of time, an "atemporal" essence. "When time and space are
conceived as homogeneous," Ermarth argues,

– that is, the same universally – then it becomes possible to chart both the
differences and similarities in nature which give rise to those generalizations in science and art that we call laws. In formulating such laws no
attempt is made to save the appearances. In fact, we might say that in

reducing the welter of particulars to some abstract regularity, scientific and realistic generalizations represent an attempt to save the essences. (1983: 17–18)

Atemporal "essences" replace sacred "eternity" as the opposite to time in Enlightenment secularization and result in the homogeneity of past and present. Such essences take the form of "invariant form" (Ermarth 1983: 34) and "hidden wholes" – "wholes, or identities, which are independent of any particular form of visual apprehension or, as in the novel, of apprehension by a single consciousness in a single moment" (1983: 16) – such as the "mankind as a whole" Lyotard mentions in the epigraph. In post-Enlightenment thinking, past and present are not "homogenized" by atemporal essences, but rather confront one another in ways that do not preclude the abstract regularities of science and art, but make those abstractions *momentary* (as opposed to the reduction of temporal moments to atemporal infinitesimals in Newtonian and Leibnizian calculus [see chapter 4]), inhabited and complicated by time.

For the Newtonian tradition of the Enlightenment, the homogeneity of time allowed for secular simplicity: every moment is "original"; every moment presents the subject of experience with a new beginning, a clean slate. This is why Descartes can assert that reason is closely associated with the individual: thus he writes that "I have never contemplated anything higher than the reformation of my own opinions, and basing them on foundations wholly my own" (cited in Gellner 1992: 3).[2] Moreover, the mind and soul of the Cartesian man stand "outside" time, "ghosts" in the machine of a wholly secular and mechanical world. Descartes' great description of this situation – one I am very reluctant to describe to students since it might lead them astray – is that his philosophy began when he realized he did not have to get out of bed in the morning to do his intellectual work.

The mode of thought about time that characterizes Enlightenment modernity has serious implications for the three areas of concern I am examining in *Modernism and Time*: material life, intellectual life, and daily experience. First of all, such a conception of time as an autonomous, homogeneous flow in a single direction separates people from the past absolutely, without confrontation or collision. The past becomes a storehouse of images, to use Yeats's figure, and while we might take advice from the past, there is no way that we can affect what has already happened. To use a phrase from

Walter Benjamin, there is no way we can "redeem" the past. Thus, despite the furious Enlightenment controversies over theology, Newton's absolute and formal conception of time is ultimately a thoroughly secular conception.[3] Moreover, as I have suggested, the conception of an atemporal subject of history, as embodied in Descartes' description of the organization of human life as what has been called the ghost in the machine, presents a thoroughly materialist conception of the world.

It is precisely such materialism that Swift parodies in *Gulliver's Travels* in the repeated references to Gulliver's bodily functions. A generation ago, Norman O. Brown argued in a chapter of *Life Against Death* entitled "The Excremental Vision" that Swift's theme, like that of Descartes, "is the conflict between our animal body, appropriately epitomized in the anal function, and our pretentious sublimations, more specifically the pretensions of sublimated or romantic-Platonic love" (1959: 186). Brown uses *Gulliver's Travels* as a vehicle for his sweeping rereading of psychoanalysis, yet it seems clear to me that there is a remarkable anachronism in his discussion – Freudian psychoanalysis is precisely a product of the late nineteenth-century culture that Jameson described.[4] Rather, Swift's effect in his repeated depictions of Gulliver's excremental functions is to demonstrate that Gulliver is such a materialist that *any* material event in his travels is worthy of note. Thus, after describing how he "discharged the necessities of nature" in Brobdingnag, he says: "I hope the gentle reader will excuse me for dwelling on these and the like particulars, which however insignificant they may appear to groveling vulgar minds, yet will certainly help a philosopher to enlarge his thoughts and imagination ... which was my sole design in presenting this and other accounts of my travels to the world" (1960: 107). For Gulliver every "matter of fact" is worthy of note because every temporal event is unique and, as a material event, atomistically important.

I say "atomistically" because it is precisely Gulliver's inability to connect events and gather them into a whole that is the object of Swift's satire. The clearest example of this is Gulliver's description of the foundering of the *Antelope*, the ship of his first voyage. Although he was the ship's surgeon, Gulliver describes the ship going down because "twelve of our crew were dead by immoderate labour and ill food, the rest were in a very weak condition" (1960: 26) without any recognition that as a doctor he might have some responsibility for this situation. Throughout the *Travels* Gulliver presents himself as an outside observer: even the sentence structure of subject, verb, object reinforces this position as a knowing subject without any connection to or responsibility for the temporal events recorded. Moreover, his relationship to the past is no different. Gulliver reports that he has read "the best authors, ancient and modern" (1960: 26), but his reading fails to "answer" his experience: throughout his account he repeatedly quotes such authors inappropriately. For instance, he wishes he had the eloquence of Demosthenes and Cicero to praise his country (1960: 141) even though both of these authors were eloquent precisely in attacking injustice in their countries; and in the end he quotes Sinon, the great liar of the *Iliad*, to buttress his claim that he strictly tells the truth (1960: 314). Swift, Hugh Kenner has argued, "is interested in a special idiosyncrasy of Gulliver's, which is to be aware of nothing but incremental evidence" (1978: 4; see also Kenner 1968 where he educes many of the examples I am presenting here); among other things, Kenner says, we are presented with "the Gulliverian principle that time has no forward loopings, and that an eyewitness ... will recount what he observed in the sequence in which he observed it" (1978: 8).

Swift's critique of the new attitude toward the world foregrounds three basic assumptions that govern Enlightenment humanism as it arises in the early modern period, assumptions concerning reason, the individual subject of reason and experience, and the absolute opposition between matter and spirit. I have already articulated two of these assumptions: that the sequence of time is absolute and that both reason and the individual reasoning subject are atemporal. The corollary to this second assumption is that the atemporal subject of knowledge and experience is fully conscious. Swift underlines the weakness of this corollary when he presents, to a particular educated audience, the disparity between what Gulliver says in quoting Sinon and what that audience will know beyond Gulliver's conscious awareness. Such disparity forms the language structure of Swift's satire and occurs throughout the book, but perhaps the most glaring narrative (as opposed to verbal) example is at the end, when Gulliver describes himself spending "at least four hours every day" (1960: 312) in the stable talking to horses he recently bought, which unlike the Houyhnhnms cannot talk, without any sense of how crazy such behavior would seem.

All three of these assumptions – the absolutely unvarying nature of time; the individual and atemporal nature of the reasoning subject; and the unvarying consciousness of spirit as opposed to absolutely unconscious matter – are conditioned by dearth and parsimony rather than abundance. This is most clear in the particular notion of reason that arose in the late seventeenth century as part of Enlightenment humanism. This notion is fully embodied in Gulliver's curiosity and his ability to atomize his experience and accept particular events on face value, such as the illness of his fellow sailors, with great gullibility. The aim of the traditional or classical conception of reason was to discover and describe first principles, universal truths that governed phenomena under consideration by providing them with what churchmen often called "right reason." In this way the reasonable was the "fitting" and "proper," and Aristotle, for instance, could equate the law with "order" or "reason" and assert that reason was the highest of men's faculties because it allowed them to understand the order of the cosmos and to pursue their lives accordingly.[5]

In the early eighteenth century Leibniz subtly altered Aristotle's conception when he asserted in the *Monadology* that "the knowledge of eternal and necessary truths is that which distinguishes us from mere animals and gives us reason and the sciences, thus raising us to knowledge of ourselves and of God. This is what is called in us the Rational Soul or the Mind" (1902: 257). This knowledge, according to Leibniz, is the result of "Reflective Acts" of individuals, and it is

based upon two great principles: first, that of Contradiction, by means of which we decide that to be false which involves contradiction and that to be true which contradicts or is opposed to the false.

And second, the principle of Sufficient Reason, in virtue of which we believe that no fact can be real or existing and no statement true unless it has a sufficient reason why it should be thus and not otherwise. Most frequently, however, these reasons cannot be known by us. (1902: 258)

Leibniz goes on to distinguish the necessary truths of reason from the contingent truths of fact, that is, to distinguish, absolutely, atemporal spirit and temporal matter. What is important to my argument, however, is that these principles emphasize the simplicity or parsimony governing Enlightenment reason: the principle of Contradiction forces choices of either/or on the subject of reason (who "decides," on his own, using the principle); and the principle of Sufficient Reason satisfies itself with sufficiency rather than multiplicity – what Freud calls at the turn of the twentieth century the "overdeterminations" of multiple rather than sufficient causes in the bustling economy of our psychological life. In a word, these two principles present, simply, what is necessary and sufficient in reason itself. Similarly, Descartes presents the same simplicity in his call for "clear and distinct ideas."[6]

In these definitions Leibniz is enacting the great transformation in philosophy during the Enlightenment, "the Cartesian ... triumph of the quest for certainty over the quest for wisdom" (Rorty 1979: 61) that elevated the reductive formalism of mathematics – its pure and atemporal *method* – over the impurities of the interpretations of rhetoric, narrative, and history. Certainty, rather than the balance of sanity, the propriety of rightness, and the comfort of peace, became the object of philosophy. If sanity, rightness, and peace – in a word, wisdom itself – are worldly then the methodical epistemology in Descartes' quest for certainty is the function of an atemporal subject, one who stands outside the experience he comprehends.[7] Swift parodies such unworldliness when he has Gulliver protest that he has not had a love affair with a twelve-inch-tall woman in Lilliput.

I take the term "worldly" from the work of Edward Said. "There must be," he writes, "it seems to me, a theoretical presumption that in matters having to do with human history and society any rigid theoretical ideal, any simple additive or mechanical notion of what is or is not factual, must yield to the central factor of human work, the actual participation of people in the making of human life" (1994: 147). He goes on to say that "this kind of human work, which is intellectual work, is worldly," that it is "situated in the world, and about that world" (1994: 147) and that it is engaged with culture in an "unprovincial, interested manner" (1994: 151). What Said describes in terms of "worldliness" – both "unprovincial" and "interested" – contradicts "disinterested" Enlightenment simplicities in powerful and troubling ways. Said's contradiction of Enlightenment unworldiness – more than the easy laughter of Swift's traditionalism – is that the responsibility and ethics of post-Enlightenment "worldliness" lends itself neither to the absolute revelations of pre-Enlightenment thinking nor to the simple formulaics of Enlightenment universalism.[8]

In any case, within the Enlightenment economy of reasonable simplicity, the atemporal subject of knowledge and experience is always fully conscious: the dream of the Enlightenment is that the atemporal reasoning subject can be the source of knowledge and, indeed, of existence altogether. This is the import of Descartes' famous dictum, "I think, therefore I am." Another way to say this is to note that since the "absolute, true, and mathematical time" of Newton cannot confuse or taint the absolute (ideal) reasoning subject, that subject will always be conscious. This is because what is "unconscious," as we use the term both in Freud's sense and in a more general sense, always manifests itself in confusions of temporal contexts. Thus, the disparity between what Gulliver means at the moment he quotes Sinon and what the words meant in the temporally different contexts of Homer's and of Swift's educated audiences disrupts the equable flow of time. And when Gulliver declares that he is "obliged to vindicate the reputation of an excellent [twelve-inch-tall] lady" (1960: 77) in a book appearing half a world away from the scene of this ludicrous scandal, he is assuming that events are universally and transparently "true" – altogether certain – because time and place cannot affect the content of knowledge.

The autonomy of time, I am suggesting, is a function of its absolute continuity, the "principle of continuity" that Ernst Cassirer has argued is the basis of "Leibniz's mathematics and his entire metaphysics" (1951: 30). The assumption and conception of continuous development through time are at the heart of the bourgeois/ Enlightenment order of the eighteenth and nineteenth centuries (see Lowe 1982: 11), and within this absolute temporal continuity the necessity of the full consciousness of an atemporal subject of knowledge and experience can be discerned. Thus Michel Foucault argues that

continuous history is the indispensable correlative of the founding function of the subject: the guarantee that everything that has eluded him may be restored to him; the certainty that time will disperse nothing without restoring it in a reconstituted unity; the promise that one day the subject – in the form of historical consciousness – will once again be able to appropriate, to bring back under his sway, all those things that are kept at a distance by difference, and find in them what might be called his abode. Making historical analysis the discourse of the continuous and making human consciousness the original subject of all historical development and all action are the two sides of the same system of thought. In this system, time is conceived in terms of totalization and revolutions are never more than moments of consciousness. (1972: 12)

The "time" of liberal humanism – the Enlightenment desacralization of time that ushers in secular bourgeois society, neutral science, and the progressivist, semiotic political economy of Adam Smith – is continuous, objective, and intimately tied up with the atemporal subject of knowledge. Moreover, it is tied up with the homogeneous continuity of time: this is what Foucault means by its "totalizing" nature in which revolutions – what Benjamin calls "messianic" flashes in time, dialectics at a standstill – are only illusions. Moreover, insofar as this conception of continuous time loses nothing – no excess, no waste, no abundance – it too is a form of parsimony.[9]

MATERIAL GOODS

These assumptions – of universal reason that uncovers the necessary laws of the world, and of a fully conscious, atemporal, individual subject of that reason – are the bases of Enlightenment thinking. The third assumption, as I have said, is that there is an absolute distinction between matter and spirit – Latour describes this as the distinction between "immanence" and "transcendence" (1993: 34) – in which the world is fully material, unredeemable, and governed fully by sequential time. This last assumption creates the possibility of unconsciousness in people, but only insofar as they are "material"; only insofar as they are "machines," as Descartes says, governed by universal laws that atemporal reasoning spirit can uncover. Such unconsciousness is only "momentary" and not a necessary element of human life conceived as spirit. There is a clear example of this kind of thinking outside of literature in the cheerful economic analyses of Adam Smith's *The Wealth of Nations*, which combine the reason and individualism of the Enlightenment (see Gellner 1992). Smith embodies these assumptions in the "general semiotics" of his economics – that is, the impersonal, systematic presentation of the logic of meaning and value in his analysis of emerging capitalism – and as the "subjective idealism" of the political economy inhabited by autonomous citizens. (These two elements in Smith correspond to Latour's description of Enlightenment modernity more generally as "the double task of domination and emancipation" [1993: 10] I mentioned in the Introduction.) Smith is important for my argument because he allows us to see clearly the relationship between impersonal reason – as Leibniz says, its "eternal and necessary" nature – and the individual subject of reason sufficient for its realization. (Descartes' "clear and distinct ideas" also combines the clarity required by the individual subject of reason and the distinctions required by reason's impersonal semiotics.) What allows Smith to combine impersonal semiotics and ideal subjectivity is universal need. Each individual citizen for Smith is interchangeable with other citizens – such interchange, in fact, defines the logic of semiotic systems – precisely because material human beings have the same needs, which are simple and limited.

The greatest expression of this paradox in Smith is his famous doctrine of the "invisible hand" in *The Wealth of Nations*. This doctrine – which Mark Blaug calls "the central theme that inspires the *Wealth of Nations*" (1985: 60) – opposes the personal considerations of Royal patents, charters, and regulations of the King insofar as these considerations rely on local interests rather than the general order of "natural" goodness. Thus Smith notes, every private individual within a system of political economy "neither intends to promote the public interest, nor knows how much he is promoting it." Rather, "by directing [his] industry in such a manner as its produce may be of the greatest value, he intends only his own gain, and he is in this, as in many other cases, led by an invisible hand to promote an end which was not part of his intention" (1937: 423). In this classic statement, Smith is joining the local and individual with the general and common. For Smith, this is simply the "nature" of things, just as for his contemporary Enlightenment thinker, Immanuel Kant, there must be a "subjective principle of common sense," a "good nature" which allows for the harmony of human faculties and the harmony between the (universal) human and Nature (see Deleuze 1984: 22–23; Davis and Schleifer 1991: 12–15).

For Smith, wealth, labor, consumption – even the manifestation of all of these in money – is at once particular and general. The nation itself, in *The Wealth of Nations*, is both local and the general aggregate of unique but interchangeable individuals and the aggregate of abstract, Newtonian spaces. This is why Smith defines use-value not in terms of particular consumption, but in terms of generalized need: he thinks of "utility not as the power to satisfy a particular want ... but as the power to satisfy a generalized biological or social need" (Blaug 1985: 40). With such generalization, the "local" nature of consumption is also always general and universal, and wealth is always "national" in this particular combination of local and general. These assumptions lead Smith to argue against colonialism – this is the burden of the final pages of *The Wealth of Nations* – and they lead him to posit, absolutely, the categories of "individuals" and "semiotics," the citizens and system of political economy.

The crucial nature of universal need in this argument is clearer in Marx's analysis of political economy. At the heart of Marx's analysis of capital is the concept, borrowed from David Ricardo, of the labor theory of value. The labor theory posits that the value of a commodity can only be measured by the amount of human labor that is expended in creating that commodity. Marx argues that the creation of "surplus value" and the accumulation of capital is based on the discrepancy between the value of a day's labor as a commodity purchased from the worker at full value in terms of what it costs to produce that commodity – namely, the food, clothing, and shelter that allows the worker to live for a day – and the amount of value the laborer produces through his labor (see 1967: chs. 6 and 7). Thus, the subsistence of the laborer might require the value of six labor hours, all told, which the capitalist pays in full while he obtains the value of ten labor hours from the worker. The difference for Marx is "surplus value." At the heart of Marx's analysis, as it is at the heart of Smith's, is that workers have universal needs, "basic" needs: food, clothing, shelter. What makes these needs "basic" is precisely their simplicity. Like the parsimony of Enlightenment reason, they create the necessary and sufficient conditions – atemporal conditions – for life and labor. Similarly, the concept of use-value in classical economics is directly related to this idea of basic need. For both Smith and Marx, the value of a pair of shoes is best measured in and by the first pair of shoes we acquire, the pair we need because it answers a basic necessity.

But what about a world in which we already have a dozen pairs of shoes, pumps, hiking boots, workshoes, sneakers? What about a world of abundance? How do we measure the value of a pair of Nikes compared to Reebok when, without them, we still wouldn't go barefoot? When we focus on the "first" pair of shoes, the basic pair, we are inhabiting the position of the individual in the Enlightenment world – which is to say the postulated, rational, and above all *idealized* world of truths that exist once and for all – situated between absolute, material temporal sequence and atemporal understanding. This paradoxical situation is created by the parsimonious equation of a temporal "first" and an atemporal "basic." (Such an equation underlines Smith's assumption of the underlying goodness of the order of things.) But when we focus on the value of the "last" pair of shoes we have – what the neoclassical economics of the 1880s called the "marginal" pair – the situation of the analyst is significantly different. First of all, the "last" pair is neither necessary nor sufficient: as Imelda Marcos has shown, a "last" pair can always become the "second-to-last" pair. In this situation – it is fully a temporal situation – Marx's crucial distinction between basic (or "primary") "use-value" and secondary "exchange-value" breaks down.[10]

Moreover, under the conditions of abundance, the hierarchy of production over products also is transformed. Both Smith and Marx describe an economic world in which the means of production takes precedence over the products of those means: they embody "the productivist legacy of the Enlightenment" (Birkin 1988: 22) where above all the production of wealth is more important than the consumption of wealth. Smith even makes an important distinction between productive and non-productive labor in terms of accumulation versus consumption (1937: 314–15). For the neoclassical economists of the late nineteenth century faced with the abundances of the second Industrial Revolution, the object of analysis was not production but consumption. In their work, for the first time in economic analysis both scarcity and time became significant factors. Scarcity replaced need as the measure of value: in this way exchange value encompassed use value as a measure of worth. (See Xenos 1989 and Sassover 1990 for important discussions of "scarcity.") Moreover, time replaced production as a measure of worth as the very products of the economy – the very "wealth" Smith describes – became, for neoclassical economics, simply "indirect or delayed consumption" (Birkin 1988: 26). For Smith and Marx, production constantly and infinitely expands, just as for Newton time is an unending expansion of ongoing sequence, while the neoclassical theorists "repealed the bourgeois law of progressive development implicit in the old classical conception of an ongoing expanding production" (Birkin 1988: 26).

The transformation of economic analysis from that of need to that of desire – for this certainly is what we are talking about when the focus changes from the first or basic pair of shoes that people have to have to a focus on their last pair of shoes that they can live without – the transformation from need to desire replaces a parsimonious economics of necessity and sufficiency with a commodious economics of desire and surplus. In these circumstances, the problem of economics is not understanding the production of wealth, but understanding the distribution of products. Even the strict demarcations between disciplinary questions break down in the face of abundance just as the strict demarcations between need and production and between production and products break down into a semiotics of exchange.[11] Moreover, the enormous wealth of late nineteenth-century Europe I outlined at the beginning of this chapter – the abundances of the second Industrial Revolution – occasioned the rethinking of the basic assumptions of the Enlightenment I have been describing. The products of the first Industrial Revolution of the late eighteenth century in England and Europe were foodstuffs, furniture, and textiles – the very food, shelter, and clothing of Marx's description of the labor theory of value – while the products of the second Industrial Revolution were steel, telephones, automobiles, film, airplanes, smokeless gun powder, school teachers, finance capital, bicycles, breakfast cereals, commercial travelers, skyscrapers, office workers, electric light, and a host of other commodities answering (or provoking) desire beyond simple or basic "universal" need. A vast array of new commodities disrupted not only traditional experience of daily life but, more importantly, the settled simple hierarchy – the Enlightenment hierarchy – between production and product, principle and example, the present and the past.

## THE PROBLEM OF ABUNDANCE AND THE EXPERIENCE OF TIME

Abundance creates problems just as dearth does, but the kinds of problems it creates are different, and the reductionist methods of understanding – for surely the positivist generalizing simplicities of Enlightenment understanding are ultimately reductive in their explanations – gave way to different modes of understanding. As I argue later in this chapter and in chapter 5, Werner Heisenberg presents one such mode of understanding in post-Newtonian physics as the pursuit of multiple "alternating" descriptions and "retrospective" descriptions rather than categorizing phenomena in terms of simple reductive principles; Roman Jakobson multiplies the "levels" of understanding in linguistic analysis just as high Modernist art forms, from Cubism to stream of consciousness fiction, multiply "levels" of experience; Freud, as I have mentioned, describes the "overdeterminations" of psychological life; and Donald MacKay, in the Macy conferences that defined information theory in the 1950s, describes the multiple layers of "structural information" (see Hayles 1994). Retrospective description, alternating levels of analysis, over-determined causes, and information conceived beyond materialism and idealism are all modes of understanding that respond to phenomena – goods, ideas, experience – that do not lend themselves *at all times* to necessary and sufficient explanations. They are all post-Enlightenment modes of understanding.

What these strategies share can be gathered together – can be "constellated" – in relation to changing conceptions of time. Newton and the secularization of science in the Newtonian tradition of mathematical physics conceived time as real, ongoing, and autonomously self-consistent. In fact, these three categories articulate the parsimonious criteria governing scientific "truth" in the Enlightenment: truth is accurate, general (atemporal), and simple (see Schleifer et al. 1992: 15). Early twentieth-century thinkers, on the other hand, re-imagined the nature of time in "truths" that at times could be better comprehended as alternating (as opposed to accurate), retrospectively comprehended (as opposed to general and atemporal), and overdetermined (as opposed to simple). Thus philosophers as different in temperament as Ludwig Wittgenstein and Henri Bergson came to understand that the very definition of time was a problem. In the *Tractatus Logico-Philosophicus* (1921) Wittgenstein writes:

We cannot compare any process with the "passage of time" – there is no such thing – but only with another process (say, with the movement of the chronometer).

Hence the description of the temporal sequence of events is only possible if we support ourselves on another process. (1990: 6.3611)

*In Time and Free Will* (1889) Bergson wrote in a very different register that "our ordinary conception of duration depends on a gradual incursion of space into the domain of pure consciousness." This is "proved," he goes on, by focusing on dreaming where "we no longer measure duration, but we feel it; from quantity it returns to the state of quality; we no longer estimate past time mathematically: the mathematical estimate gives place to a confused instinct, capable, like all instincts, of committing gross errors, but also of acting at times with extraordinary skill" (1960: 126–27). These two descriptions of time – Wittgenstein's call (particularly in his later work) for a kind of analogical thinking which multiplies frameworks of understanding rather than mechanistically reducing them and Bergson's citing the overdeterminations of dream experience to define temporality – answer Leibniz's two principles of Reason with modes of nonreductive reasoning.

That is, if Enlightenment modernity is a particular mode of thought about time, then post-Enlightenment thinking disrupts that mode, but not simply and absolutely – simple absoluteness, after all, characterizes Enlightenment reason in the simplicity of non-contradiction and the absoluteness of sufficient reason. It disrupts that mode of thought by creating the "complexification of what appeared to be simple," as Gaston Bachelard says of post-Newtonian physics (1984: 45). Jacques Derrida describes this process in an odd phrase, as an "irreducibly nonsimple ... synthesis" (1982: 13). This is an odd description, I think, because it willfully avoids our simple word for "nonsimple," namely "complex." Such nonsimplicity marks a post-Enlightenment mode of thought about time, in which there is not a strict hierarchy between past and present, with either an absolute and "objective" past overwhelming the present moment of memory or the present moment simply using the "storehouse" of the past for its own purposes. In a post-Enlightenment mode of temporalized apprehension, as Bill Readings has argued, "history is not a panoply of past events, written about in an unhistorical present ... [Rather,] the time of inscription comes both *after* history and *before* it, since History is in a sense constituted by the possibility of being re-transcribed" (1991: 58–59). In this "complexification" of history and time itself, as in Wittgenstein's multiplications of processes in order to "recover" time, time is multiplied and doubled abundantly. The present inhabits the past as much as the past inhabits the present.

It does so because the subjects of time, like the subjects of value in neoclassical economics and the subjects of knowledge in post-Enlightenment apprehensions of history, are faced, actively, with overwhelming abundance. That is, the past is not something to be recovered, but something, in Benjamin's terms, to be redeemed, and such redemption necessitates the active ethical commitment of the historian, the consumer, and even the ordinary person. I say "ethical" because the problem of abundance is choice even while the problem of dearth in the Enlightenment is duty. "Duty" is a key word for George Eliot, for whom faithfulness to a past that cannot change is the highest good precisely because it entails the "truth" of parsimonious renunciation. Thus, in *The Mill on the Floss* Maggie Tulliver is completely tied to the duty to a past that cannot change rather than actively pursuing a choice about her future. The same is true in relation to Swift's Gulliver, for whom the past is de-temporalized into a form of pre-existing Nature: he gullibly accepts every visible likeness – every simple likeness – between the present and the past until he convinces himself his wife and children are animals and his horses boon companions.

Both Gulliver and George Eliot exist in economies of need, the discourse of necessity and sufficiency. The world of George Eliot is a world of great need: "the emphasis of want" that faces Maggie throughout *The Mill on the Floss* (1961: 256) characterizes human life. The "needs" she describes are "common things," reproducible, diurnal, constantly pressing, and even in the cluttered world of Victorian capitalism they are as simple as the simplicities of food, clothing, and shelter in Marx's labor theory of value. In her novel George Eliot describes the medieval monk, Thomas à Kempis, precisely in this way. His work, the narrator says,

remains to all time a lasting record of human needs and human consolations: the voice of a brother who, ages ago, felt and suffered and renounced – in the cloister, perhaps, with serge gown and tonsured head, with much chanting and long fasts, and with a fashion of speech different from ours – but under the same silent far-off heavens, and with the same passionate desires, the same strivings, the same failures, the same weariness. (1961: 255)

In this description, time is negligible, just as the differences between medieval culture and George Eliot's secular culture is negligible in the face of what is constant in human affairs. In important ways, George Eliot wants us to see and feel the interchangeability of middle-aged monk and teenage girl, the equivalence of monastic and secular desire, the fact that time itself is experienced the same way across so much time.

Such a sense of the uniformity of the past and of time itself would make little sense to Bergson or Wittgenstein. For Bergson, dream-time creates feeling and instinct that lend themselves to both error and skill. In this state, the subject is not atemporal, but is intimately immersed in the time of experience; and time itself is not wholly or simply sequential. Such temporality, as Readings suggests (1991: 59), is analogous to the "deferred action" that Freud describes, which confuses and multiplies time. Freud first used the term in the case of the *Wolf Man* in 1918. "At the age of one and a half," he writes,

the child receives an impression to which he is unable to react adequately; he is only able to understand it and to be moved by it when the impression is revived in him at the age of four; and only twenty years later, during the analysis, is he able to grasp with his conscious mental processes what was then going on in him. The patient justifiably disregards the three periods of time, and puts his present ego into the situation which is so long past. (1963: 232)

The subject of this history is altogether temporal in the abundance of a temporality of disruption, even if Freud describes here the mechanism by which the ego creates the illusion of continuity. Jacques Lacan refers to this time as a "strange temporality" in which "something other demands to be realized – which appears as intentional, of course, but of a strange temporality" (1977: 25). The "other" to be realized is the "other time" of other people's lives – even when those "other people" are our own childish selves Freud recovers from our dreams. The fact that Freud traces those selves through time is precisely a mark of both abundance and disconti- nuity: it marks the fact that a person is not simply, atemporally one self.

### POST-ENLIGHTENMENT EXPERIENCE AND POSTMODERN PANIC

Post-Enlightenment literary responses to the abundances of the second Industrial Revolution can be seen in the narratives of Virginia Woolf and James Joyce. I choose these examples both for their distinctions from Swift and George Eliot – this chapter's other literary examples – but also for their own different approaches to narrative understanding and rendering of temporality in relation to their depictions of middle-class and lower-middle-class experience. As I argue in chapter 3, the enormous increase in the lower middle class is one of the significant "abundances" of the second Industrial Revolution, and in the juxtaposition of Woolf and Joyce we can see the collision between the "past" of petty bourgeois sensibility and the "present" of lower-middle-class sensibility. (The protagonists of both *Gulliver's Travels* and *The Mill on the Floss* are members of what later came to be called the petty bourgeoisie.)

Both Woolf and Joyce (unlike George Eliot in the parsimony of her sympathetic reason) offer rhetorical examples of abundance in the "language structure" of their narratives. In *Mrs. Dalloway* abundance takes the form of linguistic "offerings" – the extraordinary gifts that constellate themselves throughout the novel. Characters speak the same language to such a degree that they can speak as one another consciously and unconsciously: the subjects of narrative discourse explode into abundance. As Daniel Albright has noted, "the nineteenth century prepares us for many of the characteristic forms of the twentieth, but not, I think, for this tumult [in Virginia Woolf], this agony of identity, these dubious characters merging into each other or splitting ... When reading her novels," he concludes, "we feel that her world's dynamics are impossible, exaggerated" (1978: 96). In *Dubliners*, on the other hand, rather than in Woolf's cacophonies of subjectivity, abundant rhetoric finds competing voices wherever it turns in a kind of Foucauldian or Bakhtinian world of multiplied discourses that Hugh Kenner has described as "Joyce's voices" (1978). In the terms developed in the next chapter, Woolf and Joyce pursue discursive strategies analogous to the "dialectical image" and "quotation without quotation marks" that Benjamin articulated in the early decades of the twentieth century. In both strategies, language betrays panic in its easy recourse to cliché and, below cliché, a sense of the aimlessness of its choices, the gnawing feeling that in the midst of abundance, as Kafka expresses it in *The Castle*, "there was nothing more senseless, nothing more hopeless, than this freedom, this waiting, this inviolability" (1974: 139).

The upper-middle-class world of London Woolf portrays resolves itself into self-conscious spatial and temporal constellations. When Clarissa Dalloway thinks about the party she will hold at the end of the novel, for instance, she images it in terms of the ways that she will bring people together.

But suppose Peter said to her, "Yes, yes, but your parties – what's the sense of your parties?" all she could say was (and nobody could be expected to understand): They're an offering; which sounded horribly vague. But who was Peter to make out that life was all plain sailing? – Peter always in love, always in love with the wrong woman? ...

... Oh, it was very queer. Here was So-and-so in South Kensington; some one up in Bayswater; and somebody else, say, in Mayfair. And she felt quite continuously a sense of their existence; and she felt what a waste; and she felt what a pity; and she felt if only they could be brought together; so she did it. And it was an offering; to combine, to create; but to whom? (1953: 184–85)

In a syntax of semi-colons, constellations of sentences, Clarissa attempts to bring together not only the people of her party, but analogical voices, the sayings of similar things across gender (Peter and Clarissa), classes (Septimus and Clarissa), and, above all, time (Sally and Clarissa).

Woolf, I think, goes further than creating repetitions on the level of character. J. Hillis Miller's powerful argument that *Mrs. Dalloway* offers an "All Souls' Night" at which the past of Clarissa Dalloway's life and, more generally and abstractly, the past of human life, flashes forth at Clarissa's party, is a telling analysis. Miller identifies a moment that "Woolf has unostentatiously, even secretly, buried within her novel [as] a clue to the way the day of the action is to be seen as the occasion of a resurrection of ghosts from the past" (1982: 189). That moment is Peter's encounter with an ancient ragged woman in the park – "three odd and apparently irrelevant pages in the novel," Miller says (1982: 189) – in which "a sound interrupted him; a frail quivering sound, a voice bubbling up without direction, rigour, beginning or end ... a voice of no age or sex, the voice of an ancient spring spouting from the earth ..." (1953: 122). "Through all ages," *Mrs. Dalloway* continues,

– when the pavement was grass, when it was swamp, through the age of tusk and mammoth, through the age of silent sunrise, the battered woman – for she wore a skirt – with her right hand exposed, her left clutching at her side, stood singing of love – love which had lasted a million years, she sang, love which prevails, and millions of years ago, her lover, who had been dead these centuries, had walked, she crooned, with her in May; but in the course of ages, long as summer days, and flaming, she remembered, with nothing but red asters, he had gone; death's enormous sickle had swept those tremendous hills, and when at last she laid her hoary and immensely aged head on the earth, now become a mere cinder of ice, she implored the Gods to lay by her side a bunch of purple heather, there on her high burial place which the last rays of the last sun caressed; for then the pageant of the universe would be over. (1953: 122–23)

Of this passage Miller notes "that Woolf has woven into the old woman's song, partly by paraphrase and variation, partly by direct quotation in an English translation, the words of a song by Richard Strauss, 'Allerseelen,'" that he describes as "'one day in the year' [that] is indeed 'free to the dead,' 'Allerseelen,' the day of a collective resurrection of spirits" (1982: 190). Like the ordinary clichés that, in a moment, I will describe in *Dubliners*, Woolf weaves cultural clichés into the discourse of her novel that create at least the aesthetic illusion of the moment's redemption, the "resurrection" of Clarissa's past in the present that Miller describes as "the pressure of all the other moments [lying] on the present moment Clarissa experiences so vividly" (1982: 188). Woolf enacts this pressure verbally, not visually, in sentences of semi-colons and a novel without chapters against the counterpoint of Big Ben's Newtonian time. Just as in the novel the noises of the "battered old woman with one hand exposed for coppers the other clutching her side" (1953: 123–24) – "ee um fah um so / foo swee too eem oo" (1953 : 122) – are constellated into a temporal and sexual order of the paraphrase of Strauss's "pageant of the universe," so Woolf creates an aesthetics of accumulated moments. That is, Woolf's *verbal* images – resonating sound – can be "dialectical" in ways that the overwhelmingly *visual* images of realism cannot. (Classical realism – as the discussion of George Eliot in the following chapter shows – repeatedly presents the simplicities of atemporal, visual self-evidence.)

Moreover, the sheer interruption of this scene is narrated in the metonymic language of Clarissa's experience and syntax, a narration of accretion: "she felt herself everywhere; not 'here, here, here' ... She waved her hand, going up Shaftesbury Avenue. She was all that" (1953: 231). Septimus's experience and discourse is even more dispersed across moments and attentions, so that the grounding of noises in the cultural myth of Strauss's song – like the punctuations of Clarissa's day by the ringing of Big Ben – underlines the nonsimplicity of this narrative and discourse. Woolf – and Joyce as well, with his combination of what he calls the "scrupulous meanness" of *Dubliners*' style against the voices and cultural clichés that ring out throughout the experience and discourse of his characters – enacts the combination of abundance and poverty I described in the Introduction. Unlike the unexceptional temporality of George Eliot, they create dialectics at a standstill. For Woolf, it is the *scene* of the ancient ragged woman that punctuates and complicates the narrative and experiential dispersals of Clarissa and Septimus. Such scenes, Woolf wrote in *A Sketch of the Past*, are

a means of summing up and making a knot out of innumerable little threads ... I find that scene making is my natural way of marking the past. A scene always comes to the top; arranged; representative. This confirms me in my instinctive notion – it is irrational; it will not stand argument – that we are sealed vessels afloat upon what it is convenient to call reality; at some moments, without a reason, without an effort, the sealing matter cracks; in floods reality; that is a scene ... (1985: 142)

In this description of scene – which, in its figure of the sealing matter cracking, allowing a flood of reality, seems to describe the irruption of transcendental myth into daily experience enacted in the park in *Mrs. Dalloway* – Woolf is offering an analogy for what Benjamin calls dialectics at a standstill, what he calls its "image," a momentary gathering together ("knotting") of disparate phenomena rather than the continuities and identities, from Thomas à Kempis to Maggie Tulliver, of things that George Eliot presents. Such scenic gatherings do not resolve Woolf's narratives as much as punctuate them: Clarissa's party is an alternative in time, not in substance, to her panic and that more pronounced panic of Septimus; the scenes of *A Sketch of the Past*, with the collision they present of Victorian conventions and twentieth-century war, seem only momentary in their gathering together of past and present. In these "scenes," Woolf presents the abstraction of answerability – the *semantic formalism* – I discuss in chapter 4.

The world of Dublin Joyce portrays arrests itself with words rather than scenes. It does not possess the kind of cultural cliché of myth and scene of Woolf as much as the competing discourses of free-floating cliché, a cacophonous world of Foucauldian or Bakhtinian discourses wherever you turn. In a story such as "Clay," for instance, Joyce presents a twentieth-century version of Gulliver in his character Maria, a Catholic former servant, who now lives in Dublin by Lamplight laundry that is run by the Protestants to care for poor women as an alternative to either the street or Catholic charities. Like Gulliver, she takes everything at face value – in sentences, like Gulliver's, that proceed subject-verb-object – so that she records the red face of a "colonel-looking gentleman" (1967: 103) without drawing the conclusion that his friendliness towards her is related to the fact he is drunk. Maria, like all the inhabitants of *Dubliners* – and even like Stephen Dedalus in his pretentious adolescence in *A Portrait of the Artist as a Young Man* – lives in a world of multiple discursive clichés. Thus in "Clay" the word "nice" is repeated eleven times in seven pages, and its use, like our "have a nice day," is that of a word without a meaning, whose aim is simply to eliminate silence – or, perhaps, eliminate panic, emptiness, or other thoughts. In "Clay" "the fire was nice" (99), twice the evening was "nice" (100, 102), both Joe and his wife were "ever so nice with her" (100, 104, 105), three times, and while "she used to have such a bad opinion of Protestants ... now she thought they were very nice people, a little quiet and serious, but still very nice people to live with" (100).

Such clichés, as Arthur Kroker and David Cook argue, are part of the "postmodern scene," the refusal of the "world of speech and reason." "Words," they say,

are no longer necessary; merely the seductive pose which entices the eye of the tourist. Codes are no longer required, as long as silence is eliminated ... We have the experience; we know that aspertane is bad even in Diet Coke. We don't have to wonder; we know just for the 'fun of it.' We write just for the fun of it, just as we think, make love, parody, and praise ... Besides, we are having a nice day, maybe a thousand nice days. The postmodern scene in a panic site, just for the fun of it. (1986: 27)

The panic they describe is one response to abundance, and it can be seen in the clichés of literary modernism as well as the "postmodernism" they name, in Peter's seeming endless repetitions of "love" and imagined love scenes in *Mrs. Dalloway* or in the free-floating desperations of Joyce's lower-middle-class characters – of Little Chandler, Farrington, or even Lenehan – in *Dubliners*. This is why I prefer to describe the complex of materialism, understandings, and experiences of the second Industrial Revolution as post-Enlightenment rather than postmodern. Benjamin ratifies this preference in describing such panic in the fall of experience into "bottomlessness" in the early twentieth century: "never has experience been contradicted more thoroughly than strategic experience by tactical warfare, economic experience by inflation, bodily experience by mechanical warfare, moral experience by those in power" (1969: 84). It is the bottomlessness of having neither a word nor a code that is adequate to the experience of overwhelming changes and anchorless freedom, "inflation" in every department of life, material, intellectual, human, so that neither the code of reason nor the word "I" that sustained Gulliver, George Eliot, and the great achievements of the Enlightenment can find any purchase on the world. At this time, John Maynard Keynes wrote, more cheerfully than Benjamin, that "for the first time since his creation man will be faced with his real, his permanent problem – how to use his freedom from pressing economic cares, how to occupy the leisure, which science and compound interest will have won for him, to live wisely and agreeably and well" (1931: 367).

A major aspect of this post-Enlightenment freedom is temporal, and both its freedom and its panic have to do with its discontinuous temporality. Woolf and Joyce, like Kroker and Cook, can appropriate language from any time, from any place: Woolf does so in a language of cultural cliché, the bourgeois *fin de siècle* weariness that Strauss articulates; Joyce does so in the popular cliché of the lower-middle-class music hall and popular press. That is, these clichés divorce word from both semiotic code and subjective intention so that what Kenner says of Joyce could be said of Woolf as well, despite the different register of her discourse. "In so atomizing his presentation," Kenner writes, "disjoining matter and manner, forcing against us a sheer stylistic arbitrariness, Joyce is refusing the most pervasive idea of the century in which he was born, the idea of continuity" (1978: 49). This is so, Kenner argues, because the overwhelming value of continuity for the Enlightenment was a response to "the sheer otherness of the past" – a past which was subject to the semiotics of reason and the passive mastery of the atemporal subject. Kenner argues that such "otherness" – the absolute break between past and present parallel to the absolute opposition between matter and spirit – "was a Romantic invention, and Romanticism skipped Ireland. Unless the past is other," he writes, "your relationship can never be one of continuity, nor yet of discontinuity: only identity, with the costumes altered" (1978: 49).

In *Postmodernism, or the Cultural Logic of Late Capitalism* Fredric Jameson describes the kind of quotation without quotation marks in Joyce's use of clichés – ranging through all time to constitute his discourse – as "pastiche." (Woolf's scenic gathering of verbal images functions a little differently from this.) "Pastiche," he writes,

is, like parody, the imitation of a peculiar or unique, idiosyncratic style, the wearing of a linguistic mask, speech in a dead language. But it is a neutral practice of such mimicry, without any of parody's ulterior motives, amputated of the satiric impulse, devoid of laughter and of any conviction that alongside the abnormal tongue you have momentarily borrowed, some healthy linguistic normality still exists. Pastiche is thus blank parody, a statue with blind eyeballs: it is to parody what that other interesting and historically original modern thing, the practice of a kind of blank irony, is to what Wayne Booth calls the "stable ironies" of the eighteenth century. (1991: 17)

Swift is writing parody and satire: against the blank materialism and egotistic reason of Gulliver and the new science of the Enlightenment he posits common sense, the "common actions and behaviour of life" and the "common pleasures or amusements of life" (1960: 179, 181). Both Woolf and Joyce are more difficult. The upper-middle-class people Woolf describes – Clarissa, Peter, even Hugh Whitbread and Lady Bruton – have a single register of voice floating freely among multiplied subjects of discourse who imperceptibly merge in the languages of *fin de siècle* mysticism, fragments of Shakespeare, imagined dialogue, apocalyptic images – none of which was ever available to Gulliver, for whom history is fundamentally "a-theological" (though, of course, they were available to Swift in his religious traditionalism). Such mysticism, moreover, is hardly distinguishable from the illusions of cultural cliché repeated by people whose days are filled with parties, imagined love affairs, and self-mythologizing. The lower-middle-class Dubliners Joyce describes, on the other hand, have a wealth of everyday language to choose from – the music-hall language of Eveline, the language of the Church in "Araby" that provides a vocabulary to describe what Yeats calls the "ignominy of boyhood; the distress / Of boyhood changing into man" (1969: 231), the language of Maupassant in "Two Gallants," the self-pitying clichés of Romanticism in "The Dead."

But within the blank irony born of the linguistic abundances of *Mrs. Dalloway* and *Dubliners*, Woolf and Joyce present experience that seems without anchor or bottom, experience that seems neither necessary nor sufficient in a world overwhelmed with material goods, intellectual accomplishments, and human populations. Joyce offers "ordinary" free-floating anxiety: the child's anguish at the end of "Araby" while he is surrounded by meaningless goods and meaningless talk; Maria's confusion at the end of "Clay," whose title suggests she will be dead before the year is out; the simultaneous representations at the end of "The Dead" of "the pretentious sublimations of ... romantic-Platonic love" (to use Norman O. Brown's description of Swift) and the simpler bodily activity of Gabriel falling asleep. Similarly, Woolf punctuates an upper-class party with the haunting scene of madness and suicide. All these suggest that meaninglessness inhabits abundance, and that Keynes's sanguine hope for the end of necessity at the moment of that other anti-Enlightenment phenomenon, the rise of fascism in Europe, might have been too easy a response to the transformation of necessity to desire in the abundant success of Enlightenment practices and understanding. Historically, this is true. Speaking of the vast wealth in goods, ideas, and populations created in the second Industrial Revolution that I quoted at the beginning of this chapter, Jameson goes on to say that it is precisely in the midst of this remarkable abundance, this "most completely humanized environment ... that life becomes meaningless, and that existential despair first appears ... The most interesting artists and thinkers of such a period are those who cling to the experience of meaninglessness itself as to some ultimate reality, some ultimate bedrock of existence of which they do not wish to be cheated by illusions" (1981: 251–52). Such abundance seems to suggest, if only momentarily, that basic necessities and possible sufficiencies are illusory in a world where choice overwhelms need and finding what will suffice is a daunting task.

### POST-ENLIGHTENMENT REMEMBRANCE

If Jameson describes the emptiness and panic of post-Enlightenment postmodernity occasioned by a world of abundance rather than dearth, post-Enlightenment understanding and experience cannot be quite so simple. In fact, as I have argued, post-Enlightenment understanding and experience possesses irreducible complexity that is born of abundance. This is why Benjamin's complex Marxist and Messianic reading of the culture of his time is so important. In his uncompleted *Arcades Project* he attempts to find a response to his time outside the semiotic code or subjective word of the Enlightenment. Of the project itself Benjamin wrote: "this project must raise the art of quoting without quotation marks to the very highest level" (1989: 45). Such quotation, like Jameson's pastiche (and like the analogical quotations throughout this study), erases the strict hierarchy between past and present I have described and creates the possibility – not the certainty – of post-Enlightenment wisdom in the face of palpable and unmasterable temporality. Thus Benjamin traces the "strange temporality" of discontinuity that Lacan names and the literary Modernism of Woolf and Joyce enacts not on the level of the individual subject or of particular language formations but on the level of social life – in a conception of social life that is more than aggregate individuals and that creates the possibility of gathering together different generations. Even in such gatherings, however, for Benjamin time presents each generation with what he calls its own temporally specific "experience," which he describes as capable of being passed on from generation to generation. It is "characteristic," Benjamin says, "that not only a man's knowledge or wisdom, but above all his real life – and this is the stuff that stories are made of – first finds transmissible form at the moment of his death" (1969: 94). Such experience is specific to each generation and frees each generation from envy for any time but its own (1969: 253–54).

For Benjamin, storytelling creates the possibility of recovering and transmitting "experience"; he suggests that the genius of storytelling is its ability to preserve and enact value across time by creating powerful collaborations across time. Storytelling, he suggests, is a collaboration between teller and listener whose times of experience are different. Thus he quotes Morris Heimann's assertion that "a man who dies at the age of thirty-five ... is at every point of his life a man who dies at the age of thirty-five." "Nothing," Benjamin says, in glossing this text,

is more dubious than this sentence – but for the sole reason that the tense is wrong. A man – so says the truth that was meant here – who died at thirty-five will appear to remembrance at every point in his life as a man who dies at the age of thirty-five. In other words, the statement that makes no sense for real life becomes indisputable for remembered life. (1969: 100)

Remembered life for Benjamin is a form of collaboration between ourselves and those who came before us. Benjamin describes this collaboration as "a secret agreement between past generations and the present one. Our coming was expected on earth" (1969: 254). That expectation was the faith those who came before us had that they would be understood, that their best intentions – even those only recoverable later, by us – would be acknowledged and fulfilled, that by luck or by skill they would be able to so prepare us with their experience and wisdom that we would collaborate with them to create what Benjamin calls "the chain of tradition which passes a happening on from generation to generation" (1969: 98). For Benjamin, neither the past nor the present is finished: time is not simply sequential and the subject is not atemporal.

Here's how it works. Responding in his notes to a letter from Max Horkheimer in 1937 in which Horkheimer accused Benjamin of being idealistic in his assertion of "incompleteness ... if completeness isn't included in it" since, Horkheimer says, "past injustice has occurred and is done with. The murdered are really murdered" (1989: 61), Benjamin replies:

The corrective to this way of thinking lies in the conviction that history is not only a science but also a form of remembrance. What science has 'established' can be modified by remembrance. Remembrance can make the open-ended (happiness) into something concluded and the concluded (suffering) into something open-ended. This is theology; however, in remembrance we have an experience which forbids us from conceiving of history fundamentally a-theologically, despite the fact that we are hardly able to describe it in theological concepts which are immediately theological. (Cited in Wolin 1989: 225; also translated in Benjamin 1989: 61)

The activity of remembrance – which is both temporal and non-sequential – forbids us from conceiving history as secular and a-theological, as the Enlightenment did. The "theology" Benjamin mentions here describes the context of generational temporality, of post-Enlightenment temporality – the fact that the present can change the past, give it a different issue, so that while murder remains murder and each particular death remains its material self nevertheless its meaning can flash up and be recognized in relation to its own future.

These past events, in other words, exist also within the context of their future history, the context of "human life" as a species phenomenon, temporal, transitory, comprehensive. The concept of time – the experience of time – Benjamin is enacting is not Newtonian universal time, possessing what Benjamin describes as "the miserable endlessness of a scroll" (1969: 185). Rather, it is an experience of time that possesses traces of other times, the "secret agreement" that links us to the past in a social deferral of action that, as in Freud, allows us to link the past and present together, that allows the present to redeem the past. Thus, Benjamin asserts that "the true conception of historical time is wholly based on the image of redemption" (1989: 71). Such an image is like a last pair of shoes: its value comes from its temporal position of coming later, coming after. That is, Benjamin's conception of history – like the post-Enlightenment conception of history I have presented in the appropriations of literary and cultural history in this chapter and throughout *Modernism and Time* in their attempts to find meanings beyond the intentions of Adam Smith and George Eliot, Fredric Jameson and Hugh Kenner, Bertrand Russell and Mikhail Bakhtin – this concept of history answers abundance with the possibilities (not certainties) of ethical choices.

### POST-ENLIGHTENMENT UNDERSTANDING,
### POST-ENLIGHTENMENT ETHICS

Just as abundance conditions modes of evaluation and experience in the early twentieth century, so it conditioned modes of understanding. Early twentieth-century science, as well as the arts of history and narrative, found ways of conceiving of experience outside the parsimonious reductiveness of the Enlightenment. For instance in *Physics and Philosophy* Benjamin's contemporary, Werner Heisenberg, describes the opposition between classical logic and what he calls, following Niels Bohr, the logic of complementarity. As I have already noted, Heisenberg writes that Bohr's conception of "complementarity" encourages physicists "to apply alternatively different classical concepts which would lead to contradictions if used simultaneously" (1958: 179). A generation later Norbert Wiener articulated an alternative to the Enlightenment opposition between materialism and idealism. In his book *Cybernetics*, Wiener writes: "Information is information, not matter or energy. No materialism which does not admit this can survive at the present day" (1961: 132). These two assertions – namely, the irreducible temporal aspect of subjects and objects of knowledge, articulated in Heisenberg's conception of "alternation," and the breaching of the simple binary opposition between matter and energy, articulated in Wiener's definition of "information" I will cite in a moment – can help spell out, along with Woolf, Joyce, and Benjamin, a sense of the complex relationship between Enlightenment understanding and postmodern temporality. They can do so, I think, because both Wiener and Heisenberg are describing worlds of abundance: the complementarity Heisenberg describes "complexifies" the simplicity of the principle of Contradiction; the information of Wiener multiplies the determinations of Sufficient Reason.

In the technicalities of his mathematical model Wiener presents a conception of information that presents an understanding of culture, as Heisenberg presents an understanding of the theory of subatomic physics, that is above all temporal. It is my contention that such temporalization is at the heart of post-Enlightenment "postmodernism": sometimes it's called "local," sometimes a mode of "historicizing" experience, sometimes simply an "anti-aesthetic" in both Benjamin's positive sense of redemption and in others' negative sense of panic. Post-Enlightenment postmodernism, in Foucault's words describing genealogy, focuses on "the singularity of events outside any monotonous finality; it ... seeks them in the most unpromising places, in what we tend to feel is without history... not in order to trace the gradual course of their evolution, but to isolate the different scenes where they engaged in different roles" (1971: 139).

Such genealogy offers an alternative to the "purity" of the once-and-for-all formulations of knowledge of the Enlightenment that Latour both laments and, alternatively, argues never was achieved in any case. Instead, it possesses the strange temporality of Wiener's definition of "information." "Information," Wiener argues, "is a name for the content of what is exchanged with the outer world as we adjust to it, and make our adjustment felt upon it" (1967: 26–27). In Wiener's argument, information is central to Leibniz's study of optics (which he pursued before Newton did) as opposed to Newton's study of mechanics. Optics, unlike mechanics, cannot easily situate the subject outside time because it is precisely concerned with information, messages, and communication. Moreover, communication itself cannot erase its own temporal instantiation as easily as can the reductive and reproducible principles of Reason Leibniz articulates. Finally, as in Heisenberg, the apprehensions of optics are not merely "subjective," but functions of attention – of what is attended to. In opposition to the universal and atemporal assertions of Enlightenment science, I prefer to describe this process of alternation and attention in terms of Charles Taylor's description of the "successive renewals" of cultural objects (1991: 177), which I discuss more fully in the following chapter.[12]

The renewal Taylor describes is implicit in both Heisenberg's "alternatives" and Wiener's distinction among materialism, energy, and information. In both Heisenberg and Wiener, the opposition between once-and-for-all truth and local knowledges is suspended in the face of remarkable abundance so that there is no necessity to choose between them once and for all. (One can, of course, choose between them at different moments.) The qualities of information feedback and alternation are, I believe, the aspects of post-Enlightenment thinking that allow us to suspend the opposition between the aesthetic judgment and the pure reason of the Enlightenment – Leibniz's principles of Contradiction and Sufficient Reason – that, necessarily, opposes both of these to practical reason, Kant's telling description of ethics. (He might have called it "temporal reason.") That is, Wiener's conception of information and Bohr's conception of complementarity situate understanding outside the two great (if sometimes incompatible) achievements of the Enlightenment, subjective idealism and general semiotics. Thus Wiener writes, in a manner which is clearly tutored by Heisenberg and quantum mechanics, that in contemporary science "we no longer deal with quantities and statements which concern a specific real universe as a whole but ask instead questions which may find their answers in a large number of similar universes" (1967: 18–19). Here, precisely in the analogies of other "similar universes," is another mark of abundance where the suspended singularity and pluralities of information and the negative materiality of subatomic mechanics can connect the present with the past. They allow the present to attend upon the past.

In fact, such "similar universes" present us with the ethos and ethics of post-Enlightenment postmodernity altogether. What the multiplication of examples in this chapter seems to leave out amid their specificity and clutter is the global "practical reason" of postmodern temporality, the ethics embedded in its work, in our work. The problem with ethics is precisely the problem of time, the emergences and renewals, the deferral and redemption of history in postmodernism. (I almost wrote "emergencies" instead of or along with "emergences": surely that works as well, in a panic mode.) On the one hand, ethics must deal with universal value: "what kind of ethics would there be," Jacques Derrida asks in discussing feminism, "if belonging to one sex or another became its law or its privilege?" (1982a: 73). On the other hand, the "practical reason" of ethics precisely deals in the particular case, not in order to universalize its particularity, as in Kantian aesthetics, nor to discover the value-free truth of its reality, as in Enlightenment epistemology, but, as John Dewey said in 1891, in order to discover its "real meaning." "Ethics," Dewey writes, "deals with conduct in its entirety, with reference, that is to what makes it conduct, its ends, its real meaning" (1969: 241). Such meaning, unlike the representations of Enlightenment history, exist globally everywhere within conduct even if its recovery is governed above all by time, the "end" of conduct. Moreover, to complicate things even more, such temporality cannot be simply reduced to local time.

Thus, against the systematic objectivities of the material world and the subjective idealism of aesthetic experience, Emmanuel

Levinas describes the nature of ethics in terms of the temporalities of culture I have been presenting. "Man's ethical relation to the other," he writes, "is ultimately prior to his ontological relation to himself ... or to the totality of things that we call the world ... The relation with the other is time: it is an untotalizable diachrony in which one moment pursues another without ever being able to retrieve it, to catch up with, or coincide with it" (1986: 21). The relation to the other Levinas is describing assumes the form of scattered temporal abundance found within the post-Enlightenment ethos of Woolf, Joyce, and Benjamin, of commercials and pastiche – the postmodernity we are living – and within the abundances and redundancies of "information" that Wiener opposes to the matter and energies of the world and of the self. This information exists alongside the messy alternations of modes of logic and alternations of self and other that Heisenberg suggests and, indeed, that the postmodern experience that we participate in embodies. In these complexities, the connections between our time and the past that has made us and that we can remake in turn may be discerned. That we should pursue these connections is imperative in the entirety of our conduct and the specificity of our action so that we might recover value and meaning in our knowledge, our wealth, and our experience. Such a pursuit is imperative even if, as Levinas says, we will never fully and simply – or, as Descartes says, clearly and distinctly – retrieve, catch, or coincide with things that matter in a world that seems in many ways overwhelmingly complex, senselessly free, and simply too full.

CHAPTER 2

# Temporal allegories: George Eliot, Walter Benjamin, and the redemption of time

An artist such as Goethe, for example, gravitates organically toward an evolving sequence. He strives to perceive all existing contradictions as various stages of some unified development; in every manifestation of the present he strives to glimpse a trace of the past, a peak of the present-day or a tendency of the future ...

In contrast to Goethe, Dostoevsky attempted to perceive the very stages themselves in their *simultaneity*, to *juxtapose* and *counterpose* them dramatically, and not to stretch them into an evolving sequence. For him, to get one's bearings in the world meant to conceive all its content as simultaneous, and *to guess at their interrelationships in the cross section of a single moment.*
M. M. Bakhtin, "The *Bildungsroman* and Its Significance in the History of Realism" (1986: 28)

Time is not a thing.
Martin Heidegger, *On Time and Being* (1972: 3)

This chapter aims at a description of contrary modes of representing time in narrative discourse between 1880 and 1930. Even though the problematics of time is a recurrent theme in Western discourse, in this chapter I examine a notable shift of sensibility in relation to the experience and understanding of time at the beginning of the twentieth century. Why this should be so is the burden of the following chapter, although I have touched upon some of the intellectual conditions for this experience in chapter 1. In the preceding chapter, I examined the problematics of time in relation to modes of understanding in terms of particular social and intellectual conditions that gave rise to the post-Enlightenment Modernism of the early twentieth century. Just as I demonstrated there that the intellectual problem of post-Enlightenment modernity – the problem of explanation and comprehension – is most easily isolated in the particular crises of early twentieth-century culture, manifested in neoclassical economics, post-Newtonian science, and narrative strategies in Woolf, Joyce, Benjamin, and others, in this chapter I argue that the experience of post-Enlightenment time is best captured and isolated in the discourses of literary Modernism. The discourse of twentieth-century Modernism, in the contexts of social and historical phenomena I will explore in the following chapter, makes time both a theme and a discursive or representational problem. As Daniel Bell notes, "the problem of time (in Bergson, Proust, and Joyce) was the primary aesthetic problem of the first decades of this century" (cited in Harvey 1990: 201). In fact, insofar as we see time as an aesthetic problem for George Eliot or Austen or Dickens, we do so because we have been tutored by literary Modernism. In this chapter I examine a Modernist example of Walter Benjamin's recurrent focus on what he calls the "redemption" of time that I have already touched upon in chapter 1, in contrast to George Eliot's conception and representation of time as accidental and non-essential, in order to suggest some important oppositions: the difference between George Eliot's impersonal illusionism that manipulates the reader (as in the first chapter of *The Mill on the Floss*) and Benjamin's sense of the syncopated – or what Jacques Derrida calls "intervallic" (1981: 58) – temporality that insists upon the subject's active interpretation; the difference between George Eliot's nostalgia and Benjamin's recognition of guilt; the difference between the way George Eliot's novel controls narrative through consciousness while Benjamin's work confronts the past, as Woolf does, through the textualization and the multiplication of narrative. These contrasts can help us understand the ways that cultural Modernism in the early twentieth century itself is imbricated in time, and how the successive renewal of the relationship between cause and effect, structure and event, phenomena and significance, can help us to comprehend the distinctive features of early twentieth-century Modernism – the collisions of past and present, the apocalyptic sense of the new, the radically temporal subject of experience – and post-Enlightenment temporality.

The issues of periodization, of the claim that particular authors can define particular epochs in a liminal way, are tied up with the larger questions of the representations of time. That is, a chief problem that arises in a comparison of George Eliot and Benjamin – as it arises in the kind of generalized comparison between Newtonian and post-Newtonian strategies of comprehension I outlined in the preceding chapter – is the tendency of the argument to suggest developmental linearity when, in fact, comparisons themselves are "constellated" forms and analogical representations of phenomena which do not lend themselves to reduction once and for all to continuities of development as Enlightenment canons of parsimonious understanding assume. Instead of development, the temporality of comparison follows the detours of displacement, repression, repetition, and working through Freud described in the early twentieth century, the complicated provocations of what Husserl called, in a very different register, the phenomenology of "time consciousness" (1964). Both George Eliot and Benjamin are attempting to find some global comprehension of what Benjamin calls "physical nature and significance" (1977: 166), and both represent the experience of time to achieve this end. George Eliot presents time as a theme and procedure of subjective and novelistic consciousness at the very beginning of *The Mill on the Floss*: time and the past, for George Eliot, are always with us, always accessible, always the same. As Elizabeth Ermarth says of literary realism more generally, the temporal medium is homogenized in a way that finds the "past and present mutually informative" (1983: 25). Thus, Eliot's novel begins with the narrator's representation of a remembered scene from the past. Benjamin, on the other hand, presents time as intimately caught up with communal and generational life – telling stories (as opposed to reading novels) and textualizing experience in a manner that presents or represents time in relation to consciousness in a different way, less concerned with the opposition between conscious subjects and unconscious objects, atemporal truths and timely accidents. Benjamin presents time as something that has to be confronted, recovered and, by means of that recovery, that can be transformed and redeemed.

## I THE DREAM OF NARRATION: *THE MILL ON THE FLOSS*, BOURGEOIS EPISTEMOLOGY, AND THE TRANSCENDENCE OF TIME

### THE VIEW FROM NOWHERE

Many thinkers associated with twentieth-century Modernism – Husserl, Heidegger, Wittgenstein, Bergson, Schreiner, Einstein, Freud, Bakhtin – came to see that time is not an object, something that can be described, reported and referred to in a constative utterance. They also came to see that it is not something that can be simply presented and performed. Rather, time, they discovered, must be figured and, more precisely, *articulated* by something other than itself. That is why philosophers as different in temperament as Wittgenstein and Bergson, as I mentioned in the preceding chapter, came to understand that the very definition of time was a problem. Donald Lowe, among many others who have tried to define post-Enlightenment Modernism and modernity in terms of time, situates this problem in the first decades of the twentieth century and describes it as the transformation of space and time from "the absolute framework of perception" into "mere functions within a system" (1982: 11). In this understanding, representation and temporality arise in the same movement, the movement of signification – situated in the juncture between language conceived as observation and language conceived as action.

The realism of *The Mill on the Floss* describes a moment before this crisis of representation and presents time unselfconsciously and unproblematically. At the beginning of the novel, the narrator describes a scene in which the heroine, Maggie Tulliver, stands before the mill in "rapt" attention. Towards the end of the first chapter he says, "Before I dozed off, I was going to tell you what Mr. and Mrs. Tulliver were talking about ..." ([1860] 1961: 9). In fact, *The Mill* gives no "before": the novel gives, as all narratives must, the dream of narration, the stutter of time. George Eliot's adverbial "before" marks time with a hesitation, divides it with before and after. It is just this division that effects and situates the representation of time in George Eliot without a problem. Wittgenstein, on the other hand, marks the division as a problem when he says that "We cannot compare any process with the 'passage of time' – there is no such thing – but only with another process (say, with the movement of the chronometer)" (1990: 6.3611). In other words, George Eliot makes the "past impression" of the Mill "present once more" as Foucault says of representations in general (1970: 69) by assuming that time itself – "before" and "after" – is a source of impressions fully congruent with other objects in the world. For George Eliot, as for the cluttered world of Victorian laissez-faire capitalism, time has the status of a "thing," measurable, infinitely divisible, self-same. By offering the articulation of time (before and after), narrative realism presents time as simple given, another "thing" in a world of things;

it situates temporality as something that can be simply alluded to within the discourse of a more or less omniscient narrator whose resources of observation and understanding appear to transcend time – a narrator who possesses an *unmarked* "view from nowhere" (see Nagel 1986), what Ermarth calls "the narrator as nobody" (1983: 65–66). Thus, when the narrator of *The Mill on the Floss* describes Maggie's "enthusiasm" for renunciation following her discovery of *Thomas à Kempis*, the narrator has access to all of time: "remembering" the future, the narrator notes "she had not perceived – how could she until she had lived longer? – the inmost truth of the old monk's outpourings, that renunciation remains sorrow, though a sorrow borne willingly" ([1859] 1961: 255).

George Eliot articulates a similarly unproblematic view of time in the famous passage from *Adam Bede* where she describes the virtues of homely realism. There, the chief metaphor for reality is painting – George Eliot prefers the "precious quality of truthfulness" of homely Dutch painting to more heroic paintings – and the only allusion to time is the simple measure of the pastness of the narrative of *Adam Bede*, "sixty years ago" (1961a: 178). This passage implies that objects in the world – a Dutch painting, the "divine beauty of form," "the faithful representing of commonplace things" – are unmarked by the time in which they exist. Instead, the "nature" of things – including human "nature" – is essentially separate from temporality. For this reason the narrator can "know" what Maggie will learn from experience because her development in time is simply *in* time: time is always the same, mathematical, infinitely divisible, a pure ether that conditions but does not affect experience and understanding. Objects in the world, then, can be apprehended as simple objects of representation because time simply contains the re-presentation of things. The objects of experience of the first Industrial Revolution in England – primary, basic, and interchangeable experiences of atemporal but interchangeable subjects I examined in the preceding chapter – seemed to repeat themselves in the manner of what Friedrich Nietzsche calls the "homogeneous, enduring characters of long generations" (1968: 44) that George Eliot represented in her narrative which looks back at the sixty years before.

These assumptions govern George Eliot's realism. What comes "before" the narrator dozes off in *The Mill on the Floss*, the novel's first utterance, is a sentence without a verb, seemingly a timeless vision of what is – what Jacques Derrida calls a vision of the *nous*

(1982: 253) – rather than the time-bound discourse of a speaker.[1] What comes "before" the narrator dozes is the species of linguistic activity A. J. Greimas describes from which both sender and receiver have been excluded (1983: 134): "A wide plain, where the broadening Floss hurries on between its green banks to the sea, and the loving tide, rushing to meet it, checks its passage with an impetuous embrace" (1961: 7). In this opening the very dream of narration arises in the alternation between observation and act, the observed action of the narration, and what it all means, the interpretative act of its speaker. "Before I dozed off," the narrator explains, " I was going to tell you what Mr. and Mrs. Tulliver were talking about" (1961: 9). It is precisely the separation of action and observation – the temporal materialism and the atemporal subject discussed in the preceding chapter – that grounds bourgeois realism. Such separation is accomplished by unmarking the location of the observer in time or space: giving "him" – the unmarked gender of the narrator, "George Eliot," in the novels – a view from nowhere.[2] Above all, as Bakhtin says of Goethe, is "the exceptional significance of *visibility*": "all other external feelings, internal experiences, reflection, and abstract concepts are joined together around the *seeing eye* as a center, as the first and last authority. Anything essential can and should be visible; anything invisible is inessential" (1986: 27). The "real" of realism is what can be seen by anyone: it is not the felt but unseen explosions of time Heidegger talks about, nor the language of "crisis consciousness" – of the ends of things – to which such explosions gave rise, nor the discourses of stuttering, slips and dreams in psychoanalysis subject to interpretation at a different moment from their utterance. Rather, the "real" of realism is the self-evidence of the visible, sight in Gulliver's eye.[3]

That is, for George Eliot – as well as for Gulliver, Newtonian science, and the Enlightenment – every moment is "original": every moment presents the subject of experience with a new beginning, a clean slate. This, I believe, is what makes the opening of *The Mill on the Floss* such a representative depiction of Enlightenment temporality. Included within this experience of temporality – again, in significant ways conditioning that experience – are the criteria of aesthetic "wholeness" and "objectivity" as elements of truth. In these terms – in which time is continuous, events are secular (even when they create the illusion of the sacred), and the subject of temporal experiences is simple and unitary – George Eliot's "before" is altogether different from the post-Enlightenment temporality examined in the preceding chapter. George Eliot's "before" divides action and observation in the opposing discourses of the third-person narrative and the first-person narrator, yet in its continuity it allows the *position* of the narrator (the subject of discourse) to coincide with a narrative from which the sender and receiver are erased. Such an erasure eliminates what Emile Benveniste calls the particular *instance* of enunciation from the narrative representation. This is the mark, the "distinctive feature," of the realism that characterizes the classical bourgeois narrative in the years before the second Industrial Revolution. In that narrative, as in Isaac Newton's inaugural definition of space and time in the *Principia Mathematica*, both time and space are neutral "containers" in which action occurs.

In George Eliot, though, time is more "neutral" than space: realism offers minute discriminations of spatial understanding with an almost total disregard for temporal distinctions. In *Adam Bede*, for instance, George Eliot's narrator says, "I turn, without shrinking, from cloud-borne angels, from prophets, sibyls, and heroic warriors, to an old woman bending over her flower-pot, or eating her solitary dinner, while the noonday light, softened perhaps by a screen of leaves, falls on her mob-cap, and just touches the rim of her spinning-wheel, and her stone jug, and all those cheap common things which are the precious necessities of life to her" (1961a: 180). In *The Mill on the Floss* she notes the sad necessity of the metaphorical nature of intelligence that "can so seldom declare what a thing is, except by saying it is something else" (1961: 124). Intelligence, like the paintings she describes, traffics in *things* of the world with little regard to their temporal situation. The crowd of things in the description in *Adam Bede*, like the crowd of commodities found in Victorian drawing rooms, overwhelms discourse.

Such commodities, however, exist in the Enlightenment world of necessity rather than in the post-Enlightenment world of desire. George Eliot's world, as we saw in chapter 1, is one of great *need* in which "the emphasis of want" that faces Maggie throughout *The Mill on the Floss* (1961: 256) characterizes human life. The "needs" she describes are "common things," reproducible, diurnal, constantly pressing. They inhabit what Baudrillard calls "the order of *production*" (1983: 83), where order itself is a function of repetition, objectification, and above all simplification. "Need," for George

Eliot – even in the cluttered world of industrial capitalism – is simple, just as the labor theory of value that Marx expounds contemporaneously with George Eliot defines itself in terms of the simplicities of food, clothing, and shelter, in terms of canons of the "same." This is why, as we have seen, George Eliot defines Thomas à Kempis precisely in a way that makes him interchangeable with a teenage girl living four centuries later. In a similar way Ermarth argues that "if one believes – and it is the business of realistic convention to make us believe – that an invariant, objective world exists, then consciousness is always *potentially* the same, interchangeable among individuals, because it is consciousness of the same thing. All consciousness derives from the same world and so, if total consciousness were possible, it would be the same for everyone" (1983: 66). Such interchangeability – not only between girl and monk, but between character and narrator – is the hallmark of George Eliot's sympathetic and generous imagination. In the terms of Benjamin we will encounter later in this chapter, George Eliot achieves the "legibility" of Maggie's desire at the expense of its "recognizability" by erasing its nature as a unique event and rewriting it as a general, human event. And the same happens to Thomas à Kempis as well: his sacred desire is equated with Maggie Tulliver's secular desire within this economy of equivalences.

In this discourse, as in the narrator's remarks in *Adam Bede*, time is absolutely objective and homogeneous to the point of not being noted at all. In this narrative, time conforms to Newton's description of time in the *Principia* as "absolute, true, and mathematical" as opposed to the "common time [of duration] ... such as an hour, a day, a month, a year" (1964: 17). The subsumption of "common sense" into "objective meaning" is a central tenet of Enlightenment thinking, the mode of secular humanism.[4] Gulliver repeatedly assumes this hierarchical distinction in narrating his *Travels* – it appears in the ease with which he learns foreign languages and translates foreign experience into his European experience – and it is the basis of the distinction between the limited, sensual, and above all *interpretable* discourse of characters, appearing between quotation marks, and the authoritative, objective and atemporal discourse of the narrator (MacCabe 1979: 15). Bourgeois sensibility, as Newton's reference to "mathematical time" and "duration" suggest, apprehends time in terms of formal, spatial metaphors that above all emphasize the continuity of time I have described. Such an emphasis on continuity leads both to the repetition and interchangeability of the elements of and in time and also to a sense of development, in which "discrete forms are replaced by continuities" (Ermarth 1983: 16). Swift's great joke is narrating Gulliver's fantastic adventures in the style of realism while George Eliot's great achievement is the sympathy that is provoked by narrating, in a different register of realism, the interchangeability of temporal elements, young and old subjects, past and present time. Her ability to equate Maggie and Thomas à Kempis, like the ease with which Wordsworth identifies himself with his sister in *Tintern Abbey* or the ease with which both Gulliver and Descartes substitute their experience for all human experience, is closely tied to the concept of temporal "development."[5]

The problem for George Eliot in *The Mill on the Floss* is that the protagonist of her narrative, as a female subject, could not in fact, like her male contemporaries, develop in time since, as George Eliot notes, "the happiest women, like the happiest nations, have no history" (1961: 335). In the face of this problem George Eliot compresses the time of her bildungsroman and has Maggie die before she is twenty. Yet even so, George Eliot develops Maggie within the confines of homogeneous time by means of allegories of meaning whose constant thrust is to emphasize the continuity of time and the interchangeability of its moments in the face of remarkable disruptions in the economic, personal, and social histories of her novel. Throughout the novel, the narrator repeatedly offers metaphors for Maggie in the form of parallel types and archetypes (see Schleifer 1984: 200–216), which, like the metaphorical intelligence she describes, creates her significance "by saying it is something else." In comparing Maggie's life to that of Hamlet, for instance, the narrator notes that her "destiny, then, is at present hidden, and we must wait for it to reveal itself like the course of an unmapped river: we only know that the river is full and rapid, and that for all rivers there is the same final home" (1961: 351). In this passage, George Eliot is figuring the spatio-temporal ordering – the dynamism, the structure, the transformation, and the wholeness – of Maggie's life from the vantage of the peaceful quiet of the future, a view from nowhere. That is, this description, like George Eliot's repeated metaphors and figurations of Maggie, takes place before a background of time which is always the same: flowing equably without anything but illusory revolutions, above all from the position of a quiet and peaceful future that does not affect – even in the narrator's dream – "the communicating surface between the ego and external objects" Bergson describes (1960: 126–27). The dream of narration, then, in the era of enlightened realism, bourgeois sensibility, and positive science simply assumes the ability to represent events without representing time: it is to make event an object in the world and narration itself simply a mode of observation.

### THE ACT OF NARRATION

When Newton distinguishes "absolute, true, and mathematical time" from "relative, apparent, and common time" in terms of the latter's sensible and external measure of duration, he is distinguishing between absolute time and the events that inhabit time. (George Eliot does the same thing when she distinguishes between dream and event while allowing her dream of the mill all the objectivity of her normal narrative discourse.) What permits Newton's distinction is the *position* of the observer. That position is what I have been calling "the view from nowhere" and what Ermarth calls "the narrator as nobody" (1983: 65–92): a subject of knowledge who in no way is affected by the contingencies of time. Sören Kierkegaard described this position in his diary in 1843 as, above all, *philosophical*:

It is quite true what philosophy says: that Life must be understood backwards. But that makes one forget the other saying: that it must be lived – forwards. The more one ponders this, the more it comes to mean that life in temporal existence never becomes quite intelligible, precisely because at no moment can I find complete quiet to take the backward-looking position. (1960: 111)

What Kierkegaard calls a "backward-looking position" is really an *atemporal* position designated within the homogeneity of "equable" time as some vague future so as to allow it a *secular* temporal description even though it is "outside" of time. It is the quiet position of an *atemporal* future that allows the narrator of *The Mill on the Floss* to sympathize with Maggie's youthful enthusiasm for Thomas à Kempis and to compare her life to that of Hamlet's tragedy and the flow of a river.

Such a position allows bourgeois society more generally to consider *events* as analogous to objects in the world, as things. The understanding of events, whose nature is inextricably bound up with temporality, as things that can be apprehended, understood, and

represented creates the possibility of a particular, "objective" mode
of explanation. Such understanding allows for (or calls for) the
practice of nomological science, modes of explanation that subsume
phenomena under general laws. Nomological science understands
phenomena in terms of the simplicities of necessary and sufficient
explanations. It participates in the Enlightenment modes of explanation I discussed in the preceding chapter. Thus in *Time and Narrative*
Paul Ricoeur asks,"Why are hypotheses not falsifiable in history in
the same way they are in science? Because hypotheses are not the
goal of history, only landmarks for delineating a field of investigation,
guides serving a mode of understanding which is fundamentally that
of interpretative narrative, which is neither chronology nor
'science'" (1984: 156). Interpretative narrative traffics in events, but
it presents events not as simple positive entities, but what Ricoeur
calls "configurations" – Benjamin's "constellations" and Russell's
"arrangements" – of incidents defined by the temporal sequence
grasped as a whole. "The plot of narrative," Ricoeur says, "'grasps
together' and integrates into one whole and complete story multiple
and scattered events, thereby schematizing the intelligible signification attached to the narrative taken as a whole" (1984: x). Narrative
understanding, he continues, "unifies into one whole and complete
action the miscellany constituted by the circumstances, ends and
means, initiatives and interactions, the reversals of fortune, and all
the unintended consequences issuing from human action" (1984: x).

For Ricoeur – and for Donald Davidson as well, working out of a
very different philosophical tradition – events are irreducibly
complex precisely because they *involve* the subject of understanding
in a vital way. Davidson offers a description of "event" that entails
time as well as space. An event can be understood globally (e.g., the
queen killed the king) and atomistically (e.g., the queen moved her
hand, poured the poison, and the poison killed the king a week later
by affecting his nervous system in such and such a way [which itself
can be analyzed in greater and greater detail]; see Davidson 1980:
57–61). Moreover, the decision concerning the level of understanding and consequently the *significance* of an event is never made from
the disinterested "quiet" of futurity that Kierkegaard describes.
Rather, the decision is made *prospectively* – with some end or other in
prospect – and the position from which that decision is made is the
locus of noisy conflicts of interests that mark temporality. In fact,
Ricoeur explicitly calls this decision a mode of judgment and likens

its situation – the situation of narrative and temporality – to that of a judge who unravels "the tangle of plots the subject is caught up in," by attending to "the 'living imbrication' of every lived story with every other such story" (1984: 74–75; see also Schleifer et al. 1992: 18–21, 240–43).

In this understanding, time is never "equable," never quite the "same." That is, moments of time – instances of events – are unique. This assertion of temporal uniqueness, Ricoeur says,

is false if we attach to the idea of uniqueness the metaphysical thesis that the world is made up of radically dissimilar particulars. Explanation then becomes impossible. The assertion is true, though, if we mean that, in contrast to the practitioners of the nomological sciences, historians want to describe and explain what actually happened in all its concrete detail. But then what historians understand by "unique" means that nothing exists exactly like the object of inquiry. Their concept of uniqueness, therefore, is relative to the level of precision chosen for their inquiries. (1984: 124)

The uniqueness of moments, I would say, is their comprehension *as* coherent moments, whether they are the moment of awareness of Gabriel's glimpse of himself in the mirror in *The Dead* or of the narrator's seemingly instantaneous sympathy for Maggie in her study of *Thomas à Kempis* or whether they are larger events such as Maggie's life conceived, allegorically, as tragedy.

Such comprehension involves the subjects of these moments' apprehension – it involves the very activity of "time consciousness" which became a major concern at the end of the nineteenth century – in such a way that temporality itself *cannot* be separated from intention and desire. Ricoeur notes this himself when he posits the historians' intention and desire "to describe and explain" – that is to "comprehend" – the past, and Joyce notes it, more quietly than Ricoeur, when he ironizes Gabriel's experience and subjects it to his readers' interpretations (see Kenner 1978 and MacCabe 1979, as well as chapter 1 above). Joyce underlines the reader's involvement in his narrative by leaving us at the end of *The Dead*, just as he leaves us at the end of *Ulysses*, with an incomplete event whose configuration as a single, coherent occurrence can only be accomplished in the future. If Gabriel goes West with Gretta (or if Molly makes Leopold breakfast the next morning), the significance of the "event" will be configured in very different ways than if neither of these actions occur. (See Schleifer et al. 1992: 91–94 for a Greimassian reading of this interpretation.) Joyce underlines the reader's involvement by multiplying the discourses and vocabularies that make sense of experience, in this case Gabriel's alternating irony and Romanticism. Virginia Woolf – and, in a very different style, D. H. Lawrence – both do so by means of alternating and multiplying levels of comprehension in narrative.

The key term, in this description, is Ricoeur's notion of "level." It implies an abundant, multi-leveled arrangement of phenomena and apprehension where a kind of "gestaltist" apprehension or "quantum leap" transforms elements of understanding by transforming the contexts in which they occur. At the turn of the twentieth century, multi-level modes of analysis were developed in many different intellectual disciplines: Bertrand Russell's theory of "types" in mathematics and logic, Saussure's (and then Jakobson's) "synchronic" analysis in structural linguistics, Freud's topology of mind in psychoanalysis, Wittgenstein's development of game theory, among others. J. T. Fraser, in his important work on time describes "level-specific temporalities" (1982: 29), in which one level of time – a particular way of grasping temporality – emerges from simpler levels, not to replace the earlier phenomenon of time, but to build upon them (in the mode of accumulated abundance). "The grouping of structures along hierarchically nested levels of increasing complexity," Fraser writes, "produces stability points. They make it possible for the next level of organization to emerge, because the lower levels do not get easily undone. In all cases, however, the issue is not one of simple aggregation but aggregation with communication" (1982: 24). Fraser's conception of "nested" modes of temporal awareness is intimately related to the linguistic category of markedness developed in Prague linguistics after World War I. The marks of language define levels in relation to one another as the particular situations of significance. A marking (or "distinctive") feature on one level of analysis may be a non-distinctive feature on another. Moreover, as the social, technical and intellectual history of the turn of the twentieth century described in the following chapters suggests, the multiplication of level-specific temporalities Fraser describes is a particularly Modernist conception of time that participated in and responded to the particular conditions of late nineteenth-century Europe.

Above all, the conception of multiple levels complicates and problematizes the conception of the "same" ( Schleifer 1990: 88–91). In a simple example, repeated pronunciations of a particular word can focus on similarities or differences depending on whether the level of inquiry is semantic repetition or accentual differences. As Roland Barthes notes, the rolled *r* of certain French dialects is a simple accident of pronunciation, but in particular contexts, "in the speech of the theatre, for instance," it becomes a distinctive mark of discourse that "signals a country accent and therefore is part of a code, without which the message of 'ruralness' could not be either emitted or perceived" (1968: 20). For George Eliot it is self-evident (i.e., the unmarked case[6]) that we all await "the same final home," and it is so because her definition of the "same" focuses on an origin that develops in time. For her, the *event* of death is an object that can be compared to other objects precisely because its temporal status is a non-essential accident – just as in a semantic analysis of a sentence, the rolled *r* of certain dialects is a non-essential accident. In George Eliot the accidents of experience – the difference between what is essential and what is inessential, or in Roman Jakobson's linguistic terminology, the difference between a distinctive and non-distinctive feature or mark – can be judged, once and for all, from the "objective" perspective of an omniscient and atemporal view from nowhere.

George Eliot, unlike more "objective" novelists, does, in fact, involve her narrators with their stories. But she does so without thematizing time for either character or narrator. That is, as Hillis Miller has argued, irony is "the pervasive tone of the narration" and personification is "the trope whereby the ironic discrepancy between narrator and character is given a name and a personality in the putative storyteller, 'George Eliot' " (1991: 295). With these figurative modes of discourse, the narrator pretends to learn from the experience of the characters, but in fact always knows what he (or is it she?) knows all along. Even the dream with which *The Mill on the Floss* begins does not alter the communicating surface between the ego and external objects. Rather, the novel consistently enacts the essence of classical realism, "the instrumental subordination of narrative language to narrative representations" (Jameson 1979: 7), the subordination of temporal event to atemporal truth. In fact, in its first-person constructions articulated by a named narrator ("George Eliot"), *The Mill* repeatedly uses adverbial temporal markers in transitions between the narrator's commentary and the characters' actions: the "before" of the narrator's dream in the first chapter, the "until" of the narrator's promise that Maggie would grow to understand the "inmost truth" of Thomas à Kempis (1961: 255), the "then" after the comparison of Maggie and Hamlet (1961: 351, cited in the passage at the end of this section).

What these "markers" mark is not a change in temporal situation, but the presence or absence of temporality altogether, an *atemporal* absence of temporality rather than an *eternal* transformation of temporality. Charles Taylor, in describing the opposition between nomological understanding and narrative understanding in Ricoeur, distinguishes two relations between structure and event. These two relations differ in the irrelevance and the necessity of temporality as part of each particular mode of explanation. Nomological understanding, Taylor argues, creates a relationship of "subsumption": this is the mode of physics, he says – particularly, I would add, that of Newtonian mechanics – and "it concerns a form of explanation whereby the phenomenon to be explained is completely absorbed by the law or structure which constitutes its explanation" (1991: 175). This mode of understanding, he notes, manifests the "strange mistrust of the event" of twentieth-century French historiography (1991: 175) where particular and singular events are reduced to the law or structure of that understanding (including, as in structuralism, the structural laws of the transformations of structures). Here, the "same" is defined by "law or structure" so that particular events can be equated and made "equable" precisely by erasing whatever is temporally unique.

A second mode of understanding, Taylor argues, whose "paradigmatic example is that of *langue-parole*," does not reduce each of its "'events' or 'particular cases'" to "a mere example" or to "a particular case of a regularity" (1991: 176). He uses the example of language to argue that the instances (*parole*) of the general structure (*langue*) are the only means by which the "structure has purchase on the real." Taylor designates this relationship between structure and event "successive renewals," a term fully marked by temporality. "It is a matter," he writes, "of human acts aiming (in principle) at the realization of a structure, which may, however, not succeed or which may even be directed against the structures which must (in principle) rule them. Languages live only through successive renewals, each of which is a risk, for it runs the risk of not coming through this renewal unharmed" (1991: 176). The narrator of *The Mill on the Floss* is completely separate from those involved in the novel's events and its history, Maggie, Tom, and the rest, and consequently neither the narrator nor the narrative focuses on the problem of the temporality of action, the successive renewals of the significance of time. Time for George Eliot, as it is for the bourgeois civilization in which she works, is always the same, absolute and unproblematic – which is to say, even if we can find the problem of time in her work and narrative procedure, it is not a *theme* of her narrative and its problem is not an *event* in her narrative. Rather, her theme can be understood in terms of genre – the bildungsroman or the various narrative genres such as tragedy, legend, and the melodrama of the dark heroine alluded to in the text – all of which are offered as timeless structures that comprehend her heroine, just as the desires and experience of a medieval monk define her desires and experience. In this sense, twentieth-century Modernism has answered George Eliot's description and figuration of death as "the same final home" with Maurice Blanchot's unnerving description in *The Writing of the Disaster* of "the dying which, though unsharable, I have in common with all" (1986: 23) or Georges Bataille's description of death as "in one sense the common inevitable, but in another sense, profound, inaccessible" (1988: 71). Modernism answers the unexceptional accidents of the time of bourgeois realism with what Benjamin calls the "flashes" of messianic time and the possibility of redeeming "accidents" altogether.

Throughout *The Mill on the Floss* – throughout classic realism – the world acts on the characters, and the text narrates *this* action seemingly from outside its effects. "We have known Maggie a long while," the narrator tells us,

and need to be told, not her characteristics, but her history, which is a thing hardly to be predicted even from the completest knowledge of character- istics ... Hamlet, Prince of Denmark, was speculative and irresolute, and we have a great tragedy in consequence. But if his father had lived to a good old age, and his uncle had died an early death, we can conceive Hamlet's having married Ophelia, and got through life with a reputation of sanity...

Maggie's destiny, then, is at present hidden, and we must wait for it to reveal itself like the course of an unmapped river: we only know that the river is full and rapid, and that for all rivers there is the same final home. (1961: 351)

The parallel between Hamlet and Maggie is not an analogy. Rather, in the parallel and in the distinctions between inner characteristics and outer events and between the present and the destined future,

George Eliot is offering a version of nomological understanding that Taylor describes, based fully upon the separation between observer and observed, between type and instance, between understanding and action. Understanding, in this mode of making sense of experience, erases time as a significant element of what is being understood. Since human significance, human desire, human behavior, are always essentially the same – these assumptions, after all, are the foundation of the great sympathetic power of George Eliot's Victorian humanism – "the phenomenon to be explained," as Taylor says, "is completely absorbed by the law or structure which constitutes its explanation" (1991: 175). For George Eliot, that law or structure is the law of human development: such development exists in time, but its aim and realization are not in any important ways temporal. Both this passage and the ending of her novel, where Maggie dies in the flooding Floss, demonstrate how separate and accidental temporal events are in relation to character, destiny, and understanding.

This conception of development is figured by Maggie's repeated urge to drift throughout *The Mill on the Floss*. It is also, I think, figured in Newton's metaphor of the equable "flow" of "absolute, true, and mathematical time." In her scandalous adventure floating down the river with Stephen (fiancé to her friend, Lucy), in her death in the flood, even in her dream of St. Ogg (1961: 412–13), Maggie is carried along relentlessly, so that she remains helpless in the face of time and experience. Her dream of St. Ogg is particularly striking, because she dreams of waking up at home at the mill on the Floss as "a child again in the parlour at evening twilight, and [her brother] Tom was not really angry" (1961: 413). This dream repeats the narrator's opening dream of the pastoral mill, but for Maggie it is false: she wakes to the "terrible truth" that "she was alone with her own memory and her own dread" (1961: 413). Her immediate response is to recognize "the clew to life" that she had lost, "renunciation." Renunciation is the choice to order her life by memory rather than desire – her term here is "dread," not desire – so that she can find that impossible "home" where sympathy and self can be joined in a kind of personal fulfillment that is also "archetypical," governed wholly by a *prior* type (that is, a law or structure), the atemporality of realized humanity. It is the secular *atemporality* of humanity – not only in George Eliot's sympathetic understanding, but in the curious combination of science and

theology in Newton – that conditions the good and great success of
Enlightenment culture, its human sympathy, its nomological science,
its actual achievements of social and historical progress.

## II WALTER BENJAMIN AND THE REDEMPTION OF TIME

If the great achievement of the Enlightenment is the combination of
subjective idealism and general semiotics – the emancipation and
domination embedded in Enlightenment understanding and evaluation – then the narration of realism achieves at least the illusion of
this seemingly impossible combination in the transcendental subjectivity of its narrator, its atemporal subjectivity positioned on the
"infinitesimal" horizon of future time. For Benjamin the event of
death disrupts this combination as the most powerful site of temporality conceived not as a place, an atemporal "final home," but above
all as a moment of time. For Benjamin, the event of death punctuates
historical, mythological, and subjective time, the time of material
life, intellectual comprehensions, and subjective experience of these
chapters. When it is narrated, it "thickens" time and creates the
possibility of meaning in the context of repeated but non-transcendental closures – what Benjamin's contemporary, M. M. Bakhtin
calls the "finalized structuredness" of discursive genres which exist
but which are "reborn and renewed in each [particular author] in
[their] own way, that is, in a unique and unrepeatable way" (1984:
159) that I discuss in chapter 6. Thus in his essay on Baudelaire,
Benjamin describes "the *durée* from which death has been eliminated
has the miserable endlessness of a scroll" (1969: 185). Such "miserable endlessness" describes Newtonian time, the very "flow" that
accidentally ends Maggie Tulliver's life. Throughout his work Benjamin is attempting to respond to the positivism of Newtonian
mechanics that implies such repetitions. In the 1920s Georges
Bataille redefines the "materialism" of positivist mechanics as an
"intransigent materialism" of "base matter" that is not susceptible
to traditional representations, but is "external and foreign to ideal
human aspirations" (1985: 51). Like Benjamin, Bataille redefines the
received Enlightenment assumptions about time and space in the
face of the experience of modernity – and especially the experience
of time – at the turn of the twentieth century, which was conditioned
by the abundances of the second Industrial Revolution. The

problem, arising in the face of this experience that Benjamin and his contemporaries address, is most clearly apprehended in incongruence between the concept and event of death and the multiplicity of approaches – avoidance, repetition, metonymy, particularized descriptions of historical moments and events – that this incongruence occasions. For Benjamin, this problem gives rise to his attempts to forge a new conception of representation in the face of the temporality of Modernism: the poetics of fragmentation, materialist temporality, redemption, and above all a conception of allegory very different from George Eliot's nomological allegory.

Benjamin accomplishes this rethinking of representation by marking the difference between historical and semiotic analyses, the "jagged line of demarcation between physical nature and significance" (1977: 166). For Benjamin the relationship between historical event and understanding defines in large part the problematic relationship between time and representation that inhabits twentieth-century Modernism. Such incongruence is completely absent in George Eliot: it remains unthematized and exists, if at all, only unconsciously. The very ambiguity of what is "unconscious" for the Enlightenment marks this fact: what is unconscious remains comprehensible only as accident, only as something excluded by the necessary and sufficient simplicities of atemporal understanding just as the historical event of Maggie's death in *The Mill on the Floss* is purely accidental. It is precisely the unrolling of examples without possibilities of simplifying generalization and coherence, atemporally, once and for all – the unrolling of a fissure between history and semiotics – that cannot be thought by Enlightenment discourse and cannot be avoided by post-Enlightenment Modernism. Such "unrolling" is, above all, temporal. It encompasses the incongruence of history and meaning that contributed to the crisis of representation in the early twentieth century, the "crisis consciousness" I discuss at the end of the following chapter. In the early twentieth century, Benjamin attempted, more fully than many of his contemporaries, not simply to describe and respond to this crisis but to devise representational tactics that might offer possibilities, in the face of it, of recovering meaning in history. Benjamin attempted to comprehend base matter and intransigent materialism by creating a mode of representation for the semantic void of material violence and the miserable endlessness of time. This attempt, I believe, presents a tactics and a rhetoric to grasp what many of Benjamin's contemporaries thought to be ungraspable, the experience of time, multiplicity, and overwhelming change in the modern world. The combination of Marxism and Messianic Judaism is a sign of Benjamin's tactics.

### THE TEMPORALITY OF MODERNITY: MULTIPLICITY, MEANING, AND ATHEMATIC DEATH

> Just as in its most uncompromising representatives modern music no longer tolerates any elaboration, any distinction between theme and development, but instead every musical idea, even every note, stands equally near the center, so too Benjamin's philosophy is "athematic." It is dialectics at a standstill in another sense as well, in that it allots no time to internal development but instead receives its form from the constellation formed by the individual statements. Hence its affinity with the aphorism. At the same time, however, the theoretical element in Benjamin always requires farther-ranging linkages of ideas.
>
> Theodor Adorno (1992: 229)

Writing in his Introduction to Walter Benjamin's *Schriften*, Theodor Adorno notes that "Benjamin's philosophy provokes the misunderstanding of consuming and defusing it as a series of unconnected aperçus responding to the contingencies of occasion." Nevertheless, Adorno writes, "each insight has its place within an extraordinary unity of philosophical consciousness. But the essence of this unity consists in its moving outward, in finding itself by losing itself in multiplicity" (1992: 222). Adorno's description of the difficulty of reading Benjamin – what he calls later, following Benjamin's own terminology, the difficulty of his "constellation of ideas" in which the concrete is "never denigrated ... to an example of the concept" (1992: 223, 224) – encompasses the difficulty of the relationship between representation and event, between representation's need to find the general case, the common denominator among disparate phenomena, and the fact that the *power* of an event is its indivisible temporal uniqueness, its existence as only what Benjamin describes as a "small, individual moment," which creates its authority (1989: 48; 1969: 94).

This is the problem in Benjamin's study of baroque *Trauerspiel* (or lamentation plays) that George Steiner describes in his "Introduction" to the English translation, *Origin of German Tragic Drama*:

"How can there be a general and generalizing treatment of artistic-literary objects which are, by definition, unique?" (1977: 23). Adorno describes this focus in Benjamin in terms of fully determined and irreversible temporality. Benjamin's philosophical interest, he says (unlike the discourse of George Eliot's narrators, I might add),

is not directed to the ahistorical at all, but rather to what is temporally determined and irreversible. Hence the title *One Way Street*. Benjamin's images are not linked with nature as moments of a self-identical ontology but rather in the name of death, of transience as the supreme category of natural existence, the category toward which Benjamin's thought advances. What is eternal in them is only the transient. (1992: 226)

Focus on the temporally irreversible produces the difficulty of representation insofar as representation, in Foucault's telling definition, possesses "the obscure power of making a past impression present once more" so that an impression can "appear as either similar to or dissimilar from a previous one" (1976: 69). When transience is the supreme category of existence, then the "self-identical ontology" that allows for judgments of similarity and dissimilarity – that allows for representation itself – becomes a problem. Nowhere is this problem more pronounced, as Benjamin suggests, than in the category or conception of death. For like the isolated ideas in modern music that Adorno describes, the particularity of the *event* of death can never be encompassed by its conception, its historical specificity by a generalizing semiotics. The particular event of death is never simply "an example of the concept" in the way George Eliot makes Maggie's desire an example of general human desire.

This situation, for Benjamin, is a touchstone for his understanding of representation, allegory, and meaning. "Socrates," he writes in *The Origin of German Tragic Drama*,

looks death in the face as a mortal – the best and most virtuous of mortals, one may insist – but he recognizes it as something alien, beyond which, in immortality, he expects to return to himself. Not so the tragic hero; he shrinks before death as before a power that is familiar, personal, and inherent in him. His life, indeed, unfolds from death, which is not its end but its form. For tragic existence acquires its task only because it is intrinsically subject to the limits of both linguistic and physical life which are set within it from its very beginning. (1977: 114)

In this passage, Benjamin is describing the paradox that death is both inherent in the life of the tragic hero and also its limiting other. Socrates, in this narrative, sees death as fully alien from himself, something "beyond" which he can situate himself in an immortal and *atemporal* home where he expects to return to himself. For the tragic hero, however, death is familiar, personal, quotidian, yet at the same time a limit to life in both its meaning and its base materiality. It is a concrete event that can never be reduced to an example of the concept of death. This is the import of Maurice Blanchot's description of "the dying which, though unsharable, I have in common with all" (1986: 23) and Bataille's description of death as "in one sense the common inevitable, but in another sense, profound, inaccessible" (1988: 71) that I have already mentioned. Benjamin's fascinated contemplation of this situation provokes the power of his discourse. "What Benjamin said and wrote," Adorno says, "sounded as if it came from the depths of mystery. It received its power, however, from its quality of self-evidence" (1992: 221). George Eliot's pronouncements, on the other hand, present themselves as if they come from the common experience all share in the "self-evidence" of eye rather than ear.

The post-Enlightenment modernity that Benjamin encounters (or at least finds himself thrown into) includes the *materiality* of death, a "base" materiality, as Bataille says, "not implying an ontology, not implying that matter is the thing-in-itself" (1985: 49). "Base matter," Bataille says, "is external and foreign to ideal human aspirations, and it refuses to allow itself to be reduced to the great ontological machines resulting from these aspirations" (1985: 51). For Bataille, base matter – and death itself – is not the "opposite" to life in a system of spatial and mechanistic representations in which the same and the opposite play together in a homogeneous system of meaning. Rather, Bataille argues, "matter, in fact, can only be defined as the *nonlogical difference* that represents in relation to the *economy* of the universe what *crime* represents in relation to the law" (1985: 129). These phenomena – excessive, unique, powerful events rather than objects of knowledge – he describes as the "heterogeneous," but are better described, as Benjamin describes them, as possessing the inalienable temporality of events. For Bataille – and, as we shall see, for Benjamin as well – the materiality of the *event* disrupts objectivity, representations, and knowledge conceived as nomological science. In this discussion Bataille shares with Benjamin, as his translator has noted, an attempt "to find an alternative to both idealism and traditional materialism (which starts out with material facts but then goes 'beyond' them to construct an abstract, conceptual edifice)"

(Stoekl 1985: xxv; see also Tiedemann 1989: 176). For Bataille traditional materialism is simply a variant of the same "metaphysical scaffolding" as idealism. "Two verbal entities are thus formed," he writes: "an abstract God (or simply the idea), and abstract matter" (1985: 45).

The alternative to idealism and abstract materialism fully acknowledges irreversible time and its unique moments; it "exposes," as Benjamin says, "the passing moment in all its nakedness" (1969: 185). Unlike Bataille, however – or, at least, more systematically and self-consciously than Bataille – Benjamin attempts to recover such events for comprehension. Bataille, as Foucault argues, attempted "through every detour and repetition of his work" simply "to circumscribe" an *experience* (1977: 36) of what might be called the sacred but really cannot be comprehended in a concept or an idea. That is, for Bataille, the alternative to idealism and traditional materialism is precisely "ungraspable": "Christianity," he writes, "has made the sacred *substantial*, but the nature of the sacred ... is perhaps the most ungraspable thing that has been produced between men: the sacred is only a privileged moment of communal unity, a moment of the convulsive communication of what is ordinarily stifled" (1985: 242). For George Eliot – as for the Enlightenment humanism she embodies – *nothing* is "ungraspable." Benjamin implies, as I have already suggested, that the "ungraspable" can be realized and perhaps momentarily *renewed* in the analogical differences of transgenerational life. For Bataille, however, Christianity attempts to tame and master the sacred once and for all by making it a "substance." In this analysis, Bataille implies that what he calls "Christianity" repeats the conjunction of the subjective idealism and general semiotics of bourgeois humanism I described in chapter 1 and in the narrative realism of George Eliot. In analyzing Bataille, Steven Shaviro argues that "there are no limits to idealization. We can always move self-reflexively to a higher level, take our own limits and presuppositions into account, create a metalanguage" (1990: 20). Greimas, in more technical terms, describes this *linguistic* process as one of "substantivizing" relationships, "freezing all intentional dynamism into a conceptual terminology" (see Schleifer 1990: 7, 118–19).

These descriptions of "substance," "idealization," and "substantivization" – descriptions of objects, ideas, and a hidden order of discourse – all present the ubiquitous power of generalizing representation. *Anything*, as Shaviro argues, can serve representation's obscure power of erasing time and reducing things to markers for other things, of creating relationships of example and concept, of establishing a synecdochical order of meaning. This is because, meaning itself, as Jakobson says, is synecdochical insofar as language is a phenomenon in which the whole is always greater than the sum of the parts (1987: 432). (Paul de Man uses this fact to argue for the "absolute independence" of the hermeneutic and the poetic, grammar and meaning, and the symbol and what is being symbolized in his discussion of Benjamin [1986: 89].) Implicit in the synecdochical order of meaning are the assumptions of Enlightenment modernity I described in the preceding chapter, and such an order *needs* to repress, hide and exclude aspects of material and intellectual experience in order to create its hierarchy of meaning.

What is left out is precisely the "nonlogical difference" Bataille describes, a form of metonymy that both is and is not the opposite of synecdoche (see Schleifer 1990: ch. 1). "Nonlogical difference" organizes itself in effective temporality and temporal subjectivity, and in this economy metonymy becomes a figure for death and time insofar as "death" locates or gestures towards a kind of irreducible abundance of base matter and intransigent materialism beyond what Derrida calls in his essay on Bataille the "restricted economy" of meaning (1978: 252). As such, then, it creates the effects of hauntings, free-floating anxiety, and even an "aura" and the sacred alongside quotidian experience that so interested Benjamin (on the levels of politics, experience, and philosophy) and, as I argue in chapter 6, Bakhtin as well (on the level of aesthetics). It is precisely the provocation of such free-floating anxiety that distinguishes T. S. Eliot from George Eliot and Wordsworth. The anxiety T. S. Eliot expresses and provokes shares with Bataille a lack of concern for comprehension in favor of attempts to provide experience: "Bataille's writing," Shaviro argues, "neither designates objects, nor signifies ideas, nor manifests a hidden order of reality. Rather it charts the *expérience-limite* (*limit-experience*), as Blanchot puts it, of a 'détour de tout visible et de tout invisible [turning away from every visible and every invisible]' " (1990: 85–86).

Yet the recovery, comprehension, and redemption – in a word, the *organization* – of unique and unrepeatable moments in what he calls "legibility" and "recognizability" (1989: 50) is precisely Benjamin's project. In the instance I have already given, where he describes the tragic hero in the *Trauerspiel* book, he seeks to discover in "tragic existence" an alternative to both philosophical idealism and the idealism that inheres in traditional materialism. The power Adorno describes in Benjamin's language, ringing with the "depths of mystery" yet possessing the quality of self-evidence, is a function of his attempt, beyond that of Bataille and Blanchot (and even that of T. S. Eliot), not simply to describe and provoke the energy and disruption of the base materiality of time and death (which are, I am suggesting, analogous to the energy and disruptions of the second Industrial Revolution), but to harness it to human ends. Benjamin attempted to develop an alternative to idealism and to idealized materialism. Unlike Bataille or Blanchot and more explicitly than Derrida, Benjamin attempts this alternative by redefining the notion of "idea" against "concept," so that a material idea is imaginable.

Benjamin argues in *Origin of German Tragic Drama* that the idea "belongs to a fundamentally different world from that which it apprehends" (1977: 34), a world of what he calls "nonsensuous similarity" (1978: 334; Buck-Morss translates the same phrase as "non-representational similarity," 1977: 90). Speaking of the "ideas" of the Renaissance or the baroque, he notes that "as ideas, however, [they] perform a service they are not able to perform as concepts: they do not make the similar identical" (1977: 41). The making of the similar identical is precisely the work of concepts; it is the work of the parsimony of nomological science and George Eliot's humanism. Ideas, on the other hand, "exist in irreducible multiplicity" (1977: 43). They are, above all, the basis of what I am calling analogical thinking. The figures Benjamin uses for such multiplicity are astral and family *constellations*.

Ideas are to objects as constellations are to stars. This means, in the first place, that they are neither their concepts nor their laws. They do not contribute to the knowledge of phenomena, and in no way can the latter be criteria with which to judge the existence of ideas ... Whereas phenomena determine the scope and content of the concepts which encompass them, by their existence, by what they have in common, and by their differences, the relationship to ideas is the opposite of this inasmuch as the idea, the objective interpretation of phenomena – or rather their elements – determines their relationship to each other ... Just as a mother is seen to begin to live in the fullness of her power only when the circle of her children, inspired by the feeling of her proximity, closes around her, so do ideas come to life only when extremes are assembled around them. Ideas ... remain obscure so long as phenomena do not declare their faith to them and gather round them. It is the function of concepts to group phenomena together, and the division which is brought about within them thanks to the distinguishing power of the intellect is all the more significant in that it brings about two things at a single stroke: the salvation of phenomena and the representation of ideas. (1977: 34–35)

This is a difficult passage – Steiner has called the whole "Prologue" to *The Origin of German Tragic Drama* "one of the more impenetrable pieces of prose in German or, for that matter, in any modern language" (1977: 13), and the editors of Benjamin's collected works call it "the most esoteric text that Benjamin ever wrote" (cited in Moses 1989: 233–34). Its opacity resides in the manner in which Benjamin *analogizes* understanding. In this passage the analogies of "constellation" and "mother" do not function as *examples* of the principles being explored in the way, for example, Thomas à Kempis's experience becomes an example of all experience or Adam Smith's individual need becomes an example of human need in general. Rather, they offer what Benjamin calls elsewhere in the *Trauerspiel* book an "allegorical" understanding, an understanding in which different realms confront one another without reduction of one to the other. As Buck-Morss has noted, "like atoms, like cells, like solar systems [constellations] each had their own center: without hierarchy, they stood next to each other 'in perfect independence and unimpaired'" (1977: 94; the citation is Buck-Morss's translation from *Origin* 1977: 37). In these cases, Benjamin unfolds his discussion of ideas without the reduction of astrology to a debased species of knowledge and without the reduction of the family life to a species of abstract relationship.

Allegory achieves the independence of its elements, Benjamin argues, by marking time in "the jagged line of demarcation between physical nature and significance" (1977: 166); like the *Trauerspiel* which Benjamin is studying, it presents "reality in the form of the ruin" (1977: 177), meaning allegorized in the destructions of time. (It is the destructions of time that lead to what I described in the Introduction as the "abstractions" of answerability; such temporal destructions delineate the state of non-transcendental disembodiment I describe in the following chapter. As such Benjamin's allegory has little to do with George Eliot's allegorical substitution of Hamlet or Thomas à Kempis for Maggie.) "Where in the symbol," he notes,

destruction is idealized and the transfigured face of nature is fleetingly revealed in the light of redemption, in allegory the observer is confronted with the *facies hippocratica* of history as a petrified, primordial landscape. Everything about history that, from the very beginning, has been untimely, sorrowful, unsuccessful, is expressed in a face – or rather in a death's head ... This is the heart of the allegorical way of seeing ... The greater the significance, the greater the subjection to death, because death digs most deeply the jagged line of demarcation between physical nature and significance. (1977: 166)

In the allegory of constellated significance, the "center" of meaning (as in the novel, 1969: 99) or the "kernel" of thought or the "heart" of an idea does not exist. Rather, like the "slow piling one on top of the other of thin, transparent layers ... of a variety of retellings" in the story (1969: 93), the fullness of a mother's power Benjamin describes balanced between the independent power of children and parent, the power of *analogous* generations, is the result of the nonlogical difference that is intrinsically subject to the ineluctable and irreversible time of generations.

In these analogies Benjamin creates representations that do not have the "obscure power" of erasing time that Foucault describes. Analogies *mark time*: they underline the very "power of recall" Foucault mentions (1976: 69) that inhabits – unconsciously, without a mark – the generalizing abstractions of idealism and the traditional materialism of classical realism. Analogies bring together two fundamentally different orders: by marking similitude with an "as" or a "like." By more fully inscribing time in its figure, Benjamin's analogy of generations, more than the astronomical figure of constellations, combines the mystery and self-evidence – "recognition" and "legibility" – that Adorno asserts constitutes Benjamin's power and, I might add, that distinguishes itself from the self-evident legibilities of realism. Thus in describing the relationship between capitalism and nature in *One-Way Street*, Benjamin offers the analogy of generational relationships. "Who would trust a cane wielder who proclaimed the mastery of children by adults to be the purpose of education?" he asks. "Is not education above all the indispensable ordering of the relationship between generations and therefore mastery, if we are to use this term, of that relationship and not of children?" (1978: 93). In this passage "mastery," like "power" describing the mother in the *Trauerspiel* book, is a form of quotation, which, like the bringing together of different generations in one household or community, underlines the temporal disparity encompassed by allegory (see de Man 1969). In *One-Way Street* this is

particularly clear because Benjamin is quoting the sentence preceding this passage: "The mastery of nature, so the imperialists
teach, is the purpose of all technology" (1978: 93).

Death itself, the unique fate of every generation, becomes in the
unfolding of allegory a figure for a mode of representation that
avoids, to some degree, the *reductiveness* of nomological representation. But it avoids it only in its base materiality or what Benjamin
calls the "creaturely guilt" associated with "the core notion of fate"
(1977: 129). Such materiality, guilt, and fate are not only – or not
*simply* – the opposite to ideality. In the end, Benjamin argues,
allegory "loses everything that was most peculiar to it: the secret,
privileged knowledge, the arbitrary rule in the realm of the dead
objects, the supposed infinity of a world without hope. All this
vanishes with this *one* about-turn, in which the immersion of allegory
has to clear away the final phantasmagoria of the objective and, left
entirely to its own devices, re-discovers itself, not playfully in the
earthly world of things, but seriously under the eyes of heaven"
(1977: 232). The "turn" Benjamin describes is allegory's turn on
itself, accomplished by "displaying" rather than representing its own
"transitoriness" (1977: 232). Geoffrey Hartman says that "allegor-
izing, though driven by a desire for transcendence, remains skeletal,
grimacing, schematic" (1980: 90). Yet for Benjamin this mode of
sublunary understanding, with its reified, commodified, and substan-
tivized semiotics, "turns" and emerges, in its very transitoriness,
under the "eye" of heaven, into something else.

The complexity of allegory – and above all its temporal complexity of turns and changes – is a scandal to the simplicities of
Enlightenment understanding that govern George Eliot's discourse
and that I described more abstractly in chapter 1. In an analogous
way, the "*one* about-turn" of death itself is irreducibly complex. It is
an event that exists within a series of events and also as a singular
occurrence (Eagleton 1981: 35; Schleifer 1990: ch. 1). "The characters of the *Trauerspiel* die," Benjamin writes, "because it is only thus,
as corpses, that they can enter into the homeland of allegory" (1977:
217). In these instances – not examples, but particular allegorical
moments – death loses its power of representation even while its
connection to the world and to meaning is asserted. "Allegory,"
Benjamin says at the conclusion of the *Trauerspiel* book, "loses
everything that was most particular to it" and "goes away empty-
handed" (1977: 232, 233).

## THE LOGIC OF ABUNDANCE: ANALOGICAL FIGURES

All this, though, seems to have returned us to the uncomprehensible materiality of Bataille and Blanchot, what Benjamin describes in the *Origin of German Tragic Drama* as "soulless materiality" in "an empty world" (1977: 230, 139), the world opposite to that of the narrator of *The Mill on the Floss* who finds nostalgic meaning everywhere. In what ways, as Benjamin says, can the idea redeem the material world? In what ways can the unique event of death be represented without empty-handedness, ruination, or the idealizations of traditional metaphysical materialism? How can allegory re-discover itself, "seriously," under the eye of heaven? The modes of understanding Benjamin uses in his uncompleted *Arcades Project* to suggest alternatives to idealism and traditional materialism are those of quotations and that of the image, the narrative strategies of Joyce and Woolf discussed in the preceding chapter. The *Arcades Project*, he wrote, "must raise the art of quoting without quotation marks to the very highest level" (1989: 45); elsewhere, he said that the *Trauerspiel* book "consists almost entirely of quotations. The drollest mosaic technique one can imagine" (cited in Smith 1989: xxxix, n. 111). Both his use of unascribed quotations and his peculiar ideas of the image and of allegory punctuate the miserable endlessness of time.

The "mosaic technique" of quotations creates a form of radical metonymy, allowing for analogical presentation of material without abstracting a theme: it creates the possibility of "athematic" representation, in which, as Derrida has said, "the part is always greater than the whole" (1976: 96). In such analogies, the figure used, ostensibly as an example, takes on a life of its own because it *has* a life of its own insofar as the temporality of its existence is not extrinsic to it. It takes on this "other life" in the same way that Benjamin argues translation is "only a somewhat provisional way of coming to terms with the foreignness of languages" (1969: 75) since even the most commonplace words – the German *Brot*, the French *pain*, and the English *bread* – lead different lives in their respective languages (see de Man 1986: 87). Translation is an instance of quotation that is at once minute and global, and in it the irreducible differences – above all, *temporal differences* – inherent in all quotation are markedly pronounced. Similarly, the analogical figures in Benjamin – "constellation," "mother," even his figure of "mosaic" (1977: 28–29) – cite and translate different contexts of meaning to arrest discourse and transform it into what Benjamin calls "irreducible multiplicity" (1977: 43). In quotations, time is not quite succession and its subject is never quite atemporal.

That is, quotations (including the quotation of translation) are other versions of the analogical figures that function like "monuments in the discontinuous structure of the world of ideas" (1977: 33). "With every idea," he writes later in the *Trauerspiel* book, "the moment of expression coincides with a veritable eruption of images, which gives rise to a chaotic mass of metaphors" (1977: 173). The analogical figure takes on this life of its own because, as a version of quotation possessing its own temporality, it is *other* than the progress and "life" of the discourse in which it appears. Quotation, analogue, and metonym are different from yet embedded in discourse. Both part of and other than the language they appear in, they are forms of abundance, more than the "whole," as Derrida says: they are "overdetermined," "redundant," "pastiche," "complementary," "irreducibly nonsimple" (to cite articulations of abundance mentioned in chapter 1).[7] Moreover, they allow us to apprehend language itself "abundantly," as it were, not simply as nostalgic markers of loss – markers of the simple successiveness of time – as in George Eliot. Rather, they allow the idea of language itself to be apprehended abundantly, so that, as Benjamin says, it "is in every case not only communication of the communicable but also, at the same time, a symbol of the noncommunicable" (1978: 331).

The figures and ideas of quotation arrest and complicate the progress of discourse. "Thinking," Benjamin writes in the "Theses on the Philosophy of History" (XVII), "involves not only the flow of thoughts, but their arrest as well" (1969: 262). Thus in his essay on "Progress" that focuses on Benjamin's *Arcades Project*, Adorno radically redefines the idea of progress he has inherited from the bourgeois conception of continuous development. Progress, to be meaningful at all, he argues, would be transformed precisely into that which arrests the flow of history: progress, he writes, "wants to disrupt the triumph of radical evil, not to triumph in itself" (1989: 101). By bringing together things in a nonhierarchic dialectic (pursuing different levels of meaning in examining a single object), Benjamin's metonymic mosaic technique, like Jameson's "pastiche" and even the aesthetic "answerability" of art Bakhtin describes, disrupts progressive causal explanation. It is precisely the "life of its *own*" that resists the reduction of analogue to example and history to (causal) continuity. "The materialist presentation of history goes hand in hand with an immanent critique of the concept of progress" (1989: 67), Benjamin writes in the notes for the *Arcades Project*. Historical materialism "blasts the epoch out of the reified 'continuity of history.' But it also blasts open the homogeneity of the epoch" (1989: 65).

Benjamin elaborates the ways in which discourse and progress are arrested in his description of the *Trauerspiel* book. "In the canonic form of the treatise," he writes,

the only element of an intention – and it is an educative rather than a didactic intention – is the authoritative quotation. Its method is essentially representation. Method is a digression . . . The absence of an uninterrupted purposeful structure is its primary characteristic. Tirelessly the process of thinking makes new beginnings, returning in a roundabout way to its original object. This continual pausing for breath is the mode most proper to the process of contemplation. For by pursuing different levels of meaning in its examination of one single object it receives both the incentive to begin again and the justification for its irregular rhythm . . . The relationship between the minute precision of the work and the proportions of the sculptural or intellectual whole demonstrates that truth-content is only to be grasped through immersion in the most minute details of subject matter. (1977: 28–29)

In the analogical discourse of quotation, as in the later Nietzsche (as Adorno points out), truth is not "a timeless *universal*, but rather it is solely the historical which yields the figure of the absolute" (Adorno 1981: 231). It is this "historical" – which is to say "timely" – absolute that distinguishes the abundant "mosaics" of collage and montage from strategies aiming at the reductive articulation of atemporal truth.

Still, Benjamin's focus on quotation rather than phenomena and his emphasis on the temporally-situated nature of meaning brings him closer to his contemporary, Bakhtin, than to Nietzsche. For Bakhtin, "*any true understanding is dialogic in nature*. Understanding is to utterance as one line of a dialogue is to the next" (1986: 102). This is why, in *Marxism and the Philosophy of Language*, Bakhtin/Vološinov spend so much time examining versions of quotation in discourse: direct discourse, indirect discourse, and free indirect discourse (what Bakhtin's translators call "quasi-direct discourse," 1986: 142 and part III). The kind of language Benjamin is describing – quotations without quotation marks – is a form of free indirect discourse, and much of Bakhtin's materialist analysis of language and genre attends to what he calls the "finalized wholes" of discourse, language that conveys meaning (hence, is "whole") yet *always* calls for an answer within the historical situation of its utterance. (See Kenner 1988 and Harris 1993 for a discussion of this phenomenon in relation to fractal geometry.) What distinguishes Benjamin from Bakhtin is his emphasis on the sacred within experience, discourse, and culture, "the transcendent force of the sacred image and the truth itself" (1977: 28–29). Bakhtin – especially in his work of the twenties, as I argue in chapter 6 – focuses on aesthetics as the framework of sacred experience while Benjamin attempts to comprehend the sacred in experience more widely conceived, what he calls "a conception of the present as the 'time of the now' which is shot through with chips of Messianic time" (1969: 263).

It is for this reason that death as a material, temporally situated event is important for Benjamin in ways that it isn't for Bakhtin (or, for that matter, for Nietzsche). Throughout his career – in the *Origin of German Tragic Drama*, in *One-Way Street*, in the essay on Baudelaire and, above all, in the essay "The Storyteller" – the authority of discourse and experience is realized at moments of death. This is the import of his assertion that "the *durée* from which death has been eliminated has the miserable endlessness of a scroll" (1969: 185). Quotation breaks up the endlessness of a scroll by recalling and remembering, as analogies that take on a life of their own do, another time and also "the time of the now," the "now of a specific recognizability" (1989: 50). It transforms the parsimonious logic of communication to a discourse of abundance by situating a *temporal* subject of experience and knowledge within a moment of recognition. Moreover, quotation of dying words – the *citation* of the event of death – punctuates discourse and experience with the sacred. "Today," he writes in "The Storyteller,"

people live in rooms that have never been touched by death, dry dwellers of eternity, and when their end approaches they are stowed away in sanatoria or hospitals by their heirs. It is, however, characteristic that not only a man's knowledge or wisdom, but above all his real life – and this is the stuff that stories are made of – first assumes transmissible form at the moment of his death. Just as a sequence of images is set in motion inside a man as his life comes to an end – unfolding the views of himself under which he has encountered himself without being aware of it – suddenly in his expressions and looks the unforgettable emerges and imparts to everything that concerned him that authority which even the poorest wretch in dying possesses for the living around him. This authority is at the very source of the story. (1969: 94)

The structure of quotation Benjamin is describing carries "the montage principle over into history" by detecting "the crystal of the total event in the analysis of the small, individual moment" (1989: 48). Yet as the absolute disruption of death – as apocalyptic or Messianic – such moments are sacred for Benjamin. They combine quotation and an image, legibility and recognition – here in the expression and look of the dying man – so that *something* can be passed along in history to another generation.

Such transmissibility characterizes Bakhtin's dialogics (1981: 341). So, too, in Benjamin's reading, "Kafka's real genius was that he tried something entirely new: he sacrificed truth for the sake of clinging to its transmissibility, in haggadic element" (1969: 143–44). Yet Benjamin (and, in his understanding, Kafka as well) lacks Bakhtin's *cheerfulness* about history and its metonymic repetitions that go on and on. "The concept of progress," Benjamin writes, "should be grounded in the idea of catastrophe. That things 'just keep on going' *is* the catastrophe" (1989: 64). The incongruence of transmissibility and truth, communication and language, the continuity of history and chips of Messianic time, makes death itself a constant element or "level" of his discourse and experience, hovering amid each con-stellated idea he pursues; it creates the apocalyptic necessity to blast open "the homogeneity of the epoch [and saturate] it with *ecrasite*, i.e., the present" (1989: 65). It is a shadow haunting and multiplying his discourse, just as it haunts and multiplies his "idea" of allegory.

Benjamin's use and understanding of quotation is analogous to his idea of a dialectical image that he develops in an attempt to create a mode of representing the temporality of historical events – and especially death – in his notes for the *Arcades Project*. "It isn't that the past casts its light on the present or the present casts its light on the past," he writes; "rather, an image is that in which the Then [*das Gewesene*] and the Now [*das Jetzt*] come into a constellation like a flash of lightning. In other words: image is dialectics at a standstill ... Only dialectical images are genuine (i.e. not archaic) images; and the place one happens upon them is language" (1989: 49). The vehicle for dialectical images is the analogical dialogue of quotations, and the most *authoritative* quotations are those of the dying and the dead: "the community of all the dead is so immense that even he who only reports death is aware of it. *Ad plures ire* was the Latins' expression of dying" (1978: 90). Yet it is a vehicle because it creates unique moments that are not atomistic, but shared by the community. Later in his notes, he adds that "the dialectical image is a lightning flash. The Then must be held fast as it flashes its lightning image in the Now of recognizability. The rescue that is thus – and only thus – effected, can only take place for that which, in the next moment, is already irretrievably lost" (1989: 64). Here Benjamin is describing Bakhtin's *dialogical* meaning, the temporal interplay of discourses in an ongoing conversation that one joins and leaves.

The difference, though – and this, I think, is crucial for the possibility of a representation of post-Enlightenment temporality – is that Benjamin, like Woolf, is attempting to discover the sacred within death and dying and so sees it as more than *another* event within a history of events; he sees it as a focal point for the quotations of dialectical images, like the "love," which is after all the fullness of the power of mothers (and, as I know, of fathers as well), the allegorical other of that power, the Then of (remembered) love flashing in the Now of power. Such flashing conditions Benjamin's idea of remembrance discussed in the preceding chapter. It offers a "theological" understanding of remembrance that forbids us from conceiving death as (fully, purely) the athematic excess of Bataille or Blanchot – what Nietzsche calls "the stupid physiological fact" (1968: 484). Remembrance, like "experience" itself throughout Benjamin, is a function of "collective existence as well as private life. It is less the product of facts firmly anchored in memory than of a convergence in memory of accumulated and frequently unconscious data" (1969: 157). Thus, the "eyes of heaven" Benjamin mentioned in the *Origin of German Tragic Drama* describe the context of generational temporality, of post-Enlightenment temporality – the fact that the present can change the past, give it a different issue, in the meanings that flash up and are recognized in relation to that past's future. Events, as I said in the preceding chapter, exist also within the context of their future history, the context of human life as a species phenomenon, temporal, transitory, comprehensive, so that without losing their intransigent materiality they can be examined, as single objects, on "different levels of meaning" (1977: 28).

*"Memory,"* for Benjamin, "creates the chain of tradition which passes a happening on from generation to generation" (1969: 98), and it is precisely the lack of such tradition that produces the

"issueless private character" of "man's inner concerns" in the twentieth century (1969: 158) and fills "the idea of death ... with profound terror" (1977: 139). In other words, the form remembrance takes is the constellation of a dialectic image from quotations. This is a function of human life conceived as communal as well as individual, existing in a mode of time that is not Newtonian universal time, but rather possesses "traces" of atmosphere in the same way that "traces of the storyteller cling to the story the way the handprints of the potter cling to the clay vessel" (1969: 92). (Such handprints are forms of quotation.) That is, human life realizes itself most fully when it is comprehended as constellated, mothers with children, the dying with their heirs, the dialectics of Then and Now at a standstill. In this Richard Wolin sees "a 'secret agreement' that the present generation has with the preceding generation ... that serves as the basis for the redemption of the past by the present" (1989: 225). The comprehension of redemption resists absolute distinctions between past, present, and future. Benjamin notes that human beings also possess a "general lack of envy" toward the future. "This lack of envy," he says,

indicates that our idea of happiness is deeply colored by the times in which we live our life. We can only conceive of happiness in terms of the air that we have breathed, or among those people with whom we have lived. In other words, the idea of happiness ... resonates with the idea of redemption. This happiness is founded precisely upon the despair and the forsakenness which were ours ... [T]he true conception of historical time is wholly based on the image of redemption. (1989: 71)

Such "ideas" and "images" in Benjamin – as in Joyce and Woolf – are profoundly dialectical. Thus he makes the assertion that "the idea of death fills [life] with profound terror" (1977: 139) I quoted above to describe the "element of German paganism and the grim belief in the subjection of man to fate" in the baroque Protestantism of the *Trauerspiel*. With these elements, he writes, "something new arose: an empty world" (1977: 138–39). Whether his description of the response to this world – "mourning is the state of mind in which feeling revives the empty world in the form of a mask, and derives an enigmatic satisfaction in contemplating it" (1977: 139) – is an apt description of his definition of the "image," "dialectics at a standstill," and the "power" of tradition and remembrance I am pursuing here remains an open question. If it is apt, then these things remain "masks" and the mode of representation they promise is enigmatic indeed: in this case, the "salvation," "rescue," and "redemption" that punctuate his writing become empty promises, and the very "panic" of the postmodern I described earlier fully makes sense. Yet the openness of this question – the very interchange between feeling and world, between meaning and the time of the world, the answerability or "reflective system," as Stravinsky says (1982: 147), between one and the other – marks the dialectical and momentary nature of his thinking in which the concrete is never denigrated to an example of a concept. In Benjamin there is a "nonlogical" difference between human experience and the world, sensation and being, between phenomenal temporality and the time of the world, and it is precisely this version of a dialectics of "analogical" difference – a dialectics which is neither that of Plato nor of Hegel and Marx – that creates the possibility, absent in Bataille and others, of the representation of Modernist temporality.

In Thesis II of the "Theses on the Philosophy of History" Benjamin quotes (without quotation marks and with small changes) the passage on "the idea of happiness" from his notebooks I just cited. (Another version of analogical quotation in Benjamin's writings is his self-citation. It is remarkable how often he repeats and quotes himself throughout his work.) "In other words," he writes, "our image of happiness is indissolubly bound up with the image of redemption. The same applies to our view of the past, which is the concern of history. The past carries with it a temporal index by which it is referred to redemption. There is a secret agreement between past generations and the present one. Our coming was expected on earth" (1969: 254). The secret agreement is one-way, irreversible like death itself (and unlike George Eliot's interchangeability of girl and monk), contained in the jagged line of death, in its resonating (verbal) image. This agreement creates the possibility of representing death only when the particular dead are remembered in constellations that do not denigrate past concrete events in concepts and symbols and nomological "representations," but rather expect (or hope) that others will follow us to create significance in a world of seeming barbarous meaninglessness.

The vehicle for secret agreements is transgenerational remembered life, temporally other – a past, unlike George Eliot's nostalgic past, that is not simply another version of contentless temporality – yet comprehensible in our own time. This is to say that the vehicles for such agreements are the quotation, analogy, and image that

make material representations – non-transcendental disembodiments – of time possible. Benjamin offers a final version of these in
his essay, "A Small History of Photography," in what he calls the
photograph's "caption." "The camera is getting smaller and smaller,
ever readier to capture the fleeting and secret moments whose
images paralyse the associative mechanisms in the beholder. This is
where the caption comes in, whereby photography turns life's
relationships into literature … Not for nothing have Atget's photographs been likened to those of the scene of a crime … Is it not the
task of the photographer – descendant of the augurs and haruspices
– to reveal guilt and to point out the guilty in his pictures?" (1979:
256).

## CONSCIOUSNESS, HISTORY, AND UNDERSTANDING: THE RENEWAL OF TIME

The kinds of representation whose description is scattered
throughout Benjamin is realized in modern and post-Enlightenment
narratives, such as those of Joyce and Woolf I have described. They
are multiple, dialogic, and do not oppose completeness with incompleteness or idealism with materialism as Horkheimer does in his
critique of Benjamin, but attempt to comprehend communities of
images and quotations that exist, constellated, within a field of
nonlogical differences. These representations take the form of three
modes of representation I examine more thoroughly in the following
chapter: the collision between past and present that Benjamin
describes as the confrontation of the Then and the Now; their
apocalyptic constellation in an image; and finally, reimagining the
subject of experience as communal and temporal rather than
individual and atemporal. In the context of these ideas – that is to
say, in the context of Benjamin's comprehension of the nature of
temporality in terms of discursive interruptions – the coexistence of
messianic Judaism and revolutionary Marxism in his life makes
sense.

Benjamin reimagines "dialectics" by representing the common
experience of time of post-Enlightenment modernity: it is the
reading of two times, two texts, two experiences together, analogically, so that each can redeem the other. Such redemption is
thoroughly temporal and *worldly* in the sense Edward Said defines
that term. Above all, it is conditioned by the temporality of the Now

Benjamin describes confronting a past that is other, flashing in apocalyptic images, and transforming the subject of knowledge which is no longer "disinterested." That such an interested and time-bound subject can be "unprovincial," and thus the object of representation – the constellated "images" he describes – is the great hope of Benjamin as well as Said. (Other articulators of post-Enlightenment "postmodernism" – Baudrillard, Kroker and Cook, and the species of postmodernity that Latour describes as simply the expression of despair [1993: 46], among others – are not so hopeful.) I shall choose one image of Modernist temporality to conclude this chapter: really it is a postmodern image that, in its postmodernity, offers a redemptive representation of the time of the past, the time of Modernism I am studying in Benjamin. In *Camera Lucida* Roland Barthes says "in front of the photograph of my mother as a child, I tell myself she is going to die: I shudder, like Winnicott's psychotic patient *over a catastrophe which has already occurred*. Whether or not the subject is already dead, every photograph is this catastrophe" (1981: 96). Barthes offers an instance of Benjamin's image – just as Woolf does in the "catastrophic" verbal image that can be sensed in the noises of the ancient homeless woman in the park. Barthes's instance is a caption for a remembered moment captured in a photograph and indissolubly bound up with the Now of temporality: for Barthes and Benjamin the past bequeaths the anterior future to the present, our ability to remember what happened next so that what Barthes calls "asymbolic Death, outside of religion, outside of ritual, a kind of abrupt dive into literal Death" (1981: 92) can be rescued or redeemed – that is, represented – in memory, and statements that make no sense for real life become indisputable for remembered life.

All of these instances – Benjamin and Barthes, Said and Woolf – offer precisely the opposite of George Eliot's narrative representation of time. In *The Mill on the Floss* the very bridge the narrator stands on to view the mill at the beginning of the novel is washed away in the flood at its end, yet the narrator offers no "memory" of that catastrophe which had already occurred. The narrator's view is non-temporal and without memory, simply a view from "nowhere." That is, Victorian humanism, as Carol Christ has argued (1993), constructs narratives that represent and repress the anterior future. Barthes, like Benjamin, does the opposite: he transforms narrative to image and repression to shock. "With the Photograph," Barthes writes, we enter into *flat Death*. One day, leaving one of my classes, someone said to me with disdain: "You talk about Death very flatly." – As if the horror of Death were not precisely its platitude! The horror is this: nothing to say about the death of one whom I love most, nothing to say about her photograph, which I contemplate without ever being able to get to the heart of it, to transform it. The only "thought" I can have is that at the end of this first death, my own death is inscribed; between the two nothing more than waiting; I have no other resource than this *irony*: to speak of the "nothing to say." (1981: 92–93)

But Barthes's response, his "caption," is also narrative. He gets the tenses right and tells a story beginning, like the traditional stories Benjamin describes, with "one day." Still, this story is punctuated by the collision of past and present – his death inscribed, apocalyptically, in the photograph he sees and the story he tells, the very postmodern flatness of his discourse, like "the chaste compactness which precludes psychological analysis" Benjamin describes in "The Storyteller" (1969: 91). As in post-Enlightenment literary Modernism, Barthes offers the dialectics of representation (with the repression inscribed within representation), transmission (with the flashing punctuation of time inscribed within transmission), and dialectic consciousness itself.

Remembrance and the flash of recognition – quotation and the image – define, in large part, the function of time in Benjamin. Remembrance, as we have seen, is a function of ongoing time – of transmission and bequeathment. The image, on the other hand, is momentary: time seems to stop or at least seems momentarily captured, as in the final pronouncement of a dying person. In the combination of these things – one might call them both unprovincial and interested – Benjamin believed time can be "renewed." That is, both remembrance and the image confront the otherness of the past, not in order to "subsume" it (to use Charles Taylor's word) but in order *momentarily* to complete it, "finalize" it. Remembrance forbids us from conceiving history as a-theological, which is to say, it forbids us from thinking of time as an indifferent container of interchangeable events. Instead, time can be modified from moment to moment: what comes after can *change* the past by giving it a different issue. Joyce does this with his endings in their confrontations of the Then and the Now (conceived as the present and his narrative's unarticulated futures); Woolf does it in the punctuated communal time of her discourse; and Lawrence does it in the discontinuities of his narrative.

No such possibility exists for George Eliot or her narrative. Just as the governing actions in Benjamin are remembrance and dialectical images, the governing "action" in *The Mill on the Floss* and in all of George Eliot's novels are sympathy and identification. (Each is really an attitude and an ideology rather than a particular action.) Sympathy assumes that all people are basically the "same": that Maggie's despair is equivalent to Thomas à Kempis's; that in time Tom will acquire the sympathetic wisdom of the narrator; that evil always results from remediable weakness. The great pleasure George Eliot affords us is the implication that we, her readers, are as sympathetically intelligent and generous as she is: all her gentle irony is based upon the assumption that we know and feel as much as the narrator suggests. Such sympathy is based upon the erasure of time: time is a kind of container, but it makes no real difference. Otherness – and especially the otherness of the past – is simply an illusion. Therefore, time does not need to be "redeemed," but simply "developed." That is why the dialectics of historical remembrance and apocalyptic change in Benjamin are unthinkable for George Eliot, where things are (or are not) the "same" without regard to time.

Throughout his work, Benjamin manipulates quotations, images, and even the semantics of subjectivity to arrest the reader and call attention to the temporality that cannot be disengaged from his meanings precisely because those meanings cannot solely be understood as aesthetically self-contained wholes that exist once and for all. That is, he apprehends and describes phenomena, in an *alternative* mode of understanding and representation, as essentially temporal in that they are completed as meanings only in terms of their future – in terms of the comprehension of their issue – which is not the "same" as their present. The term "alternative" has to be understood as fully temporal: even dialectics "at a standstill" exists in time as a moment preceded and succeeded by other moments. That is, Benjamin creates what Derrida calls an "intervallic" discourse, marked by continuity *and* hesitations. Neither mode of comprehension subsumes the other: rather, in the event of interpretation one or the other must be chosen, provisionally, and this choice, in fact, defines the event at its particular moment. Yet these choices are provisional in that they need not be in force for *all time*. The choices of George Eliot – if not "his" characters – are for all time. The remembrance of her narrative does not grow out of a collision, but out of nostalgia; the allegories of her narrative are not the apocalyptic lightning flashes of Then and Now, but typologies; the subject of her experience is neither communal nor transgenerational nor even marked by womanhood, but the unmarked individual subject of fully conscious – that is to say, atemporal – knowledge.

As Benjamin notes, the world changed between the time of George Eliot and his own time, during the turn of the century. Experience in the modern world, he says in "The Storyteller," had fallen into "bottomlessness." "Never has experience been contradicted more thoroughly," Benjamin writes,

than strategic experience by tactical warfare, economic experience by inflation, bodily experience by mechanical warfare, moral experience by those in power. A generation that had gone to school on a horse-drawn streetcar now stood under the open sky in a countryside in which nothing remained unchanged but the clouds, and beneath these clouds, in a field of force of destructive torrents and explosions, was the tiny fragile human body. (1969: 83–84)

These changes made the temporality of consciousness, history, and meaning a problem and called for new modes of representation. In this chapter I have examined the rhetoric and temporality of "experiences" that, like time itself, in Shaviro's description of Bataille, "neither designates objects, nor signifies ideas, nor manifests a hidden order of reality" (1990: 85). In the following chapter I examine the phenomenal history of such "experiences" at the turn of the twentieth century, and especially the vague but palpable sense of overwhelming abundance inhabiting such experience which in no way lent itself to the comforting reductions of the Enlightenment. Such abundance, I argue, made time a central concern of post-Enlightenment Modernism.

CHAPTER 3

# The second Industrial Revolution: history, knowledge, and subjectivity

If the French Revolution were to recur eternally, French historians would be less proud of Robespierre. But because they deal with something that will not return, the bloody years of the Revolution have turned into mere words, theories, and discussions, have become lighter than feathers, frightening no one. There is an infinite difference between a Robespierre who occurs only once in history and a Robespierre who eternally returns, chopping off French heads.

Let us therefore agree that the idea of eternal return implies a perspective from which things appear other than as we know them: they appear without the mitigating circumstance of their transitory nature.

Milan Kundera, *The Unbearable Lightness of Being* (1984: 4)

As I mentioned in chapter 1, the decades before and after the turn of the twentieth century have come to be described by many as the second Industrial Revolution, the transformation in Western Europe and America of the relatively small-scale industrialism of entrepreneurial or industrial capitalism to large-scale finance capitalism. This period created an enormous increase in consumable wealth – personal income among Parisian workers, for instance, increased about 65 percent in the two generations after the mid-nineteenth century, advertising revenues in the United States during the same period increased tenfold (Birkin 1988: 118, 120), and there was an explosion of technologically advanced consumer goods such as bicycles, automobiles, telephones, domestic electric lighting, and the like (Kern 1983; see also Tipton and Albrich 1987) in a period that, a generation ago, Carleton Hayes called "the climax of the Enlightenment" (1941: 328). "By 1900," Oron Hale notes, "Europe was the center of a booming world economy"; it was experiencing one of those discontinuous leaps forward in technology and invention which had marked the industrial progress since the mid-eighteenth century. Electricity, petroleum for lighting and fuel, the internal combustion engine, the automobile and the airplane, refrigeration, the wireless telegraph, and motion pictures appeared as marvels of applied science affecting directly the lives of millions of the earth's inhabitants. (1971: 55, 56)

In *The Culture of Time and Space*, Stephen Kern characterizes this period as facing a "crisis of abundance" (1983: 9) that transformed the intellectual, quotidian, and political life of Western Europe and America. Concerning this period, a wide range of different scholars working in various fields have noted, to one degree or another, what I am arguing here: namely, that the remarkable abundance of material, intellectual, and human resources associated with the second Industrial Revolution occasioned transformations in the modes of explanation inherited from the Enlightenment that I examined in the first chapter, in comprehensions of experience that I examined in the preceding chapter, and in the broadest senses of history and political economy that I examine here. Such transformations are most clearly discernible in changing phenomenologies of temporality governing explanation, conditioning experience, and apprehending value. In this chapter I examine the confrontation of past and present that, I believe, is a chief characteristic of the second Industrial Revolution, and then I explore the place of time within the political economy it produced, the modes of understanding associated with it, and the kinds and representations of subjectivity within the "classless class or half-class" (Mayer 1975: 422) that arose in this period as one of its "abundances," the new lower middle class of clerks and information workers.

### THE COLLISION OF PAST AND PRESENT

The historical moment of twentieth-century Modernism, as I suggested in the confrontation of George Eliot and Walter Benjamin in the preceding chapter, is the collision of two modes of conceptualizing and apprehending temporality: the Enlightenment view of objective temporality and a newer view, born of a world of abundance rather than need, where the particularities of temporality – like the very products created by the "means of production" – cannot be fully subordinated to atemporal mathematical formulations, hierarchies of meaning, or antecedent causal explanation. Kundera captures a strong sense of this collision in the epigraph to this chapter in the ways he describes the overwhelming sense of change and of the breakdown of traditional patterns of experience and value many, including Nietzsche, felt during the years surrounding the turn of the twentieth century. Nietzsche resists the overwhelming sense of the transitoriness of phenomena in his conception of eternal return, just as D. H. Lawrence resists it by conceiving of novelistic character as a "phenomenon ... representing some greater, inhuman will" (1966: 17); Bertrand Russell resists it, as I argue in chapter 4, by reconceiving mathematics as the science of order rather than quantities, and Bakhtin resists it, as I argue in chapter 6, by conceiving of the aesthetics of art as the jagged demarcation between ethics and knowledge. The moment of twentieth-century Modernism is marked by "crisis consciousness" – it is strikingly apocalyptic – even if one of the pleasures of Kundera's postmodern discourse is the ways which he plays with this Modernist crisis. But before I turn to the attempts in the Modernist era to reimagine and reconfigure the time of the now in relation to the curious reimagining of the materiality of goods, of knowledge, and of experience, I want to examine the figure of "collision" between past and present in the second Industrial Revolution that will govern my discussion of a constellation of historical events that conditioned the experience of twentieth-century modernity.

I am borrowing the figure of "collision" from Heidegger's analysis of the eternal recurrence of the same in volume 2 of his study of Nietzsche. The passage Heidegger is glossing is from *Thus Spoke Zarathustra* in which Zarathustra articulates the concept of the eternal recurrence of the same in the figure of a gateway called "Moment" at which two paths meet and "offend each other face to face" and "contradict each other eternally" (Nietzsche, 1954: 269–70). "Must not whatever *can* walk have walked on this lane before?" Zarathustra asks the dwarf sitting on his shoulder.

Must not whatever *can* happen have happened, have been done, have passed by before? And if everything has been there before – what do you think, dwarf, of the moment? Must not this gateway too have been there before? And are not all things knotted together so firmly that the moment draws after it *all* that is to come? Therefore – itself too? For whatever *can* walk – in this long lane out *there* too, it *must* walk once more. (1954: 270)

Confronting the superabundance of temporality in Nietzsche's narrative, Heidegger describes the bewilderment of the dwarf in this passage. How is the offense and contradiction between past and future possible, Heidegger asks, "when each thing moves along behind its predecessor, as is manifest with time itself? For in time the not-yet-now becomes the now, and forthwith becomes a no-longer-now, this as a perpetual and-so-on. The two avenues, future and past, do not collide at all, but pursue one another" (1984: 56).

The dwarf lives in Newtonian time that goes on and on with "the miserable endlessness of a scroll" Benjamin describes (1969: 185). That is to say, the dwarf situates himself, like a Victorian narrator, precisely "nowhere" in relation to time. "A collision does occur here," Heidegger writes; but "only to one who does not remain a spectator but who *is himself* the Moment, performing actions directed toward the future and at the same time accepting and affirming the past, by no means letting it drop. Whoever stands in the Moment is turned in two ways: for him past and future *run up against* one another ... To see the Moment means to stand in it. But the dwarf keeps to the outside, perches on the periphery" (1984: 56–57). Thus Heidegger concludes that in the doctrine of eternal return "eternity *is* in the Moment, that the Moment is not the fleeting 'now,' not an instant of time whizzing by a spectator, but the collision of the future and past" (1984: 57; see also 98). Discussing this passage, Genevieve Lloyd notes that for Heidegger, "the 'collision' of the two paths is something accessible only from within the temporal, only through reflection on our own being in time" (1993: 114). Like Benjamin's "redemption," Heidegger's "collision" offers the possibility of "retrieving" the past: "any genuine approach to history," Charles Bambach writes in discussing Heidegger, "... had to take into account [the] horizonal structure of the past which was not merely a *factum brutum* standing there against the [historical] researcher but an authentic possibility for future existence" (1995: 255).

The "Moment" of the advent of the second Industrial Revolution, the moment of twentieth-century Modernism, is precisely when, in history, narrative, and science, the possibility of a view from nowhere, the possibility of forgetting time and temporality by reducing it to spatial figures – of reducing time simply to an accident that can *always* be disregarded – is lost. This absolute possibility is lost because the collision Heidegger describes cannot be avoided, but clashes noisily in the abundances of material, intellectual, and

quotidian life. Still, such a loss of an absolute transcendental and
atemporal standpoint need not result in the "radically dissimilar
particulars" that Ricoeur describes as one opposite of nomological
explanation (1984: 124). It is precisely the resistance to *this* radical
alternative, I believe, that Nietzsche, Russell, and Bakhtin pursue in
their reconception of a "moment" that neither assumes the transcendental status of an infinitesimal nor is completely incomprehensible in relation to other moments. They pursue a logic of
abundance, which attempts to comprehend what is "self-exceeding,"
what I call the excess of non-transcendental disembodiment – as in
the electricity, telephones, and finance capital I examine in this
chapter, but also in Benjamin's constellations, Einstein's operational
definitions, Wiener's information, and the analogies of Heisenberg's
complementary comprehensions examined elsewhere in this book.[1]

   In any case, the "moment" of Modernism and the second
Industrial Revolution is conditioned by the historical and material
events I describe in this chapter – the confrontation of different
orders of political organization, different versions of labor and class,
different comprehensions of the uses of commodities, diachronic and
synchronic modes of analyzing experience and meaning, and, in the
rhetoric of Lawrence, different understandings of the relationship
between subjectivity and temporality. Out of the confrontation and
collision of these things come what Heidegger calls in *Being and Time*
"ecstatic temporality": Nietzsche's "self-exceeding moment" (cited
in Wood 1991: 291), which, as Gilles Deleuze says, "must be
simultaneously present and past, the present and yet to come, in
order for it to pass" (1983: 48). The transformation of the entrepreneurial individualism of industrial capital into the impersonal semiotics of finance capital – the breaking up of the combination of
subjective idealism and general semiotics that characterized
Enlightenment ethos – participates in this process of "self-exceeding" insofar as it produces commodities such as the moveable power
of electricity and petroleum, the explosion of privacy by telephonic
communication, and the "self-exceeding" natures of the petty
bourgeoisie/lower middle class and of the nation states of imperialism's Europe. These "things" – it's hard to tell if they are
"disembodied" commodities or something else – exceed themselves
in ways that the basic commodities of Adam Smith and Marx do
not.

## LABOR AND TIME IN THE FIRST INDUSTRIAL REVOLUTION

The transitions from universal to fragmented values, from uniform to contingent temporality, and from the self-evident universal human nature of realism to the scattered self-conscious discourses of Modernism are marked by the confrontation of the first and second Industrial Revolutions, the collision of past and present. This confrontation manifests itself in the emerging complicated *subjects* of experience I will illustrate with Ursula's Brangwen's ambiguous emergence into the lower-middle-class life of this period. But it also manifests itself in the *products* of this period of history – especially in Great Britain, which was the heart of nineteenth-century industrialism. The great products of the first Industrial Revolution were quotidian consumer goods: clothing, food, shelter. The manufacturing sector – which comprised the second largest sphere of economic activity after agriculture in all the countries of Europe except Great Britain (where it was first) – consisted, as Arno Mayer has shown,

mainly of four branches of consumer goods production: textiles and apparel, food processing, leather (including shoes), and wood (especially furniture). The technology of consumer manufacture was that of the first Industrial Revolution, notably the application of coal and steam as well as the ready availability of iron and steel and of rail transport. This sprawling economic sector comprised, above all, single-unit enterprises of labor-intensive small workshops and medium sized plants (below factory level) staffed by artisans and unskilled hands using simple, low-energy machinery. Because of their relatively small capitalization most manufacturing firms were family owned, financed, and managed. (1981: 20)

In their generality, the consumer goods Mayer describes are directly related to the labor theory of value described by classical economists such as David Ricardo and assumed by Marx as the basis of his analysis of capitalist expropriation of wealth in *Capital*.

The labor theory of value assumes that the *universal* measure of value is the human labor that contributed to the creation of the valued object or commodity. Thus Robert Heilbroner notes in his elegant description of Marx's analysis of profit that it is the *commodification* of labor-power that makes capitalist profit possible. "The laborer, like the capitalist," he writes,

sells his product for exactly what it is worth – for its value. And its value, like the value of everything else that is sold, is the amount of labor that goes into it – in this case, the amount of labor that it takes to "make" labor-power. In other words, a laborer's salable energies are worth the amount of socially necessary labor it takes to keep that laborer alive. Smith and Ricardo would have agreed entirely: the true value of a workman is the wage he needs in order to exist. It is his subsistence wage. (1953: 149)

Profit, in Marx's analysis, comes from the difference between this "true value" – for instance, in Heilbroner's example, the "six hours of society's labor to maintain a workingman" – and the amount of labor the workingman sells at *its* "true value," his agreement "to work a full eight-hour, or in Marx's time a ten- or eleven-hour, day. Hence," Heilbroner concludes, "he will produce a full ten or eleven hours' worth of value and he will get paid for only six" (1953: 149).

What is remarkable about Marx's analysis in the context of my discussion of the post-Enlightenment experience of time is the way that it both creates a universal standard of time congruent with Newton's universal time and, at the same time, erases time from the "energy" and "commodification" of labor. In this analysis labor is measured in time, but that time is the abstract number, "t," of Newtonian formulas. That is, time marks value, but remains itself unmarked, the homogeneous "ether" of activity: like the narrator in classical realism or the infinitesimals of Newton's mathematics, time is reduced to atemporal formalism. In the labor theory of value, time is all-important – it measures "the laborer's salable energies [which] are worth the amount of socially necessary labor it takes to keep that laborer alive," as Heilbroner says – yet insofar as labor and time itself function within a system of commodification, time is immediately de-temporalized as a commodity or fetish: labor is measured in terms of *things*, the "subsistence" of the laborer, the food, clothing, and shelter that "he needs in order to work."[2]

If food, clothing, and shelter, as Mayer notes, are the great consumer goods of the first Industrial Revolution, they are, in the classical economics of Smith, Ricardo, and Marx, the *universal standards* of humanity. Described in the abstract, their necessity are precisely what Maggie Tulliver and Thomas à Kempis have in common. As abstract values, temporality does not affect what they are. The labor theory of value in classical economic theory, as I have suggested, is based upon need. In a world of need, the specific attributes of particular time are of no account, just as the particularities of food – fish or fowl, for instance – are of no account in satisfying need. Need stands beyond time, as it were, in the simplicity of absolute necessity. This is the reason that, in the labor theory of value, time, while a factor in labor, had no effect upon the activities it contained: it is, paradoxically, a "timeless" commodity.[3] Adam Smith distinguishes between productive and unproductive labor in terms of the abstract, contentless future I have examined in relation to realism: thus he describes economic growth in terms of the "progress of improvement" (cited in Barber 1968: 28). Such an abstract future is very different from the futurity that inhabits Benjamin's sense of redemption and that characterizes Heidegger's attempt to reconceptualize temporality. For instance, Smith distinguishes between productive and unproductive employments, "the distinction between activity that results in capital accumulation and activity that services the needs of households" (Blaug 1985: 55). Activities that result in accumulation, according to William Barber, "must meet two tests: (1) that they led to the production of tangible objects, a condition prerequisite to accumulation; and (2) that they gave rise to a 'surplus' that could be made available for future re-investment" (1968: 28). This distinction assumes that time – conceived in terms of an abstract future of progress – is Newtonian mechanical time, always the same. Moreover, the opposition between productive and non-productive labor is that between re-investment and consumption. Consumption beyond need – that is to say, the emphasis of the present over the future – is, in classical economics, the great sign of moral turpitude because it destroys the future by destroying the assumption that the present and the future are of one piece. This is the economics of the principle of duty – that assumes that an unchanging past is interchangeable with the present and the future – that, I argued, characterizes George Eliot.

Unproductive labor, for Smith and even in the drama of *The Mill on the Floss*, is also the province of women. This is the importance of the masculine pronouns that Heilbroner uses to describe workers even though, as Mayer notes, most of the machines in England's textile industry "were operated by nonproletarian female labor" (1981: 35). In this regard the transformations of the protagonists of *The Rainbow* from the Brangwen family in pre-industrial England to the Brangwen men in the early nineteenth century and to Ursula Brangwen in the period of the second Industrial Revolution are significant because Lawrence represents the feminization of the "unproductive" lower middle class of clerks and teachers (Mayer 1975: 426) – a crucial aspect of the second Industrial Revolution. For the economic analysis of labor, as for more general analyses of the Enlightenment, the universal standard was abstract masculine humanity. In other words, "basic" labor power, including the *time* of labor power, is unmarked by attributes in the mathematical and mechanical analysis of wealth just as the very products of the first Industrial Revolution – clothing, food, shelter – fulfill basic human needs insofar as, in their abstraction, they are unmarked by any distinctive attributes.[4]

Norbert Wiener offers what he calls a "genealogy" of steam power, the energy source of the first Industrial Revolution, that can help us see why labor itself was standardized and universalized in a manner that is analogous to the standardization and universalization of time in Newtonian mechanics. "The first place where steam power came into practical use," he writes,

> was in replacing one of the most brutal forms of human or animal labor: pumping of water out of mines. At best, this had been done by draft animals, by crude machines turned by horses. At worst, as in the silver mines of New Spain, it was done by the labor of human slaves. It is work that can never be interrupted without the possibility of closing down the mine forever. (1967: 190)

Under these conditions the temporal aspect of labor is completely universalized: labor time becomes in these circumstances absolute, true, and mathematical time. To define labor in terms of animals and slaves faced with an unchanging *condition* of things is to make time wholly mechanical and so general as to be irrelevant as an attribute.

The very structure of the factory system in the first Industrial Revolution as opposed to that of the second Industrial Revolution – a system based, like the mine pumps, on centralized steam power – participated in the sense of *simple* universal laws of nature, standards of value, and definitions of humanity where time existed, but only on the level of an abstract "ether." The great technical change of factory production that occurred in the late nineteenth century was "the great change-over in engineering," Wiener describes, "between mechanical connections and electrical connections" (1967: 194). Earlier, in the first Industrial Revolution, the steam power that drove the great textile mills of England became the model for almost the whole course of the mechanization of industry, both in terms of the concentration of labor in the factory system and the universalization and standardization of labor-power itself. "The steam engine," Wiener notes,

used fuel very uneconomically by modern standards ... [Early steam engines] were much more economical to run on a large scale than on a small one. In contrast with the prime mover [the source of steam power], the textile machine, whether it be a loom or spindle, is a comparatively light machine, and uses little power. It was therefore economically necessary to assemble these machines in large factories, where many looms and spindles could be run from one steam engine. (1967: 193)

Wiener goes on to say that the only available means of transmission of power at that time were mechanical, and that great ingenuity was used by workers to harness the power of steam to a multitude of small machines. In this factory system, power itself is simple and standard: machines are all connected to a *basic* source of power just as labor power itself is tied to simple *basic* commodities, clothing, food, shelter.

In this way, the structure of the factory system along with the commodities produced by it in the first Industrial Revolution emphasized what was basic and universal. Above all, it emphasized *need*. "In writing the history of unfashionable families," George Eliot notes in *The Mill on the Floss*,

one is apt to fall into a tone of emphasis which is very far from being the tone of good society, where principles and beliefs are not only of an extremely moderate kind, but are always presupposed, no subject being eligible but such as can be touched with a light and graceful irony. But then, good society has its claret and velvet carpets ... how should it have time or need for belief and emphasis? But good society, floated on gossamer wings of light irony, is of very expensive production: requiring nothing less than a wide and arduous national life condensed in unfragrant deafening factories, cramping itself in mines, sweating at furnaces, grinding, hammering, weaving under more or less oppression of carbonic acid ... This wide national life is based entirely on emphasis – the emphasis of want, which urges it into all the activities necessary for the maintenance of good society and light irony ... Life in this unpleasurable shape demand[s] some solution even to unspeculative minds; just as you inquire into the stuffing of your couch when anything galls you there, whereas eider-down and perfect French springs excite no question. (1961: 255–56)

George Eliot, like her contemporary Marx, is describing a world of base and superstructure, the "basic" needs of the labor for subsistence over against the floating irony of those whose needs are fulfilled and who consume, almost without question, eider-down and

French furniture. That is, she is presenting two "logics" of "wants," one based upon need and the other, more superficial (and "unproductive"), based upon desire.

A generation later in *Heart of Darkness* Joseph Conrad describes the first of these, the bedrock of "basic" need – what I might call "absolute, true, and mathematical need, without relation to anything external" – in Marlow's remarkable description of hunger. "No fear can stand up to hunger," Marlow says, "no patience can wear it out, disgust simply does not exist where hunger is; and as to superstition, beliefs, and what you may call principles, they are less than chaff in a breeze … It takes a man all his inborn strength to fight hunger properly. It's really easier to face bereavement, dishonour, and the perdition of one's soul – than this kind of prolonged hunger" (1971: 42–43). In *Heart of Darkness*, however, such need is above all "primitive," inhabiting the earliest time of the earth: Conrad narrates the collision between the modern world of European imperialism and the "basic," primordial world of dark Africa. Thus David Spurr describes the usual conception of literary Modernism as "writing that sees itself as belated, as coming at the end of history and as thus attempting to originate itself – hence Pound's injunction to 'make it new,'" and nevertheless he argues that "this self-origination … takes the form of a *recovery* of origins in the primitive, in antiquity, in some privileged moment of the past, a retrospective moment that historicizes itself" (1994: 267). Such cultural "retrospection," joining, as we shall see, the retrospection of Eric Hobsbawm's conception of "history" and Werner Heisenberg's conception of "science," helps condition the creation of an academic anthropology (usually dated in 1871, with E. B. Tylor's *Primitive Cultures*) that seeks to define a pre-Enlightenment sense of time – the collapse, as Spurr says, of "a number of distinctions essential to rational Western thought," including the distinction "between present and past or future" (1994: 268) – even while that same anthropology participates in the "apocalyptic" marking of Modernism that attempts to make "it" new through universal imperialism.

George Eliot turns to the past of Thomas à Kempis to recover basic human attributes; Joseph Conrad turns to the past of equatorial Africa to confront pre-Enlightenment strangeness. "The earth seemed unearthly. We are accustomed to look upon the shackled form of a conquered monster, but there – there you could look at a thing monstrous and free" (1971: 36). For George Eliot the otherness of the past is immediately recovered as another version of a (universalist) present. Need is basic and universal, and she might well ratify Marx's contention that the secularization of value in Enlightenment capitalism "at last ... forced [men] to face with sober senses the real conditions of their lives and their relations with their fellow men" (*The Communist Manifesto* cited in Berman 1982: 95). For Conrad, contemporaneous Africa becomes not the universality of "real conditions," but the "base materialism," absolute otherness, the "unspeakable" profusion of a monster: a particular *moment* in history that can never be recovered as such, but that can repeatedly be apprehended as "colliding" with the present.

## PAST AND PRESENT: THE SECOND INDUSTRIAL REVOLUTION

In an important discussion of this moment of twentieth-century Modernism Perry Anderson describes what he calls Marx's conception of the historical time of capitalism as "a complex and *differential* temporality in which episodes or eras were discontinuous from each other and heterogeneous within themselves" (1988: 321–22). Such a conception, he argues, is particularly important in an analysis of "the set of aesthetic practices and doctrines [of the turn of the twentieth century] subsequently grouped together as 'modernist,'" an analysis that involves "the intersection of different historical temporalities" (1988: 324). "Modernism," Anderson argues, is "'triangulated' by three decisive coordinates": an aesthetics "dominated by aristocratic or landowning classes"; the "emergence within these societies of the key technologies or inventions of the second Industrial Revolution; that is, telephone, radio, automobile, aircraft, and so on"; and "the imaginative proximity of social revolution" (1988: 324–25). These three factors "provided a critical range of cultural values *against which* insurgent forms of art could measure themselves but also *in terms of which* they could partly articulate themselves" (1988: 325). "European modernism in the first years of this century," he concludes, "thus flowered in the space between a still usable classical past, a still indeterminate technical present, and a still unpredictable political future. Or, to put it another way, it arose at the intersection between a semi-aristocratic ruling order, a semi-industrialized capitalist economy, and a semi-emergent, or semi-insurgent, labor movement" (1988: 326).

Anderson is describing the historical period of Modernism as one that is inhabited by the collision of the past and present. This is perhaps most graphically marked in the composition of the Conservative government elected in Great Britain in 1895. Great Britain, as Barbara Tuchman notes, "was at the zenith of empire" (1967: 2) and it manifested the full power of the triumph of the bourgeois capitalist order of the second Industrial Revolution (see Jameson 1981; Kern 1983; Tichi 1987; Birken 1988; Harvey 1990; Schleifer 1990). Still, the government elected was that of the Old Regime. "The Prime Minister," Tuchman writes,

> was a Marquess and lineal descendant of the father and son who had been chief ministers to Queen Elizabeth and James I. The Secretary for War was another Marquess who traced his inferior title of Baron back to the year 1181, whose great-grandfather had been Prime Minister under George III and whose grandfather had served in six cabinets under three reigns. The Lord President of the Council was a Duke who owned 186,000 acres in eleven counties, whose ancestors had served in government since the Fourteenth Century, who had himself served thirty-four years in the House of Commons and three times refused to be Prime Minister. The Secretary for India was the son of another Duke ... The President of the Local Government Board was a pre-eminent country squire who had a Duke for brother-in-law, a Marquess for son-in-law, an ancestor who had been Lord Mayor of London in the reign of Charles II ... (1967: 2–3)

At the turn of the century, then, there was the curious conjunction of landed wealth governing a country of capital wealth that had expanded well beyond the local enterprises of industrial capitalism. It was as if the coincidence of political power with economic power awaited the wrenching transformation of the industrial capitalism of the first Industrial Revolution into the finance capital of the second Industrial Revolution effected by the great wars of the twentieth century. As I will suggest later, as long as positivism remained the ruling assumption of the bourgeois intellectual order, on the level of politics the aristocracies of real estate – value based upon the self-evident positive "reality" of land – would not be superseded by (the "unreal" semiotics of) aristocracies of finance (see Brantlinger 1996.)

But it was precisely the collision of land and capital manifesting the collision of the past and present, most notable in the advanced capitalism of nineteenth-century England, that characterizes the emergence of the second Industrial Revolution and informs twentieth-century Modernism. In 1884 Nietzsche described this very collision in *The Will to Power*, setting "the former means for obtaining homogeneous, enduring characters for long generations: unalienable landed property, honoring the old (origin of the belief in gods and heroes as ancestors)" against "the breaking up of landed property [which] belongs to the opposite tendency: newspapers (in place of daily prayers), railway, telegraph. Centralization of a tremendous number of different interests in a single soul, which for that reason must be very strong and protean" (1968: 44). The "tremendous number of different interests" is the mark of abundance, and it is both the cause and effect of experience inhabited by different temporalities. The time of landed wealth – of "real" estate – is "long," "homogeneous," and possesses the simplicity of a single "interest." That of capital wealth is short, heterogeneous ("protean"), and possesses the complex abundances of "different interests." Under the regime of capital, to use a phrase from *The Communist Manifesto* that Marshall Berman takes for the title of his study of Modernism, "all that is solid melts into air" (1982).

The "experience of modernity" that Berman describes is "a state of perpetual becoming," a "maelstrom" that has "come to be called 'modernization'" (1982: 16). The experience of modernity at the turn of the twentieth century is closely related to the second Industrial Revolution as technological and conceptual changes are informed by and inform different and *alternating* temporalities, experiences, and interests. Thus, in his richly detailed social history of this period, *The Culture of Time and Space*, Kern examines the great technological and intellectual changes of this period that transformed the experience of time and space, but not once and for all as different *kinds* of experiences and understanding alternated with one another in "collisions" of past and present. In this way, Kern demonstrates, through the examination of memoirs, scholarship, art, and other documents, how the phenomenology of everyday life was transformed by the very products Anderson mentions: telephones, automobiles, radios, standardized time, aircraft, finance capital itself. In Europe and England at the beginning of the nineteenth century banks were institutions to a greater and lesser degree owned by individuals or families that served local communities. By the end of the century single families could not capitalize banks, which had become impersonal corporations accumulating the huge amounts of capital necessary for the second Industrial Revolution. As Rudolf Hilferding argued, a new form of capitalism developed "characterized by the emergence of banker control, increased monopolization and growing state regulation of the economy" (cited in Hansen 1985: 51). For example, the number of corporations in England rose from 700 in 1855 to 7,900 in 1883 (Edwards 1938: 29).

More strikingly, as Kenneth Hudson observes, the second Industrial Revolution differs from the first in two important ways. The first way, he notes, is that the vast majority of the technological innovations of the second Industrial Revolution, unlike the first, were made and developed outside of Britain. Secondly, he writes, "the First Industrial Revolution was the period of bankruptcies whereas the Second has been typified more by mergers and take-overs." For these reasons, he continues,

The history of industry and commerce becomes increasingly complicated after c.1870 as licensing agreements, cartels, international groups, import controls, and government direction and intervention have increasingly to be taken into account. All combine to produce a situation which makes the world of Watt, Brunel and their contemporaries seem very small and simple ... If one is concerned with the history of iron-making between c. 1700 and c. 1850, all the essential developments can be documented by studying British sites. If, however, the field is cornflakes, tractors or telephones then the early shrines are to be found in North America. The same is true regarding most electrical appliances, safety razors, escalators, passenger lifts, linotype and monotype printing, roll-film cameras, aero-planes, cinemas, petroleum extraction and refining, incandescent lamps, typewriters and refrigerators. (1983: 12)

Hudson is describing the "tempestuous advance" of capitalism (Hobsbawm 1987: 34), the solid objects of positivism "melting into air": telephones, electricity, escalators, lifts, roll-film cameras, aero-planes, cinemas, incandescent lamps, even cornflakes – all create what I am calling non-transcendental disembodiments of solid goods, experiences, and even understanding. If the first Industrial Revolution universalizes need into a horizon for atemporal human-ity, the second Industrial Revolution disembodies desire through the very abundances of consumer capitalism. This non-transcendental disembodiment is accomplished through dispersal: the mergers and takeovers of finance capital and the very commodification of com-munication, information, and power in the products of the second Industrial Revolution.

The transformation of the motor of industrial change from bank-ruptcies to takeover, combination, and merger at a time in which, as Eric Hobsbawm notes, the "traditional moral foundation" of the bourgeoisie "crumbled under the very pressure of its own accumulations of wealth and comfort" (1987: 10) is marked through and through by problems and indeed a crisis of abundance. Such a crisis creates problems of understanding, such as those discussed in the first two chapters of this book and those occasioned by the new sciences of Cantor, Einstein, Heisenberg, Jakobson, and Bakhtin that I examine the following chapters. The very form these problems assume is also one of abundance. If, as David Harvey argues, "the Enlightenment project ... took it as axiomatic that there was only one possible answer to any question" (1990: 27), then post-Enlightenment understanding is more complicated. This is why Hobsbawm can question the very category of the second Industrial Revolution. "And yet," he writes, "before we hail this impressive crop of innovations as a 'second industrial revolution', let us not forget that it is so only in retrospect. For contemporaries, the major innovation consisted in the updating of the first industrial revolution by improvements in the tried technology of steam and iron: by steel and turbines" (1987: 53). In his specialized history of artificial light in the eighteenth and nineteenth centuries, Wolfgang Schivelbusch similarly describes the non-simple complications of the second Industrial Revolution. "Lighting technology," he writes, "appears to have progressed in logical steps from the hearth flame via the torch, the candle and the Argand lamp to gaslight, without faltering or looking back. But technical progress is more than a resolute stride forward; it also involves the developmental stages that have been left behind." "In all these cases," he concludes, "the old technology was infiltrated, as it were, by elements of a new technology" (1988: 49, 50). Hobsbawm's description of the "reinforcement" rather than the "replacement" of the first Industrial Revolution by the second can also be described under Schivelbusch's category of "infiltration." In both cases, they offer characterizations of the difference between (complicated) merger and (simple) bankruptcy Hudson notes in industrial development at this time. The parallel or analogy with post-Newtonian science is striking. As we will see in chapter 5, Werner Heisenberg notes the thoroughly *retrospective* orientation of quantum physics (1952: 56–57). Such retrospective understanding – in history, in physics, and, as we shall see in Lawrence, in literary narrative – underlines temporality as a constituent element in experience, understanding, and comprehension that cannot be simplified as a background or container of phenomena.

Conceptual terms like "infiltration," "reinforcement," and "retro-spection" emphasize the special palimpsestic sense of temporality that many people who lived through this period discovered in their experience. Such experiences and understanding created and embo-died the maelstrom of modern life that Berman describes. In 1896 the President of the National Electric Light Association commented in this fashion. "What in the days of our childhood was scarcely more than a toy," he wrote,

– at best the interesting, the mysterious phenomenon of the scientist's laboratory – is in these closing years of the century the mightiest agent known to man. By its means the news of the world is gathered from its four corners in less than a second's time ... [N]ight is turned into day, darkness into light; the waste forces of nature are harnessed and wafted like spirits, unseen and instantaneously, over mountains and rivers, miles upon miles, to turn the busy wheels of distant industry; the hidden secrets of nature are laid bare by the ray that pierces dense matter with the ease of a shaft of sunlight traveling through thin air. (cited in Marvin 1988: 207)

In this description nature itself seems transformed. Such a trans-formation, as Susan Buck-Morss argues, is a central theme in Benjamin's work, the comprehension of what she calls a "new nature." She uses this term, rather than "the Marxist term 'produc-tive forces,' because Benjamin meant by it not just industrial technology but the entire world of matter (including human beings) as it has been transformed by that technology." Buck-Morss con-cludes that "there have been, then, two epochs of nature. The first evolved slowly over millions of years; the second, our own, began with the industrial revolution, and changes its face daily" (1989: 70; compare this to the remarks of John Maynard Keynes 1931: 360–61). The second epoch, terrifying in its later stages to those who experienced it, transformed space and time in ways that the President of the National Light Association expressed.

That is, transformations in technology, experience, and under-standing conditioned one another and resulted in, among other things, enormous changes in the intellectual and everyday experi-ence of time. Hobsbawm's suggestion that retrospective comprehen-sion is the only way that the second Industrial Revolution can be discerned, like Heisenberg's assertion that "quantum theory always enables us to give full reasons for the occurrence of an event after it has actually taken place" (1952: 57), is one such transformation, a mark of the superimposition of temporalities and not simply "one answer." Similarly, in one striking instance of everyday experience, Kern notes that

Stefan Zweig recalled the slow-paced and secure world of his childhood in Austria before the introduction of the new technology. "It was a world with definite classes and calm transitions, a world without haste." The adults walked slowly and spoke with measured accents; many were corpulent at an early age. He could not remember his father ever having rushed up the stairs or done anything in a visibly hasty manner. "Speed was not only thought to be unrefined, but indeed was considered unnecessary, for in that stabilized bourgeois world with its countless little securities, well palisaded on all sides, nothing unexpected ever occurred ... The rhythm of the new speed had not yet carried over from the machine, the automobile, the telephone, the radio, and the airplane, to mankind; time and age had another measure." (1983: 127–28)

The measure of time and age was, above all, that of self-evident "nature," not a "second nature" of social development, but the simplicities of truths that existed once and for all: time followed the rhythms of life, which were a function of *universal* laws, values, human nature. Such universals followed the pattern of Newtonian time; they manifested themselves in the value of the "countless little securities" of bourgeois and aristocratic life Zweig describes; and they made it possible for George Eliot to narrate, in the tone of presenting self-evident truth, what a young girl and a middle-aged monk, separated by centuries, had in common.

Thus in the 1920s Guido de Ruggiero described the crisis of liberalism precisely in terms of the loss of universal standards in the foundations of the middle-class order, in law and politics, which led to "the bitterness of modern social conflicts, which, precisely because all universal standards have been overthrown, cannot be moderated and controlled by principles belonging to a higher and unchallenged sphere" (1959: 428).[5] Similarly, the bitterness and "crisis" of the present – what Berman calls the "maelstrom" of modernity and what Heidegger describes as a pervasive "crisis consciousness" in the new century – can be seen in the attitude toward the past altogether. The sense of nostalgia can be felt in Kern's citations from Zweig's memoirs. Comparing eighteenth- and nineteenth-century autobiographies, Richard Sennett notes that while both were nostalgic, "two new elements" appear in the nineteenth-century memoir: "in the past one was 'really alive,' and if one could make sense of the past, the confusion of one's present life might be lessened" (1977: 168).

The confusions of the present, at the turn of the twentieth century, are the confusions of disembodiments that are not the transcendental disembodiment of a view from nowhere, the realist narrator as a "nobody" that is "not intelligible as a corporeal existence" (Ermarth 1983: 66). Rather, such disembodiments are as vague as the subtle rhythms of experience, haunting not quite "positively" the edges of things. This is clear in Virginia Woolf's narrator, whom she describes as anonymous, but whose anonymity, like Clarissa Dalloway herself, exists in the position of dispersal rather than a transcendental future: the narrator is "everywhere; not 'here, here, here'" and "spreads wide" (1953: 231, 232) sharing the thoughts of Peter, Clarissa, and even Richard Strauss, but not quite *transcendentally* wide. The narrator in Woolf, as Woolf wrote of herself in her diary, is "20 people," but rummaging "in the bran pie" (1954: 33) is hardly out of this world. (Yeats's fear for himself in the *Autobiography* and elsewhere is that of dispersal, which is precisely the opposite of his transcendental aspirations.)

The language structure of Woolf – the unceasing metonymies of her semi-coloned prose, her characters to whom *always* other attributes can be added, her narrative scenes in which Then and Now can be apprehended and read – answers and repeats, but also discovers and redeems her thing-filled world. Such non-transcendental disembodiment is announced in the very linguistic deictic, "there" – what Barthes, following Jakobson, calls the subversive "shifters" of language (1977: 166) – with which *Mrs. Dalloway* ends:

> "I will come," said Peter, but he sat on for a moment. What is this terror? what is this ecstasy? he thought to himself. What is it that fills me with extraordinary excitement?
>
> It is Clarissa, he said.
>
> For there she was.
>
> THE END                                         (1953: 296)

Woolf's adverb, spatial but also strangely temporal, marks a time and place imbricated with other times and other places in its "finalization": it creates the illusion of wholeness of person, day, story, and even the illusion of a novel (which Benjamin argues is characterized, structurally, by the word "Finis" at the end [1969: 100]) and underlines its illusoriness with the felt possibilities that there is simply another thing or person or scene by which we could understand Mrs. Dalloway a little better. Peter's terror and ecstasy, like the terror and catharsis of the tragic hero (whose life, Benjamin says, like that of Septimus Smith in Clarissa's understanding and like that of the ancient ragged woman for whom the narrator speaks, "unfolds from death, which is not its end but its form" [1977: 114]) is both personal and impersonal. Such a combination of personal and impersonal also characterizes the very dispersal of consumerist desire among the material repetitions and semiotic uniqueness of the commodity that is very different from the basic, specific, universalist need of George Eliot and Karl Marx.

Similarly, even the speed Zweig remembers as a positive and "positivist" speed, experienced as solid, measured, "corpulent," is remembered in the context of new "rhythms" of speed experienced in relation to technological transformations that cannot be pinpointed in a (parsimonious) one-on-one causal relationship to that phenomenological transformation. The speed of Zweig's present is disembodied through dispersal, not transcendence, and leads to the *apprehensions* – panic, emptiness, confusion – occasioned by abundance. Such disembodiment is effected by multiplication of phenomena not reducible to the simplicities of Enlightenment comprehension.

A similar transformation – or "non-transcendental disembodiment" – can be seen in the changing class structure of the second Industrial Revolution. That is, even the structure of social life – the life of political economy – conceived in terms of the organization of a tripartite division of the polity from classical times seemed to melt into dissipation, multiplication, and panic. This is clear in the emergence of the lower middle class in Britain in the late nineteenth century, which repeated the confrontation between past and present – the confrontation of landed "real estate" and the semiotics of finance – in its opposition between what Geoffrey Crossick describes as "the classic [and long-subsisting] petty bourgeoisie of shopkeepers and small businessmen," who, in fact owned "petty" versions of the means of production, and "the new white collar salaried occupations, most notably clerks but also managers, commercial travelers, school teachers and certain shop assistants" (1977: 12). This " 'new' lower middle class of dependent clerks, technicians, and professionals expanded quickly," Mayer writes, as "a by-product of the rapid development of industrial, commercial, and financial capitalism" in the last decades of the nineteenth century (1975: 417). Hobsbawm analyzes the "enormous expansion"of this class, whose work was both clearly subaltern and remunerated by wages (even if they were called 'salaries'), but which was also clearly non-manual, based on formal educational qualifications, if relatively modest ones, and above all carried out by men – and even by women – most of whom specifically refused to consider themselves as part of the working-class and aspired, often at great material sacrifice, to the style of life of middle-class respectability. (1987: 172)

This "class" distinguished itself from the working class in two ways: although its members were "often barely a financial hair's breadth above the better-paid skilled workers," they did not perform manual labor; and "they certainly belonged to what British social observers called the 'servant-keeping class'" (Hobsbawm 1987: 180; see Mayer 1975: 424 for a more extended definition). In other words, insofar as petty bourgeois and new "white collar" workers identified with one another – and Crossick argues that "in many parts of Europe at this time old petty bourgeois groups and new salaried occupations came to see each other as *in some ways* in a similar situation" (1977: 13; see also Mayer 1975: 411, 418) – they complicated the simple received distinctions between production and consumption and consequently the basic definition of people in terms of their relationship to the means of production. Such "non-manual employees ... at the margin, were distinguished from workers who might earn as much as they only by the would-be formality of their working dress (the 'black-coated' or, as the Germans said, 'stiff-collared' proletariat), and by a would-be middle-class style of living" (Hobsbawm 1987: 183). This definition of the lower middle class was further complicated by the influx of women into this class, especially as clerks and teachers. Classical theories of class had great difficulty dealing with women as workers, with the family taken to be the unit of analysis and the male "head of household" defining the unit's relationship to the economy (Crossick 1977: 18).

It is not even clear whether the lower middle class of "'black coated' or 'white collar' workers," this "middle class proletariat" (McLeod 1977: 61), could even be classified as a social class. That is, the complicated conception of a "lower middle class" – which Mayer describes as a "classless class or half-class of quasi workers and quasi bourgeois" (1975: 422) – like the dissociation of capitalist and entrepreneur that characterized the international banking system of late nineteenth-century finance capital, effected what I am calling a non-transcendental disembodiment of classical class demarcations by means of dissipation, multiplication, and merging. "What constituted 'the bourgeoisie,'" Hobsbawm writes, "was always more difficult to determine than what, in theory, defined a nobility (e.g. birth, hereditary title, land-ownership) or a working class (e.g. the wage-relationship and manual labor)" so that "the boundaries between the bourgeoisie and its inferiors were ... far from clear" (1987: 172, 171). This was less a concern for what he calls "the 'old' lower middle class or petty bourgeoisie of independent artisans, small shopkeepers and their like" – the "class" whose relation to the means of production is clear – than the "new" class of clerks, commercial travelers, and teachers whose numbers exploded in the last decades of the nineteenth century. This group, especially on the continent, faced "erratic and intermittently frenzied politicisation" based "essentially on insecure panic" (Crossick 1977: 41): the great and constant fear of white collar workers was the constantly imminent absorption into the lower class. In England this group was less politicized and more characterized by a strong focus on domestic life – a kind of intense turn towards the privacies of suburban home life and non-conformist religion (McLeod 1977: 71, 74) characterized by an "isolation to which they were condemned by their life-style and aspirations" (Crossick 1977: 28) – but even so, Crossick argues, "the paradox of the expansion of the salaried workforce in Britain was that as it grew so its frustration increased, based most concretely on a sense of unfulfilled ambition" (1977: 31).

The concerns of this class are probably most fully expressed in the combination of the rhetoric of realism and transcendentalism in Lawrence's fiction I examine at the end of this chapter – this combination is another version of the confrontation of past and present. The problem of the ambiguities of this new class – the difficulties it presented of distinguishing between material and social life, between "base" and "superstructure," between objective position and subjective aspiration – is a manifestation of the kinds of problems occasioned by abundance rather than dearth. Thus Ursula Brangwen describes herself in *The Rainbow* as "a half stated question," "an unfixed something-nothing, blowing about like the winds of heaven, undefined, unstated" (1915: 267). Moreover, the anxieties and the ambiguities of this class are a recurrent focus on Anglo-American literary Modernism more generally.[6] In *The Waste Land*, for example, T. S. Eliot saves perhaps his nastiest description for a member of this class, "the young man carbuncular, ... / A small

house agent's clerk, ... / One of the low on whom assurance sits /
As a silk hat on a Bradford millionaire" (1964: 60). Similarly, Yeats
saves his nastiness for the new lower-middle-class Catholics who
betray "Romantic Ireland," and in *Howards End* E. M. Forster offers
the collision between the bourgeois life of the Schlegels, based upon
stocks and bonds, and the lower-middle-class aspirations of Leonard
Bast, based upon social aspiration and imperfect education. In these
examples, the high Modernist Anglo-American writers are performing a kind of rear-guard defense of the aristocratic values Anderson
describes in cultural Modernism. Even Forster's usual generosity
falters into a kind of snobbery in his descriptions of Bast, just as
Virginia Woolf's generosity falters in her descriptions of Miss
Killman in *Mrs. Dalloway* (whose economic position in the lower
middle class she hardly distinguishes from Dr. Holmes's petty-
bourgeois self-satisfactions). Eliot, himself, was a bank clerk and a
member of the lower middle class – though the fact that he was also
a scion of a St. Louis family with aristocratic pretensions underlines
what Nietzsche called the phenomenon of a "tremendous number of
different interests in a single soul, which for that reason must be very
strong and protean" (1968: 44) – while Forster maintained himself,
like the Schlegels, on a small legacy and Woolf, with the Hogarth
Press, was actually a member of the petty bourgeoisie.

On the other hand, Joyce and Lawrence grew up more or less
intimately connected with the new lower middle class: *Dubliners*,
more than *Ulysses*, offers narratives of young men who are clearly
(and, to some degree, sympathetically) positioned in the "new"
lower middle class and who constantly feel the pressure to plunge
back into the working class. A striking example is Lenehan in "Two
Gallants." Waiting for his friend, Corley, Lenehan "paused at last
before the window of a poor-looking shop ... He eyed [the food in
the window] earnestly for some time and then, after glancing warily
up and down the street, went into the shop quickly" (1967: 57).
Lenehan's wary glance betrays his anxiety of being seen entering a
working-class restaurant, in which "the mechanic and the two work-
girls examined him point by point before resuming their conversation in a subdued voice" (1967: 57). "Two Gallants" is a story about
"simony" – Corley has the servant "work-girl" he is courting steal
money for him – and the whole of this story, perhaps most strikingly
in *Dubliners*, presents the anxiety of slipping back into the working
class from the lower middle class. "The Boarding House" and

"Counterparts" also depict the anxiety of lower-middle-class clerks – and Leopold Bloom is himself a commercial traveler – but Lenehan, unlike these others, is a "pure" manifestation of unproductive labor: he does not even have a job and exists on the whims of his economic betters. Unlike the panic and emptiness Joyce depicts in his characters, however, Lawrence repeatedly attempts to find kinds of post-Enlightenment values for members of this ambiguous class, in which an ideology of individualism, a situation of felt isolation attending upon family, religious, and other "private" modes of developing a "self," and an underlying sense of anxiety were constant factors. Ursula Brangwen, in *The Rainbow*, grows into this class from her rural, farm background, and throughout that novel, as we will see, Lawrence attempts to find a vision and a rhetoric for a person cut off in significant ways from the interests and solidarity of this or any "class." Both Lawrence and Joyce, however, situate members of this class within a precarious moment that is opposed to the "traditional moral foundation" of the bourgeoisie Hobsbawm describes (1987: 10). Moreover, the very anxiety attendant upon this class is a product of abundance, not dearth, of choice rather than need.

My larger point here, however, is that the very opposition between transcendental value and material goods that is so clear in the sense of "duty" of George Eliot and her contemporaries – based as it is upon an opposition between a past and a present that are both homogenous and clearly distinguishable – seems to melt into air in the overwhelming sense of crisis associated with the explosion of products and the bureaucratization of work in the second Industrial Revolution. Thus Lewis Coser writes that "modern industrial society has created so complicated a division of labor and so differentiated and fluid a status system that any simple classificatory scheme such as prevailed till the eighteenth century could no longer be adequate" (1973: 444). In a world of abundance, the simple logic of Aristotle's description of the organization of society comprised of "the very rich, the very poor, and those who are between them" (cited in Coser 1973: 443), like Leibniz's necessary and sufficient truths, breaks down into isolation, panic, confusion, and crisis.

The emergence of "abundances" of social and class positions and of calculuses of private and social value accompanied, in the second Industrial Revolution, the abundances of commodities beyond the food, shelter, and clothing of the first Industrial Revolution. These included abundances of energy in the burgeoning of electrical and petroleum energies that replace the stable fixities of the material power of steam; the rise of the telephone that replaced the stable fixities of the epistolary culture of Enlightenment knowledges; and the remarkable explosion of imperialism in the last decades of the nineteenth century that replaced the experiential fixities of the time and space of that other element of Enlightenment culture, the nation state. All of these things confused received ideas and experiences of time as they conditioned transformations of quotidian experience, narrative discourse, and canons of understanding.

## CONSUMPTION AND TIME IN THE SECOND INDUSTRIAL REVOLUTION

Just as the private experience of subjectivity within the civilization of England for Ursula Brangwen manifests itself in the disordered temporality of repeated charged moments of Lawrence's prose,[7] so the more or less public experience of Africa Marlow expresses is an encounter with a world that is too full, a world, as he says, that is monstrous and free. The freedom Marlow and Conrad describe is that of overwhelming abundance. The very landscape of Africa signifies abundance without hierarchy. "Trees, trees, millions of trees," Marlow says; "massive, immense, running up high; and at their foot, hugging the bank against the stream, crept the little begrimed steamboat, like a sluggish beetle crawling on the floor of a lofty portico. It made you feel very small, very lost, and yet it was not altogether depressing, that feeling" (1971: 35). Such an abundance of *things* – the very transformation of need to desire that resulted in the development throughout the late nineteenth century of a consumer society – occasioned its own kind of "crisis." The enormous growth of capital resulted in an explosion of consumer goods by the turn of the century: bicycles, automobiles, cinema (whose consumption is wholly temporal, leaving nothing behind – what David Harvey calls the production of "events" rather than substantial goods [1990: 157]), radio, telephones, electric motors, electric lights, etc. This explosion conditioned the transformation of experience in its details – electric light transformed the relationship between day and night; bicycles made travel of distances of more than ten miles, extremely difficult for Jane Austen's gentry, within the power of working people; and even the capitalization of education, in what Fredric Jameson calls "the experimental triumphs of positivistic science and its conquest of the university system" at the end of the nineteenth century (1981: 251), allowed for the "socialization" of science in Copenhagen, in Vienna, in Menlo Park and Princeton and for the multiplication and employment of lower-middle-class people such as Ursula Brangwen or D. H. Lawrence himself. One telling example is the transformation of labor and labor time precipitated by the replacement of steam by electricity. If steam required a central, factory-based source of energy mechanically connected to machines by "long lines of shafts suspended from the rafters, and pulleys connected by belts to the individual machines" (Wiener 1967: 193), electricity allowed the construction of machines each of which had its own motor. Electricity transformed the factory system by multiplying the sites of energy, "complexifying" production (Bachelard 1984: 45), allowing at once the maintenance and the dissolution of the factory system (Wiener 1967: 195–96).

Electricity transformed everyday life as well. As Carolyn Marvin notes in her social history of electric communication in America at the turn of the twentieth century, *When Old Technologies were New*, "electricity was the transformative agent of social possibility ... Electricity had the vitality of a natural force" (1988: 63). Electricity gave rise to "apocalyptic theories of disaster" (1988: 119); it functioned as a "healing agent" (1988: 129); and it became central to understandings of bodily life and public spectacle (1988: 151, 174). "The period of electrification," Schivelbusch argues,

also witnessed changes in the economic structure of capitalism. The transformation of free competition into corporate monopoly capitalism confirmed in economic terms what electrification had anticipated technically: the end of individual enterprise and an autonomous energy supply. It is well known that the electrical industry was a significant factor in bringing about these changes. An analogy between electrical power and finance capital springs to mind. The concentration and centralization of energy in high-capacity power stations corresponded to the concentration of economic power in the big banks ... To cling to entrepreneurial autonomy and energy independence in the new world of the second Industrial Revolution would have been a quixotic act. (1988: 73–75)

Electricity gave rise to systems of abundances – of energy, of commodities, indeed, of ways of apprehending experience – that themselves called for the kind of analogical thinking that Schivelbusch pursues.

Such analogies, as I am arguing, constitute the "logic" of abundance. This logic disrupts the staid relationship between base and superstructure, principle and example, production and consumption, that governed Enlightenment comprehension. It disrupts the staid linear relationship between past, present, future. In the telephone, for instance, time as well as distance is transformed. When Marcel calls his grandmother in *Remembrance of Things Past*, electric communication presents him "a real presence" in "that voice so near – in actual separation" and, at the same time "a premonition also of an eternal separation!" Without "seeing her who spoke to me from so far away," he writes,

it has seemed to me that the voice was crying to me from depths out of which one does not rise again, and I have known the anxiety that was one day to wring my heart when a voice should thus return (alone, and attached no longer to a body which I was never more to see) to murmur, in my ear, words I would fain have kissed as they issued from lips for ever turned to dust. (1934: 810)

The temporalities of this passage – present voice, future voice, Roland Barthes's anterior future I mentioned in the preceding chapter – alternate and collide in the context of a telephone conversation. Here in Proust we can apprehend "the character of 'having been' [arising] ... from the future" that Martin Heidegger writes about in *Being and Time* (1962: 373) in a vein very close to that of Benjamin I have discussed.

In her study of late nineteenth-century electronic communication, Marvin traces the effects telephones had on everyday life events such as courtship, conceptions of work, the transformation of class and social distinctions, politics, and what she calls "cognitive imperialism" (1988: 192). Of remarkable importance is the sense of abundance she describes. "The idea that more communication would render cultural differences meaningless," she writes, "was closely related to the idea that productive abundance would render politics superfluous" (1988: 205). "Predictions that strife would cease in a world of plenty created by electrical technology," she continues,

were clichés breathed by the influential with conviction. For impatient experts, centuries of war and struggle testified to the failure of political efforts to solve human problems. The cycle of resentment that fueled political history could perhaps be halted only in a world of electrical abundance, where greed could not impede distributive justice. (1988: 206)

Hand in hand with this sense of what she calls "the end of politics in a thing-filled world" (1988: 205), however, are the actual uses of new technologies of electricity and communication within late nine-teenth-century imperialism. The uses of technology participate in the transformation of the nation-state into something far different at the end of the nineteenth century. As Hobsbawm notes, the era from 1875 to 1914 "was probably the period of modern world history in which the number of rulers officially calling themselves, or regarded by western diplomats as deserving the title of, 'emperors' was at its maximum" (1987: 56). Hobsbawm goes on to name the rulers of Germany, Austria, Russia, Turkey, and Britain in Europe; China, Japan, Persia, Brazil, and – "perhaps with a larger element of international diplomatic courtesy" (1987: 57) – Ethiopia and Morocco.

The complicated relationship between the transformations of technology in the second Industrial Revolution and the experience of time can be discerned in the coincident emergence of the "new" lower middle class and "new" – one might say "post-Enlighten-ment" – conceptions of nation and nation-state in the last decades of the nineteenth century, parallel in significant ways to the trans-formation of the motor of capitalist development from bankruptcies to take-overs. Hobsbawm identifies "the novel and quite non-tradi-tional classes and strata now rapidly growing in the urbanizing societies of developed countries" (1990: 109) as one of three factors in the rise of nationalism from the 1870s to 1914. (The other factors were "the resistance of traditional groups threatened by the onrush of modernity" and "the unprecedented migrations which distributed a multiple diaspora of people across the globe" [1990: 109]. All three factors are manifestations of abundance.) Hobsbawm describes this new lower-middle-class stratum as "the lesser examination-passing classes" (1990: 118) who "saw themselves as embattled and endan-gered" (1990: 121). Above all, like Ursula Brangwen in *The Rainbow*, they are "a half stated question" (1915: 267) with no clear sense of their identity. "If they already lived in a nation-state," Hobsbawm writes,

nationalism gave them the social identity which proletarians got from their class movement. One might suggest that the self-definition of the lower middle classes – both that section which was helpless as artisans and small shop-keepers and social strata which were largely as novel as the workers, given the unprecedented expansion of higher education white-collar and professional occupations – was not so much as a class, but as the body of the most zealous and loyal, as well as the most 'respectable' sons and daughters of the fatherland. (1990: 122)

Such a search for a stable identity in a world of overwhelming change – which most historians identify with the strong support rising fascist movements received from the lower middle class in the early decades of the twentieth century – manifested itself as well in the individualism, conservatism, and religiosity of the lower middle class (Crossick 1977: 39, 28). The "crisis" of this class, manifesting itself in these assumptions and impulses, we shall see, are answered and reflected in the language structure of a "momentary" aesthetic of self and art that enacts the collision between secular and spiritual, base and superstructure, nature and culture, and past and present in Lawrence's fiction.

### UNDERSTANDING IN THE SECOND INDUSTRIAL REVOLUTION

If the second Industrial Revolution made complex the simplicity of the factory with a single source of power (no matter how complex the transmission of that power became), the simplicities of face to face communication and its representations in epistolary communication, and the simplicities of "nation" embodying ethnically unified peoples, territorially unified places and clearly recognizable classes, it also made complex the simplicity of need. Classical economics, as I have suggested, is based upon the interchangeability of the subjects of economics – laborers, who all worked as generalized (male) humanity in a scale of labor measured but not informed by time; capitalist entrepreneurs, who competed with other entrepreneurs faced with problems of scale and temporality that were constant and universal; consumers, who all shared the same basic needs. The professionalization of work, the transformation of entrepreneurial capital to finance capital, and the creation of desire rather than need as the motor of consumption are all functions of abundance. The latter can be seen in the neoclassical or marginalist economics of the late nineteenth century I mentioned in chapter 1. The vocabulary economics developed was that of "marginal utility" which analyzed consumption rather than production. That is, just as Marcel's telephone conversation in *Remembrance of Things Past* is, in Heidegger's word, "futural," so these economists studied the last rather than the first item a consumer bought: for instance, the eighth rather than the first pair of shoes. The last pair is bought, not out of necessity, but from desire. Moreover, as the *last* pair, it makes time a factor in economic life in a way different from the silent and universal measurement of classical economic thought. This is why, as David Harvey says, the leading English neoclassical economist, Alfred Marshall, "could confidently assert in the 1870s that the influence of time is 'more fundamental than that of space' in economic life" (1990: 265).

It is also why, as Barber says, in the theoretical structure of neoclassical economics "market behaviour within carefully delimited spans of time supplied the organizing principle of thought. Meanwhile, the grand themes of long-period development faded far into the background" (1968: 163). These "grand themes" assumed, above all, the endless sense of progress in homogeneous time common to Newton, Adam Smith, and even Marx. Thus, as Birken has argued, the work of these neoclassical economists focused on the transformation of constant and basic need to endlessly changing desire in the remarkable transformations of experience in the second Industrial Revolution. For classical economics, Barber argues, "demand" was

constructed largely in a 'logistical' sense: i.e. to refer to the quantities of goods required for particular purposes. In was on this basis that classical economists could assert that population growth would increase the 'demand' for subsistence goods ... The effects of consumer preferences on transactions received little attention; in the main the dominant classical assumption had been that the tastes of the bulk of the population (i.e. of the working class) were fairly rigid ... (1968: 171)

The marginalist economists "insisted that the point of an economic system was not the production of commodities, but the production of satisfactions" (1968: 173). Thus Marshall explicitly defines "*labour* as any exertion of mind or body undergone partly or wholly with a view to some good other than the pleasure derived directly from the work" (cited in Barber 1968: 173). Labor is measured in precisely the *difference* between the present moment and other (subsequent) moments, a "collision" of moments. And that *temporal* difference, as both Freud and Lacan have shown, inhabits, in an essential way, desire.

At the time of the second Industrial Revolution, then, experience and understanding were re-constellating themselves outside of essentialist or positivist vocabularies. In fact, reading neoclassical economics against the classical economics of Adam Smith, David Ricardo, and Karl Marx presents the opposition of synchronic and diachronic modes of analysis insofar as diachronic analysis assumes the universal homogeneity of time. Smith and Marx emphasize the *progressive* nature of economic life, which inhabits the world of Newtonian time, in the very essentialist vocabularies they use. Such vocabularies inhabit even Marx's oppositions between base and superstructure, between means of production and products, between the labor theory of value and the theory of surplus value, between use value and exchange value. For all of these, time is absolute, true, and mathematical: it is the realm of superstructures reducible to basic structures of universal needs, the realm of consumption reducible to structures of production measured by homogeneous labor-time, value reducible to the "equable" time of labor. The neoclassical economists, on the other hand, present small-scaled analyses of "carefully delimited spans of time" (Barber 1968: 163), which allowed them to focus on short-term satisfaction rather than long-term production, to focus on abundance rather than need, and even to make scarcity a central concept of analysis (see Xenos 1989; Sassover 1990). Scarcity is a concept closely tied to consumption – it is closely tied to exchange value rather than use value, and like abundance itself, as I have mentioned, it is not altogether an absolute or monumental category. (Though unlike abundance, scarcity approaches such monumentality as it approaches absolute – "basic" – need, as in Marlow's description of hunger.) At this time Saussure was developing what A. J. Greimas later called a linguistics of "perception and not of expression" (cited in Schleifer 1987: xix), Freud was attempting to define normal psychology on the basis of the subject's own sense of his or her ability to function, and Einstein was developing his "operational definitions" of the basic concepts of physics. In all these disciplines, received ideas of the hierarchical nature of organization, of spatial rather than temporal configurations of truth, and of the atemporal nature of agency and subjectivity confronted questions about their self-evidence. In politics, economics, and just the experience of everyday life the present collided with the past.

The very multiplication of ways of understanding experience is a mark of this collision and this abundance. That is, classical explanations – in physics and aesthetics as well as economics – are not superseded by the Modernist explanations of marginal economics or the post-Newtonian physics and the momentary aesthetics I describe in part II of this book. Rather, different modes of explanation stand side by side, "alternating" (in Heisenberg's figure) at different moments. Abundance and desire do away with need only momentarily, just as the collisions of the conceptions of time inhabiting value I am describing here do not do away with the particular differences of linear-progressive time and the phenomenologies of momentary time I have mentioned. This is why Heisenberg's figure of alternation is such a useful description: it inscribes time in explanation, emphasizes the border-lines between conceptual worlds, yet doesn't require choices to be made – simple, *atemporal* choices – once and for all. Such atemporal choices characterize the "classical" modality of time that grows out of the secular logic of the Enlightenment, "the by now well accepted fact," Harvey describes, "that Enlightenment thought operated within the confines of a rather mechanical 'Newtonian' vision of the universe, in which the presumed absolutes of homogeneous time and space formed limiting containers to thought and action" (1990: 252).

In the second Industrial Revolution, these things were exploded by the abundance that Conrad, Joyce, and Woolf dramatize and help us to feel and understand. The "clichés breathed by the influential with conviction" that Marvin describes (1988: 206) are recoverable – and *redeemed* – in the language of Proust and Joyce, in the very narrative spread wide, "everywhere," of Woolf. That is, Benjamin's description of history in terms of image and dialectics at a standstill – his struggle to recover and redeem the past – is also an aesthetics of the moment that allows, as Joyce does, cliché to become a powerful signifier and even the seeming omniscience of Woolf's narrator to describe – and even tutor – what I am arguing electricity, telephones, the imperial nation-state, and finance capital describe, a non-transcendental disembodiment.[8]

CRISIS CONSCIOUSNESS, NEW SUBJECTIVITY, AND THE
LOGIC OF ABUNDANCE

D. H. Lawrence's early novel, *The Rainbow* (1915), gathers together in a different register from Joyce and Woolf, many of the aspects of the examination of history, understanding, and consciousness in this chapter because his novel comprehends many of the historical, scientific, and experiential aspects of what I have been describing in its depiction of Ursula Brangwen's assumption into the new lower middle class. Like the confrontation of past and present Heidegger describes, Lawrence's chronicle of the Brangwen family history from the late eighteenth century to the early twentieth century describes the confrontation of past and present, especially in the contrast between the communal history of the family and the career of Ursula Brangwen in the early twentieth century. Moreover, Ursula's university education presents her with a sense of the century's new science, a sense of the limits of mechanical science. And her quotidian experience – her position as a lower-middle-class worker, her intellectual experience, and her emotional experience – is conditioned throughout by the abundances of the second Industrial Revolution. Finally, and perhaps most strikingly, Lawrence's novel straddles the discourses of realism and twentieth-century Modernism I have described in the preceding chapters by alternating and confronting, in his very language, different levels of discourse.

This is apparent in an often-cited and important letter to Edward Garnett in 1914 in which he outlined some of his intentions for his novel and questions received conceptions of narrative and character:

I don't so much care about what the woman *feels* – in the ordinary usage of the word. That presumes an ego to feel with. I only care about what the woman is – what she IS – inhumanly, physiologically, materially – according to the use of the word: but for me, what she *is* as a phenomenon (or as representing some greater, inhuman will), instead of what she feels according to the human concept . . . You mustn't look in my novel for the old stable *ego* of character. There is another *ego*, according to whose action the individual is unrecognisable, and passes through, as it were, allotropic states which it needs a deeper sense than any we've been used to exercise, to discover are states of the same radically unchanged element . . . You must not say my novel is shaky . . . it is the real thing . . . (1966: 17)

From one point of view, Lawrence's intention for *The Rainbow* is that of Enlightenment knowledge, seeking to depict some sort of order and significance amid the welter of experience, to find the reality of the "same radically unchanged element" through the appearance of its "allotropic states." Yet from another vantage Lawrence's intentions destroy the traditional expectations we bring to a novel. Unlike *The Mill on the Floss*, in which narrative and significance are generated in the ironic tension between appearance and reality, realized in a narrator who has simply lived longer than his characters, knows more, and expresses both irony and sympathy for the past events depicted, *The Rainbow* attempts to deal, unironically, with a "new" reality; it tries to render a vague sense of being overwhelmed by abundance in the language of traditional secular humanism, to deal with the unknown in terms of the known. Even in the letter in which Lawrence announces his intention, the struggle between vision and language is already begun: by means of the "ordinary usages" Lawrence is trying to intimate some "deeper sense." Thus, the same word, *"ego,"* is used to describe opposite attributes of human being according to human and inhuman "concepts," and the passage itself opens up into the metaphoric use of scientific analogy to express itself. At once the analogy asserts the reality of Lawrence's vision and his necessity to find or create a language to express it. The use of the allotrope/element metaphor reveals this double tendency: on the one hand, it asserts a strict scientifically factual analogy to his conception and, given his interest in the non-human "physic," the "inhuman will, call it ... physiology of matter" (1966: 17, 18), it asserts the physical reality of his vision as well; yet at the same time the ubiquitous "call it ..." reveals his necessary struggle with his language, the same struggle Benjamin describes in "The Task of the Translator." The rhetoric Lawrence seeks is one that would mark the intersection of his novelistic and extra-novelistic concerns; within the novel, it would confront "weekday" and "Sunday" experience, rendering the latter as real as a physical presence;[9] within the context of my discussion, it would mark the "collision" of Enlightenment and post-Enlightenment temporalities.

In *The Rainbow* this problem of articulation is almost immediately translated into a problem of subjectivity rather than problems of social organization and ideology. Just as the emergence of the "middle-class proletariat" of the lower middle class in the late nineteenth century fractured the concept of class and emphasized for its members the seeming class-free categories of identity, religion, and nation, so Ursula's problem immediately becomes one of the private fulfillments of subjectivity. "How to act," she asks, "that was the question? Whither to go, how to become oneself? One was not oneself, one was merely a half stated question. How to become oneself, how to know the question and the answer of oneself, when one was merely an unfixed something-nothing, blowing about like the winds of heaven, undefined, unstated" (1915: 267). These questions about speech and action are the questions that discontinuous experiences – of understanding, of self, of class – raise in what Lawrence calls the "weekday world of people and trains and duties and reports" as opposed to the "Sunday world of absolute truth and living mystery"(1915: 266–67). In the face of these questions, for Ursula and ultimately for Lawrence himself, the ironies of Enlightenment – born of the opposition between once-and-for-all truths and local misapprehension – pale before desperation and engagement. Stable irony, we might say, sustains classical realism in a tense self-contradictory balance of action and meaning, feeling and thought, narration and significance: stable irony is the mode of discourse of Enlightenment secularism insofar as abstract detachment is the position of Enlightenment secularism. It is the "light and graceful irony" George Eliot both mocks and participates in (1961: 255). Yet Lawrence creates conflict in his novel between poles of experience which, in terms of "the living fabric of Truth" the novel itself raises (1915: 467), cannot be resolved in some abstract "once and for all." Thus, in one striking instance Tom finally responds to this conflict at Anna's wedding with *momentary* "bewilderment," rage, and an "unconscious" anguish that is not "timeless," as is Freud's unconsciousness, but exists, momentarily, in a temporality of charged moments that does not take its place within a stable hierarchical order (1915: 124–25).

Lawrence creates what I have called a disordered temporality of charged moment: in his figure of "allotropic states" he is trying to describe differences that are not fully reducible to the same, just as, I argue in chapter 5, Heisenberg is seeking a discourse of analogy rather than example. Such analogical thinking – in Lawrence, Heisenberg, and even the historiography of Benjamin, Schivelbusch, and, locally, in the "retrospections" of Hobsbawm – attempts to create a sense of presence inhabited by time, the non-transcendental disembodiments of the second Industrial Revolution. This is why in this spacious novel Lawrence seems so much more interested (and so much more successful) in rendering the physical rhythms of life and death, birth and growth, than in creating character. In one sense, Lawrence's intention makes him more distant from his characters than any novelist I know, perched, atemporally, like Nietzsche's dwarf, outside the experience that is represented: he puts word against word and uses his characters' experience for some "inhuman" end which is completely detached from their conscious lives. Yet this detachment is far from the atemporal detachment of the stable ironies of classical realism. Rather, Lawrence is seeking the same end as his characters, not love or feeling or social and class action, "but something impersonal" as Ursula says (1915: 448), so that his goal is not disinterested nor intellectual nor "personal" in any way. Rather, it is the same as his characters': what one is and how to act are the questions with which the novel grapples and which it must settle for itself in a world that seems strangely too full of explanations, things, and other people, too full of time.

The most striking example of this is the passage which ends Chapter 10, in which the seeming omniscient narrator of *The Rainbow* responds to the novel's narrative in the first person. At first glance this passage seems to be the narrator's response to his own narration, an identification of fiction and reality parallel to the identification of metaphor and fact his rhetoric repeatedly achieves. As the Christian year "was becoming a mechanical action now" for the whole Brangwen family, the narrator's voice enters the narrative to articulate questions about the failure implicit in such a "mechanical" understanding of experience and to imply answers. In this passage the narrator explicitly assumes the role of Christ in the present tense: "Why shall I not rise with my body whole and perfect, shining with strong life? Why, when Mary says: Rabboni, shall I not take her in my arms and kiss her . . . ?" (1915: 264). At the same time, however, the narrator is also assuming the role of the Brangwen children who "lived the year of christianity, the epic of the soul of mankind" (1915: 263). This epic creates the "rhythm of eternity in a ragged inconsequential life" (1915: 264), so that the assumption of Christ's role is also the assumption of that of the Brangwens.

The intrusion reveals the discontinuous method of narration – a confrontation of past and present – which ratifies an "inhuman" subjectivity over the clear social, political, and intellectual implications of his novel and of the received novel of classic realism. In important ways, Lawrence is attempting to transform the atemporal subjectivity of transparent consciousness and individual and transcendental knowledge into a "rhythm of eternity" that is plural, temporal, and inhumanly, physiologically, and materially *unconscious*. Such an intrusion is striking precisely because Lawrence doesn't pursue the Modernist strategies of Joyce's free indirect discourse or of the pluralization of subjectivity in Woolf's cultural clichés. Instead, Lawrence embeds within the rhetoric of the solid subject position of an omniscient narrator (who is far more "transcendental" that the named narrator of *The Mill on the Floss*) another *kind* of subjectivity felt within the rhymes of his prose, its repetitions, its very abundant "thickness" created when Lawrence alternates and confronts different modes of apprehension in the very same word.

Thus, at the end of *The Rainbow*, as in Lawrence's letter to Garnett, the narration uses the same word to describe different levels of experience: Ursula "*knew* there was something else ... she did not want *to know* they were there ... she *knew* without looking ... she was *aware* ..." In this way the scene creates a double sense of reality: not a reality which is informed by a larger atemporal meaning, but rather the confrontation of two modes of temporality, two ways of *knowing*, different kinds of subjectivity that alternate with one another. Discussing Freud's death drive, Jacques Derrida describes this kind of "translation" from one modality to another, as a "translation" of a language into itself "with the 'same' words suddenly changing their sense, overflowing with sense or exceeding it altogether, and nevertheless impassive, imperturbable, identical to themselves" (1979a: 4–5). Benjamin makes a similar assertion about "meaning" in "The Task of the Translator," an attempt to present and represent the overwhelming abundances and disordered temporality of a charged moment in a post-Enlightenment rhetoric.

Lawrence's rhetoric – in his discontinuous style, that so quickly jumps from the world to "eternity," that identifies vision with truth, and that valorizes the "inhuman" in place of the democratic humanism of Enlightenment values, and in its very sense of *crisis* inhabiting every department of life – presents us with implications that are much more sobering than Woolf's aestheticism. The limitations of vision in Lawrence repeat, in important ways, the limitations of the lower middle class that emerged in the second Industrial Revolution. This "class" – which does not quite fit a definition of class insofar as Marx or Weber understood class to be a category that combined interests and consciousness – can help us to comprehend, intellectually, materially, and phenomenologically, the experience of time in relation to abundance as it manifested itself in a particular mode of consciousness, what Heidegger and his contemporaries called the "crisis consciousness" of the turn of the century. This sense of crisis was pervasive throughout the years from the 1880s until the postwar years in the 1920s, what Bambach describes as "a generational mood of crisis." "In England, France, and elsewhere on the continent," he writes,

one spoke of the "economic crisis," the "world crisis," the "crisis of liberalism," the "crisis of Western civilization," and other popular conceptions. In Germany, crisis-consciousness also flourished; but we need to ask whether we can explain intellectual changes in mathematics, physics, philosophy, sociology, and other fields in the human sciences in terms of a generational mood of crisis. (1995: 49)

Lawrence's "momentaneous" aesthetics (1966: 109) takes its place within the mood of crisis – as do post-Newtonian sciences and, indeed, the very sense of "retrospective" historicism I have described in this chapter – as well as the larger senses of insecurity, isolation, and what Fredric Jameson calls "the experience of meaninglessness itself" (1981: 252) within the petty bourgeoisie and lower middle classes.

This crisis, in large part, involved the transformation of the sense and experience of time. Just as Lawrence wants to abandon the humanism of character conceived in terms of "realism" – that is, in terms of consistency and consciousness, "according to the human concept" as he says (1966: 17) – so a host of thinkers felt a "crisis of historicism" during these years. "Historicism," Bambach writes, "was synonymous ... with the logic of linear narrative and dia- chronic succession which authorized the humanistic reading of the past from the position of a transcendental subject: the self-conscious, autonomous *cogito* of Cartesian metaphysics" (1995: 3). The narrative and rhetorical strategies of *The Rainbow* I have described break from these assumptions (in ways that the discursive strategies of *Sons and Lovers* do not), in the novel's attempt to redeem time and experience within the crisis of the overwhelming abundances of things, ideas, and possibilities.

Heidegger's word for such "redemption," according to Bambach, is "retrieval" – "a 'retrieval' of the past within the horizons of the present and the future" which "discovered that the past exists not *as* past but as a futural possibility" (1995: 211) – in the same way that Ursula's experience in *The Rainbow* "retrieves" and redeems – punctuates with meaning and "felt" knowledge – the past experi- ences of her forebears. Bambach's description of Heidegger's "*Dasein*" offers a vocabulary to grasp the kind of experience that Lawrence is attempting to represent within the bewildering welter of the second Industrial Revolution. "What he tried to communicate with his new term *Dasein*," he writes, "was something nonsubjective, something that destructures the anthropological sense of a person or the humanist understanding of an individuated ego. *Da-sein*, literally, is a place, a *topos*, a 'there' *in* being, an event marked by temporality rather than a thing weighted down with substance" (1995: 230). Heidegger's and Lawrence's "there" is far more crisis-ridden, more anxious than *Mrs. Dalloway*'s aesthetic adverb insofar as the "temporality" they represent seems the only way the explosion of goods, social positions, and experiences themselves can be marked when they are untethered from the solid simplicity – the "positivities" – of parsimonious understanding.

In a sense, Heidegger is describing, as Lawrence does, a "new" subjectivity – "nonsubjective," "inhuman," and fraught with crisis and "free-floating" anxieties – responding to the transformed "objectivities" arising in the second Industrial Revolution. I am describing such free-floating experiences of this epoch as nontranscendental. By this I mean that experience seems not to anchor itself in events weighted by "substance": the abstractions of the metaphysics of positive science – including the metaphysics of a transcendental conception of time that makes it a substance without attributes, the "ether" of mechanics – the metaphysics of the economics of positive need, and the metaphysics of secular humanism. Instead, events are marked by temporality insofar as they do not occur "once and for all," but lend themselves to repetitions of redemption and retrieval, but also – and more darkly – to more or less meaningless repetitions of events, in Derrida's description, "suddenly changing their sense, overflowing with sense or exceeding it altogether, and nevertheless impassive, imperturbable, identical to themselves" (1979a: 4–5). The crisis of Enlightenment values that Lawrence and Heidegger even more than Woolf embody in the narrative and philosophical "logics" of abundance they present is that of the confrontation and strife of an "inhuman" response to the logic, hopefulness, and secular humanism of Enlightenment ethos beset by the power of its own success at the limits of a world of necessary and sufficient truths. The sciences of the new century – mathematics, physics, linguistics, and aesthetics – also confronted abundance and created logics of representation, analogous to those of Lawrence and Benjamin, Woolf and Joyce, for the new century, logics of abundance I explore in the following chapters.

# Logics of abundance

CHAPTER 4

# *The natural history of time: mathematics and meaning in Einstein and Russell*

If he had smiled, why would he have smiled?
To reflect that each one who enters imagines himself to be the first to enter whereas he is always the last term of a preceding series even if the first term of a succeeding one, each imagining himself to be first, last, only and alone, whereas he is neither first nor last nor only nor alone in a series originating in and repeated to infinity.

James Joyce, *Ulysses* (1961: 731)

In "Development of Concepts in the History of Quantum Mechanics," Werner Heisenberg discusses the relationship between what he calls "simple mathematical schemes" for quantum mechanics and the elaboration of those schemes discursively. In this chapter, I explore the relationship between mathematical formalism and the semantic concepts that are associated with that formalism, especially in relation to the conception and experience of time. To put it differently, I want to explore the question of whether the mathematical formalism of post-Newtonian physics can be comprehended by a natural history, whether, as Heisenberg says, it can be comprehended by means of a "plain language, understandable to anybody" (1958: 168). A certain kind of formalism, as Stravinsky's observations about the relationship between the "language structure" of art and the "structure" of the phenomenal world (1982: 147) suggest, governs analogical thinking, and both here and in the following chapter I examine this in what I am calling "semantic formalism."

The larger question, here and elsewhere throughout this study, concerns the effects that the changing phenomenology of time had upon the possibilities of representation in the early twentieth century. If, as I argue in chapter 1, Enlightenment understanding was governed by the necessary and sufficient truths that Leibniz articulated at the turn of the eighteenth century, then the narratives of "natural history" – and the reconception of the "natural history" of time – at the turn of the twentieth century forces the reconsideration of sufficient truth, what Leibniz called "the principle of Sufficient Reason, in virtue of which we believe that no fact can be real or existing and no statement true unless it has a sufficient reason why it should be thus and not otherwise. Most frequently, however, these reasons cannot be known by us" (1902: 258). The extreme case of the reconsideration of "sufficient reason" is what Bertrand Russell calls, in *Mysticism and Logic*, the "stupendous fact" of the possibility of "the creation of the exact science of the infinite" by Georg Cantor and others in mathematics (1917: 61). In the following chapter, which focuses on Heisenberg's uncertainty principle in relation to linguistic negation, I examine the reconsideration of Leibniz's "necessary truth," the "first" of his "two great principles," "that of Contradiction, by means of which we decide that to be false which involves contradiction and that to be true which contradicts or is opposed to the false" (1902: 258). Thus, these two chapters examine the criteria of (empirical) "accuracy" and (logical) "simplicity." The third chapter of this section, focusing on Bakhtin's work on aesthetics roughly contemporaneous with Russell and Heisenberg, examines "wholeness," the last of the criteria of Enlightenment science. As I have suggested throughout this book, the "logic" of abundance calls these criteria of accuracy, simplicity, and wholeness into question, not necessarily to replace them, but to supplement them or, as I said in the preceding chapter, to "exceed" them.

The starting point of the discussion of this chapter is Bertrand Russell's popularization of Einstein's work, *The ABC of Relativity* (1925), and his earlier books, *The ABC of Atoms* (1923) and *Mysticism and Logic* (1917). These studies – especially the first two – fall within the category of natural history insofar as natural history presents scientific data, as Greg Myers argues, without erasing narration, self-conscious interpretations, and the subject of experience – the observer – from its account (1990: 195–206). In these books, Russell directly and indirectly historicizes the physics and mathematics of the early twentieth century, not simply in tracing their histories but in suggesting ways in which they responded to historical events. That is, he is responding not only or simply to historical events understood as intellectual history, but also to the larger and vaguer sense of the historical changes in the scale of ideas, experiences and things I have been examining. In *Relativity*, Russell narrativizes (to use a term from the semiotics of A. J. Greimas) Einstein's mathematic descriptions of gravity, especially his use of tensor calculus. In *Atoms*, he is less inclined to narrative, offering instead a more abstract vocabulary to set forth his interpretation of the new science of subatomic physics. In *Mysticism and Logic* – and also in *Introduction to Mathematical Philosophy* (1919) – he examines mathematics in terms of arrangements rather than quantities, implying the importance of the observer.

These three elements of natural history – narrative, interpretation, and the observer – are closely related, and in this chapter I examine their conjunction in the context of the impulse to narrative in Einstein's work as well as Russell's. (Latour has argued persuasively the ways in which Einstein's work is a species of narrative [1988].) Quantum physics, as I argue in the following chapter, calls for a rethinking of negation rather than narrative as a modality of interpretation, which itself might profitably be considered – again in Greimas's semiotic terminology – as narration's other or "contradictory." Bakhtinian aesthetics, as I argue in chapter 6, calls for a rethinking of series and sequence in terms of the *momentary* comprehension of wholes by an observer, and it might profitably be considered narration's "contrary." In any case, Russell's mathematical philosophy, Heisenberg's categorical analysis, and Bakhtin's comprehensive aesthetics all participate in the phenomenal transformation of time in the new century. The ultimate aim of these chapters is to suggest some particularly Modernist modes of understanding – logics of abundance – that can be traced in mathematical physics, linguistics, and aesthetics along with more humanistic enterprises of literature and history explored in the first three chapters. Reading post-Newtonian science in relation to narrative and linguistics analogically corresponds to the readings of experience and discourse of the new century examined in the first part of this book. The chapter on aesthetics in relation to the work of Mikhail Bakhtin corresponds to the intellectual (or "theoretical") aspects of the enormous reassessment of time in the twentieth century in philosophy and thought that I also examined earlier.

COMPLICATIONS OF FORMALISM: EXPOSITIONS OF RELATIVITY

The central issue, not only in Russell's popularization of the special and general theories of relativity, but also in Einstein's own work in the mathematical formalism of post-Newtonian physics, involves the translation of phenomena into narrative discourse. That is, the problem that faces Russell in *The ABC of Relativity* – as it has faced all expositors of relativity, including Einstein in his 1905 publication, "On the Electrodynamics of Moving Bodies" – is how to create a comprehensible exposition of the meaning of mathematical formulations. To put this in terms that concern Greimas and, indeed, the synchronic structural linguistics that arose at the same time as Einsteinian physics, it is the problem of finding some relationship between logic and semantics. As Russell himself says in *The ABC of Relativity*, "one of the purposes of the method of tensors, which is employed in the mathematics of relativity, is to eliminate what is purely verbal ... in physical laws" (1925: 177). Its purpose, as we shall see, is to reduce difference to the same.

This is all further complicated by the aim of relativity, which is to circumscribe, at least, a definition of time. This aim is intimately tied up with the narrative comprehensions of natural history. That is, in the early twentieth century, time itself is the site of contending logical and semantic definitions. "What is time?" St. Augustine asked in the *Confessions* in a passage that Russell's great student, Ludwig Wittgenstein cites; "If no one asks me I know; if I want to explain it to someone who does ask me, I do not know" (Wittgenstein 1958: § 89; trans. Augustine 1960: 287). Augustine is perplexed by the inability of discourse, whose very nature is to *mark* phenomena in order to encompass them within its languages, to deal with the phenomenology of time consciousness. For Augustine, as for Wittgenstein, the problem of time is the problem of the non-congruity of experience and representation.[1] But since the time of the Newtonian tradition "flows equably without regard to anything external" (1964: 17), without regard, that is, to anything besides time – since, as J. T. Fraser says, time measurement always requires two "usable clocks" (1987: 59) – there is no formal metalanguage that would allow precise definition. For this reason time is felt as a particular thing or experience, but it cannot be explained, as Augustine says, to someone else. In *Mysticism and Logic* Russell similarly asserts that time exists only locally, marked by "a direct time-relation of before and after" in the experience of particular individuals (1917: 161). Freud offers an analogous description in the confusion of time and the asymmetry of experience and representation in neurotic symptoms, and Saussure makes the problematical nature of received nineteenth-century ideas concerning time the starting point of his work. Why these contemporaries – Russell, Freud, Saussure, and Einstein – felt the need to rethink nineteenth-century notions of time and representation can help us to understand cultural Modernism and the logic of abundance.

Einstein offers one response to the problem of the non-congruence of experience and representation by presenting an operational rather than a formal or conceptual definition of time.[2] If the formalism of Newton's "mathematical time" emphasizes representation over experience, and if Augustine's conceptual definition assumes the priority of experience over representation, Einstein's operational definition underlines the noncongruence of experience and representation. "If we wish to describe the *motion* of a material point," he wrote in his famous 1905 paper,

we give the values of its co-ordinates as functions of the time. Now we must bear carefully in mind that a mathematical description of this kind has no physical meaning unless we are quite clear as to what we understand by "time." We have to take into account that all our judgments in which time plays a part are always judgments of *simultaneous events*. If, for instance, I say, "That train arrives here at 7 o'clock," I mean something like this: "The pointing of the small hand of my watch to 7 and the arrival of the train are simultaneous events." (1905: 38–39)

Einstein's need to relate "mathematical description" and "physical meaning" is especially remarkable in the context of the formalism of Newtonian physics. As Ivar Ekeland notes, "Newton himself considered gravitational attraction more as a mathematical convenience than as a physical reality" (1988: 15).

The "mathematical description" Einstein mentions, as opposed to Augustine's conceptual description and even the "physical meaning" he also mentions, allows for a great deal of complexity. It does so through the formalism of mathematics. This is because mathematics *aims* at difficulty: mathematical symbolism, Russell says, "is useful because it makes things difficult." "New and difficult symbolism, in which nothing seems obvious," he writes, forces us to question the obvious and self-evident (1917: 73). Elsewhere, Russell says more generally "every advance in a science takes us farther away from the crude uniformities which are first observed, into greater differentiation of antecedent and consequent, and into a continually wider circle of antecedents recognized as relevant" (1917: 182). Such differentiation is a result of the formal mathematization of under-

standing: "No doubt the reason why the old 'law of causality,'"
Russell writes,

has so long continued to pervade the books of philosophy is simply that the
idea of a function is unfamiliar to most of them, and therefore they seek an
unduly simplified statement. There is no question of repetitions of the
"same" cause producing the "same" effect; it is not in any sameness of
causes and effects that the constancy of scientific law consists, but in
sameness of relations. And even "sameness of relations" is too simple a
phrase; "sameness of differential equations" is the only correct phrase.
(1917: 188)

In a similar register, Gaston Bachelard, we have seen, describes
relativity as the "complexification of what appeared to be simple."
Like Augustine, Bachelard focuses upon the self-evidence of the
experience of time. Relativity, he says, "challenges the intuitive
notion of simultaneity. It does this by insisting that before we assert
the simultaneity of events occurring at two different locations in
space, we specify how we have determined that they are simultaneous. From this novel requirement relativity was born" (1984: 45).
Relativity, he concludes, "complicated a simple notion by giving a
mathematical structure to what had been concrete" (1984: 48).

Such a structure allows for a description of phenomena which is
curiously abstracted from the semantics of meaning: as Fraser says,
mathematical description in physics "consists of identifying symbols
whose mathematical behavior corresponds to the behavior of instrumental observations" (1987: 244). By means of these descriptions,
Russell says in *The ABC of Relativity*,

we want to express physical laws in such a way that [even with] ...
reference to two different systems of coordinates ... we shall not be misled
into supposing we have different laws when we only have one law in
different words. This is accomplished by the method of tensors. Some laws
which seem plausible in one language cannot be translated into another;
these are impossible as laws of nature. The laws that can be translated into
*any* coordinate language have certain characteristics ... Combined with
what we know of the actual motions of bodies, [this translation] enables us
to decide what must be the correct expression of the law of gravitation:
logic and experience combine in equal proportions in obtaining this
expression. (1925: 178)

Mathematics, as Russell's discussion of "the method of tensors"
suggests, is the logical expression of these laws. "It is impossible," he
writes earlier in *The ABC of Relativity*, "without mathematics to
explain the theory of tensors; the non-mathematician must be

content to know that it is the technical method by which we eliminate the conventional element from our measurements and laws, and thus arrive at physical laws which are independent of the observer's point of view" (1925: 142–43). Similarly, in 1934 Gaston Bachelard wrote:

The new science shuns naive images, however, and has in a sense become more homogeneous: It stems entirely from mathematics. Or rather, it is mathematics that sets the pattern of discovery. Without mathematics science could not even conceptualize the phenomena of relativistic physics. As the noted physicist Paul Langevin (1872–1946) put it some years ago, "tensor calculus knows physics better than the physicist does." Psychologically, tensor calculus is the matrix of relativistic thinking. Contemporary physical science has been created by this mathematical instrument, much as microbiology was created by the microscope. None of the new knowledge is accessible to anyone who has not mastered the use of this new instrument. (1984: 55–56)

The issue of "accessibility" that Bachelard mentions is crucial to the question of whether the formal mathematical descriptions of time and "space-time" (as it is called in the General Theory) can be rendered in a natural history.

This is particularly important in relation to "tensor calculus" because this formal calculus is precisely the mathematics of "translation": it is, as Banesh Hoffmann has written, "the mathematical tool ... for writing equations valid for all coordinate systems" (1973: IV, 89). In this, it – and, in Russell's discussion, mathematics more generally – has a double and seeming self-contradictory aim: it aims at both complication *and* reduction. As Russell says, tensor calculus is the mechanism by which the "verbal" and "conventional" are eliminated so that invariant "laws" can be maintained across "different systems of coordinates," different frames of reference. More generally, mathematical symbolism, Russell argues in *Mysticism and Logic*, creates "certain rules for operating on the symbols [so that] the whole thing becomes mechanical. In this way," he concludes, "we find out what must be taken as premiss and what can be demonstrated or defined" (1917: 73). For Russell the premisses of both logic and pure mathematics are absolutely arbitrary (1917: 71). These mechanical "rules" allow calculation in "chunks": the logic of demonstration allows "lemmas" or sub-demonstrations that can be formally assumed by the demonstration at hand. It is precisely this formalism in mathematics that allows for the "complexification" Bachelard describes.

For example, in Hoffmann's exposition of the "ten years [it took Einstein] to find the way from the special theory of relativity of 1905 to the general theory of relativity" Hoffmann presents several abstract mathematical formulas "analogous" to previous formulas in his exposition and other versions of "convenient mathematical short-hand" (1973: IV, 89). Thus, after giving a formula to describe "the space-time interval $ds$ between events $(x, y, z, t)$ and [other events in space-time] $(x + dx, y + dy, z + dz, t + dt)$" in special relativity, he complicates it for general relativity's "reference frame writhing and accelerated" in relation to special relativity (1973: IV, 88) in which the coefficients of $g$ (e.g., $g_{00}$, $g_{11}$, $g_{22}$, etc.) "change from place to place" (1973: IV, 87). Hoffmann then notes that the ten coefficients of the complicated formula,

by which one converts coordinate differences into space-time distances, are denoted collectively by the symbol $g_{ab}$ and are referred to as components of the *metrical tensor* of space-time. A convenient mathematical shorthand lets ([the complicated formula] 11) be written in the compact form:

$$ds^2 = g_{ab}dx^a dx^b.$$

With the principle of equivalence Einstein had linked gravitation with acceleration and thus with inertia. Since acceleration manifests itself in $g_{ab}$, so too should gravitation. Einstein therefore took the momentous step of regarding $g_{ab}$ as representing gravitation, and by this act he gave gravitation a geometrical significance. (1973: IV, 88–89)

Even if we cannot grasp the details of the "difficult" mathematics of his discussion, Hoffmann's conclusion is striking. The "momentous step" of identifying acceleration ($g_{ab}$) with gravitation he describes in Einstein is a form of interpretation imported in the heart of his technical description.

The concept of "interpretation" that emerged in the early twentieth century – which I examine more closely in a moment – is not easily separated from the logical formalism of mathematics in post-Newtonian physics, even if it is difficult to articulate their formal relationship. As Russell says in *The ABC of Relativity*, "the formulae giving the motions of the planets are almost exactly the same in Einstein's theory as in Newton's, but the meaning of the formulae is quite different. It may be said generally," he concludes, "that, in the mathematical treatment of nature, we can be far more certain that our formulae are approximately correct than we can be as to the correctness of this or that interpretation of them" (1925: 217–18; see also 1919: 55). This example is an illustration of what Russell calls in the *Introduction to Mathematical Philosophy* "the general principle that what matters in mathematics, and to a very great extent in physical science, is not the intrinsic nature of our terms, but the logical nature of their interrelations" (1919: 59). Talking about the possibility of reintroducing "aether" in place of the "atomic character of matter" in a passage I quoted in part in the Introduction, he writes in *The ABC of Atoms* in a similar vein: "If the possibility should be realized, it would not mean that the present theory is false; it would merely mean that a new interpretation had been found for its result. Our imagination is so incurably concrete and pictorial that we have to express scientific laws, as soon as we depart from the language of mathematics, in language which asserts much more than we *mean* to assert. We speak of an electron as if it were a little hard lump of matter, but no physicist really means to assert that it is. We speak of it as if it had a certain size, but that also is more than we really mean" (1923: 153). Because, as he says elsewhere, "mathematics may be defined as the subject matter in which we never know what we are talking about, nor whether what we are saying is true" (1917: 71) – because, in other words, abstract formalism, implicit in the equation of mathematics and logic, cannot give what Einstein calls "physical meaning" – what is crucial about mathematical physics (Hoffmann's adjectives are "profound," "momentous," "powerful") are precisely its interpretations.

### SYMBOLIC FICTIONS, NATURAL HISTORY: THE TIME OF "EVENTS"

But if mathematics makes understanding difficult and complex by means of its formal reductiveness, then *interpretation* – that is, the mode of semantic understanding – simultaneously simplifies and expands. Narrative and "natural history" are modes of semantic understanding that are very different from the mode of explanation which is so complicated that it requires, as Russell says, the precise mechanisms of mathematical formalism to achieve its goal. In *Time and Narrative*, Paul Ricoeur examines three modes of understanding and explanation, what he calls "configurational," "theoretical," and "categoreal" modes of comprehension. (In an interview in 1929,

Einstein said "the meaning of the word 'truth' varies according to whether we deal with a fact of experience, a mathematical proposition, or a scientific theory" [1982: 261]. These three categories correspond to the experience, description, and abstraction of chapter 3, the accuracy, simplicity, and generalization of Enlightenment science.) "According to the theoretical mode," Ricoeur writes,

objects are comprehended in terms of a case or as examples of a general theory. The ideal type of this mode is represented by Laplace's system. According to the categoreal mode, often confused with the preceding one, to comprehend an object is to determine what type of object we are dealing with, what system of apriori concepts organizes an experience that otherwise would remain chaotic. Plato aims at this categoreal comprehension, as do most systematic philosophers. The configurational mode puts its elements into a single, concrete complex of relations. It is the type of comprehension that characterizes the narrative operation. All three modes do have a common aim, which is no less implicit in the configurational mode than in the other two. Comprehension in the broad sense is defined as the act "of grasping together in a single mental act things which are not experienced together, or even capable of being so experienced, because they are separated by time, space, or logical kind. And the ability to do this is a necessary (although not a sufficient) condition of *understanding*." (1984: 159; Ricoeur is citing Mink 1970: 547)

Laplace's method is that of formal mathematics: Laplace, more than anyone else in the history of physics, pursued the "general theory" of Newtonian mechanics as it is *formally* articulated in differential calculus to its logical extreme. The Platonic mode of comprehension is thoroughly *conceptual*: it deals with experience organized into concepts. Finally, the narrative configurations Ricoeur describes accomplish the comprehension of temporal wholes and elemental "events" from serial and disparate phenomena or data, the superimposition of what Ricoeur calls the various "circumstances, ends and means, initiatives and interactions, the reversals of fortune, and all the unintended consequences" of action (1984: x).

I am taking the term "superimposition" from Bruno Latour's brilliant discussion of Einstein's narration of the theory of relativity in his 1921 book, *Relativity* (1988: 20). Einstein claimed that this "popular" exposition cost him more trouble than the special and general theories themselves. The superimpositions of narrative frameworks Latour analyzes in relativity possess a distant formal similarity to tensor calculus. The "distance" here is between visualizable and self-evident semantic and narrative content and the unvisualizable formality of mathematical schemes. Still, like the expansive superimpositions of narrative, tensor calculus *calls for* interpretations rather than seeming to present interpretations, as Ricoeur's other modes do. This is, in part, because the "difficult" complexity – the unvisualizability – of the formal "superimpositions" of its matrices and repetitions does not immediately present the simplicities of formal and conceptual interpretation.

Both the similarity and dissimilarity between narrative understanding and the mathematical formalism of tensor calculus may be clearer if we examine Russell's repeated term, "interpretation," itself. Interpretation exists in the "two very different" modes of interpretation A. J. Greimas and J. Courtés describe in *Semiotic and Language*. In the first mode, "every system of signs may be described in a formal way that does not take into account the content and is independent of possible 'interpretations' of these signs" (1982: 159). In this conception, "semantic interpretation" comes after and follows from abstract formalism, as in the "general theory" of the abstract logic of Newton's "mathematical convenience" or in Augustine's *a priori* concepts of "knowing" and "explanation." This first mode of interpretation describes both the formal/logical definitions of Ricoeur's "theoretical" understanding and the conceptual definitions of his "categoreal" understanding.

The second mode, Greimas and Courtés argue, "is completely different." Within this perspective, "interpretation is no longer a matter of attributing a given content to a form which would otherwise lack one; rather, it is a paraphrase which formulates in another fashion the equivalent content of a signifying element within a given" system of meaning (1982: 159). In this second mode, interpretation offers an analogical paraphrase of something which *already* signifies within a different system of meaning in the full force of the temporality of the adverb. It is precisely this mode of interpretation that Einstein pursues when he takes the "momentous step" of identifying acceleration with gravitation in his mathematical term "$g_{ab}$." The force of this analogy as a form of interpretation – as the generation of meaning and comprehension – is clearer in what Russell calls his "qualitative description of Einstein's law of gravitation": "just as geometry has become physics," Russell writes, "so, in a sense, physics has become geometry. The law of gravitation has become the geometrical law that every body pursues the easiest course from place to place" (1925: 129–30). It is also clear in what

Hoffmann describes as Einstein's earlier "profound insight": "that physical measurements are essentially the observation of *coincidences* of events, such as the arrival of a particle when the hands of the local clock point to certain marks on its dial" (1973: IV, 88). By grasping in a single mental act formal geometry and gravitational dynamics or the simple "concept" of time and a complex "idea" of events, Einstein is participating in a mode of interpretation that pursues both the simple concept of physical meaning and complex formal precision without reducing one to the other, once and for all.

Such interpretations form the *natural history* of Einsteinian time, the "time" of the second Industrial Revolution. In these terms, Ricoeur's third mode of understanding – that neither satisfies itself with the simple accountings of contingencies and accident nor reduces difference to the same – *alternates* in Einstein's work with Laplacean calculation and Platonic conceptualization. In this alternation Einstein creates, as Greg Myers argues that natural history does, a "sense of an immediate encounter with nature" (1990: 194): not "action at a distance," which Russell shows Einstein's law of gravitation disrupted, but "the geometrical law that every body pursues the easiest course from place to place" (1925: 130). "Natural history," Myers writes, is the opposite of "developed theory" because it presents "a written account of actions of particular animals at a particular place or time, recorded by particular observers" (1990: 195). Such narrative texts, Greimas has argued, narrate neither the pure contiguity of accidental events – the *arbitrary* conceptual premisses Russell describes – nor the logical implications of mathematical "theory." Instead, in natural history, Myers says, "things happen. Such events are indicated in natural history texts ... by the use of the past tense. In contrast, the present tense usually indicates, in scientific texts, the general nature of the phenomenon being described, asserting that it is true at all times" (1990: 196). Besides the past tense, natural history offers apparently gratuitous details, the treatment of animals as individuals who are often "like characters in novels," and the characterization of the human observers of nature (1990: 196–201). Above all, Myers says, "natural history texts seek out the singular, whereas biology texts seek out the typical" (1990: 204). By "type" here he means Ricoeur's systematic concepts; he also means the allegorical types we encountered in George Eliot. I could add that the texts of mathematical physics seek out the formalism of Ricoeur's "general theory."

This kind of "natural history" is apparent in Russell's accounting of tensor mathematics for non-mathematicians. In *The ABC of Relativity* he attempts to narrate an understanding of gravity as it is presented in the tensor calculus of the General Theory of Relativity. Russell had just described the so-called "force" of repulsion exerted by a tiger let loose "in the middle of a bank holiday crowd." "The 'force' exerted by the sun," Russell writes,

only differs from that exerted by the tiger in being attractive instead of repulsive. Instead of acting through waves of light or sound, the sun acquires its apparent power through the fact that there are modifications of space-time all round the sun. Like the noise of the tiger, they are more intense near their source; as we travel away, they grow less and less. To say that the sun "causes" these modifications of space-time is to add nothing to our knowledge. What we know is that the modifications proceed according to a certain rule, and that they are grouped symmetrically about the sun as center. The language of cause and effect adds only a number of quite irrelevant imaginings, connected with will, muscular tension, and such matters. What we can more or less ascertain is merely the formula according to which space-time is modified by the presence of gravitating matter. More correctly: we can ascertain what kind of space-time *is* the presence of gravitating matter. When space-time is not accurately Euclidean in a certain region, but has a non-Euclidean character which grows more and more marked as we approach a certain center, and when, further, the departure from Euclid obeys a certain law, we describe this state of affairs briefly by saying that there is gravitating matter at the center. But this is only a compendious account of what we know. What we know is about the places where the gravitating matter is *not*, not about the place where it is. The language of cause and effect (of which "force" is a particular case) is thus merely a convenient shorthand for certain purposes; it does not represent anything that is genuinely to be found in the physical world. (1925: 204–05)

This passage contains many of Myers's elements of "natural history": it has anthropomorphized agents – the tiger, the sun – as well as the human "travelers" circulating in the solar system along with the planets, who all function "like characters in novels." It offers gratuitous details, such as its mention of a bank holiday and all its talk about knowledge and forms of representation. It presents what Ricoeur calls the "miscellany" of "circumstances, ends and means, initiatives and interactions, the reversals of fortune, and all the unintended consequences" of action (1984: x) within its par-ticular example of the solar system without reducing the elements of that miscellany – the congeries of "circumstances" and "events" enumerated – to *simply* the formal "unity" of the metrical tensor of space-time, $ds^2 = g_{ab}dx^a dx^b$.

Above all, it presents order, action, and events. Earlier Russell asserts that in the context of relativity theory "we are concerned with *events*, rather than with *bodies*," and that "when we know the time and place of an event in one observer's system of reckoning, we can calculate its time and place according to another observer" (1925: 69). The whole of relativity transforms bodies into events (in a manner analogous to Bambach's description of *Dasein* as "an event marked by temporality rather than a thing weighted down with substance" [1995: 230]) just as subatomic physics, as we shall see, transforms energy into action: the work of "the *metrical tensor* of space-time" Hoffmann describes is to transform "coordinate differences into space-time distances" (1973: IV, 89). Moreover, such transformations require that the first mode of interpretation Greimas and Courtés describe – a mode combining Laplacean formalism and Platonic conceptualism – is capable of being understood as also, "alternatively," the second mode of interpretation. The second mode is that of narrative, which as Ricoeur says, "puts its elements into a single, concrete complex of relations" (1984: 159). Ricoeur's description here, in fact, defines *event*. "In the old view," Russell writes,

a piece of matter was something which survived all through time, while never being at more than one place at a given time. This way of looking at things is obviously connected with the complete separation of space and time in which people formerly believed. When we substitute space-time for space and time, we shall naturally expect to derive the physical world from constituents which are as limited in time as in space. Such constituents are what we call "events." An event does not persist and move, like the traditional piece of matter; it merely exists for its little moment and then ceases. A piece of matter will thus be resolved into a series of events ... The whole series of these events makes up the whole history of the particle, and the particle is regarded as *being* its history, not some metaphysical entity to which the events happen. (1925: 208–09)

In this description of "events," Russell is articulating what has come to be called Minkowski "world-lines" which apprehend temporality as a constituent of "particles" (see Penrose 1989: 193). Thus, in this narrative even the most abstract formulas describing relativity *are* its natural history, the natural history of time. For the natural history of time embodied in relativity calls for precisely what Russell denies:

the "compendious accounting" of semanticization, what Einstein himself says in "On the Electrodynamics of Moving Bodies" allows equations and formulas to be "clothed in words" (1905: 54).

Such "clothing," as I have been suggesting, are forms of interpretation and semanticization that inhabit in local moments all three of the modes of understanding Ricoeur describes, theoretical, categoreal, and configurational. These modes follow with more or less precision the books of Russell I have cited: *The ABC of Relativity* begins with the complexity and reductions of mathematical formalism manifested in tensor calculus – Laplacean abstractions. Russell's earlier book, *The ABC of Atoms*, begins with categoreal theory – the "Platonic" systematization – of the Periodic Law. The third book I have cited, *Mysticism and Logic*, examines without naming the "logic" of set theory, what he calls "classes or series of particulars, collected together on account of some property which makes it convenient to be able to speak of them as wholes"; they are, he says, "what I call logical constructions or symbolic fictions" (1917: 124). All three participate in the semanticization of natural histories.

The "symbolic fictions" Russell names are closely related to the concept of interpretation he discusses in both *The ABC of Relativity* and *The ABC of Atoms* and to Ricoeur's concept of "configuration." Moreover, they are closely related to the "natural history" that is presented, not only in Russell's discussions of post-Newtonian science, but also in the verbal and mathematical symbols of Einstein's discussion of time. "Natural history," as Walter Benjamin asserted in the 1920s, calls for the reconception of both nature and history and possesses, as Susan Buck-Morss argues, "a 'logical structure' different from that of traditional philosophy, where concepts like nature and history, myth and transiency had been distinguished from one another by 'invariants' in their meaning" (1991: 66). Buck-Morss writes in the chapter entitled "Natural History: Fossils" in *The Dialectics of Seeing*, her book on Benjamin's "Arcades Project," that "not only nature, but all the categories in Benjamin's theoretical constructions have more than one meaning and value, making it possible for them to enter into various conceptual constellations" (1991: 66). "Constellations," as we have seen, is a key term in Benjamin that paraphrases in "another fashion" what Russell means by "logical constructions or symbolic fictions." Russell offers the symbolic fiction of such a "natural history" of time itself. He accomplishes this history in *The ABC of*

*Relativity* by means of what I have called (following Greimas and Courtés) the "analogical paraphrase" of "geometry" and "physics" or, more generally, "matter" and "events." In *The ABC of Atoms* it occurs in the analogical transformation of the complexity and reductiveness of the atemporal Periodic Law into the temporality of quantum mechanics or, more generally, the transformation of the universals of "energy" and "force" into the local temporalities of the technical term "action" Russell closely defines (1923: 145–46). And in *Mysticism and Logic*, such analogical paraphrase occurs in the reconception of the mathematics and physics of continuous "quantities" as "order" and "the investigation of kinds of series and their relations" (1917: 87). More generally, this is the reconception of "matter" in terms of what Russell calls "a whole assemblage of particulars, existing at different times" in a world packed "much fuller than it could possibly hold" (1917: 132).

Einstein, too, packs the world full with multiple frames of reference, unvisualizable mathematics, and configured temporalities. This is *his* "natural history," as well as Russell's, and in it the concepts of "nature," "history," and even "time" are transformed by means of his "momentous" interpretations bringing together – that is, interpreting, arranging, and constellating – geometry and gravitation, mathematical formalism and physical meaning. With relativity, Russell writes, "just as geometry has become physics, so, in a sense, physics has become geometry" (1925: 129). The "sense" Russell imports is the temporalities of analogy – of different systems of meaning existing before and after, in time – in which even the "invariants" of mathematical and conceptual time are occasionally comprehended and configured within the "natural history" of events, action, and momentary order, as in Einstein's operational definition of time.

PERIODICITY AND TEMPORALITY: THE TIME OF "ACTION"
AND DISCONTINUITY

The function and reconception of time implicit in the transformations in physics in the early twentieth century – a post-Enlightenment conception of time – will be clearer if we look more closely at Russell's earlier book, *The ABC of Atoms*, in which he attempts to describe the new science of subatomic physics. If *The ABC of Relativity* begins with the complexity and reductions of mathematical form-

alism manifested in tensor calculus, then *The ABC of Atoms* begins
with the systematization of the Periodic Law, the transformation of
"the haphazard multiplicity of the chemical elements" into "something more unified and systematic" (1923: 19–20). The Periodic Law
is a great "combinatory," as the French call it, a systematic ordering
of elements in relation to their properties and their atomic number.
It is analogous to Saussure's synchronic systematization of the
phonological elements of language. Saussure's formal analysis of
Indo-European vowels, *Mémoire sur le système primitif des voyelles dans les
langues indo-européennes*, which he published in 1878 – his only
published book – described an element of language which did not
exist among recovered ancient documents. "What makes Saussure's
work so very impressive," Jonathan Culler has argued, "is the fact
that nearly fifty years later, when cuneiform Hittite was discovered
and deciphered, it was found to contain a phoneme, written *h*, which
behaved as Saussure had predicted. He had discovered, by a purely
formal analysis, what are now known as the laryngeals of Indo-
European" (1976: 66). Similarly, Russell says of the Periodic Law –
which, first articulated by Mendeleyev in 1870, is contemporaneous
with Saussure's work – that "when the periodic law was first
discovered, there were a great many gaps in the series, that is to say,
the law indicated that there ought to be an element with such-and-
such properties at a certain point in the series. Confidence in the law
was greatly strengthened," Russell concludes, "by the discovery of
new elements having the requisite properties" (1923: 23–24). Both
Saussure's phonemic studies and the Periodic Law combine systematic ordering and detailed empirical observation in their formal
analyses, the reduction and complexity I have been discussing.

That is, the Periodic Law – like structural linguistics (Saussure's
*Course in General Linguistics* was published in 1915), Russell and White-
head's *Principia Mathematica* (1903), and indeed the organization of
higher education into professionalized faculties and disciplines in the
late nineteenth century – is a culmination of the Enlightenment's
double quest for reduction and complication that Russell describes
in mathematics. This seeming self-contradictory project is a version
– an "analogy" – of Latour's description of the definition of
Enlightenment modernity, "the double task of domination and
emancipation" (1993: 10). In *The Philosophy of the Enlightenment*, Ernst
Cassirer calls this double project of systematization and empiricism a
wider sense of "calculus," which "thus loses its exclusively mathe-

matical meaning" (1951: 23). Such a "calculus" is what he describes
as Leibniz's great goal:

to arrive at an "alphabet of ideas," to resolve all complex forms of thought
into their elements, into the last simple basic operations, just as in the
theory of numbers every number can be understood and represented as a
product of prime numbers. Thus here again the unity, uniformity,
simplicity, and logical equality seem to form the ultimate and highest goal
of thought. All true statements, so far as they belong to the realm of strictly
rational "eternal" truths, are "virtually identical" and can be reduced to
the principle of identity and contradiction. (1951: 28)

The Periodic Law is an "alphabet of ideas" that pursues the
Enlightenment "method of formulation of scientific conceptions
[that] is both analytical and synthetic" (1951: 10), the "method of
reason" that "consists in starting with solid facts based on observation, but not in remaining within the bounds of bare facts" (1951: 21).
    Rather, it combines complexification and reduction: "The phe-
nomena of nature," Cassirer argues,

present themselves to perception as uniform events, as undivided wholes.
Perception grasps only the surface of these events, it can describe them in
broad outline and in the manner of their taking place; but this form of
description is not sufficient for a real explanation. For the explanation of a
natural event is not merely the realization of its existence thus and so; such
an explanation consists rather in specifying the conditions of the event, and
in recognizing exactly how it depends on these conditions. This demand
can only be satisfied by an analysis of the uniform presentation of the event
as given in perception and direct observation, and by its resolution into its
constitutive elements ... The method of formulation of scientific concepts
is both analytical and synthetic. It is only by splitting an apparently simple
event into its elements and by reconstructing it from these that we can
arrive at an understanding of it. (1951: 10)

The double project of analysis and synthesis – what Nietzsche calls
the "doubling" within the action of interpretation (1969: 45) examined in the following chapter – gives rise to a notion such as "force,"
which, as we have seen, Russell finds "does not represent anything
that is genuinely to be found in the physical world" (1925: 205), but
which, for Leibniz, is a "fundamental conception" (Cassirer 1951:
32).
    "Force" is fundamental for Leibniz – and central to Enlighten-
ment understanding – because it allows him to transform "the
analytical identity of Descartes and Spinoza" into "the principle of
*continuity.*" "Leibniz's mathematics and his entire metaphysics,"

Cassirer argues, "is based on this principle. Continuity means unity in multiplicity, being in becoming, constancy in change" (1951: 30). The Periodic Law is the "culmination" of this project – the complexification and reduction of phenomena – precisely in the way that it erases the *differences* marked by time[3] and presents the Enlightenment conception of time as essentially continuous and, like "aether," a purely *formal* category. What makes the Periodic Law "periodic" is the systematic recurrence of properties among its elements: "Mendeleeff (and at about the same time the German chemist, Lothar Meyer) observed," Russell writes, "that an element would resemble in its properties, not those that came next to it in the series of atomic weights, but certain other elements which came at periodic intervals in the series" (1923: 22). The Periodic Law transforms difference into continuity, and it does so – in the "combinatory" of the Periodic Table – by erasing the very temporal element suggested by the term "period." It accomplishes this by its very inscription, the emphasis it puts on the formalism – the "language structure" – of its *notational* devices. Einstein himself devised his own notational conventions in articulating the Special Theory of Relativity, and it is precisely the way in which he noted tensors in his formulas that allowed him kinds of simplicity – and semanticization – of his formulas, the "momentous step of regarding $g_{ab}$ as representing gravitation" denied to Maxwell. Thus, Russell writes, "it has been found that, when the order derived from the periodic law differs from that derived from the atomic weight, the order derived from the periodic law is much more important" (1923: 23). The erasure of "commonsensical" temporality from the "periods" of elements – and thus *not* "remaining within the bounds of bare facts," which Cassirer describes as central to the "method" of Enlightenment science (1951: 21) – permits the complexifications and reductions of formalism. Here again, as in the Enlightenment economics examined in chapter 1, a temporal category such as "first" is comprehended as an atemporal category such as "basic."

The periodicity Russell describes in relation to quantum mechanics does not erase temporality from its calculations in the same way that the Periodic Law does; it fully retains its temporal determination, which becomes a constitutive rather than a formal category. Thus, in discussing the "wave-theory" of light, Russell argues that

The quantum-theory has to do, not with what is happening in a point at an instant, but with what happens to a periodic process throughout its whole period. Just as the period occupies a certain finite time, so the process occupies a certain finite space; and in the case of a light-wave traveling outward from a source of light, the finite space occupied by the process grows larger as it travels away from the source. For the purposes of stating the quantum principle, one period of a periodic process has to be treated as an indivisible whole ...

It must be confessed that the quantum principle in its modern form is far more astonishing and bewildering than is its older form. It might have seemed odd that energy should exist in little indivisible parcels, but at any rate it was an idea that could be grasped. But in the modern form of the principle, nothing is said, in the first instance, about what is going on at a given moment, or about atoms of energy existing at all times, but only about the total result of a process that takes time. Every periodic process arranges itself so as to have achieved a certain amount by the time one period is completed. (1923: 150–51)

In this discussion, periodicity is fully temporal and, like the "event" Russell described in *The ABC of Relativity*, its "time" itself is not fully interchangeable with other "times." As in the later book, Russell asserts in *The ABC of Atoms* that "the ultimate facts in physics must be events, rather than bodies in motion" (1923: 163). Russell explicitly denies the universalist notion of time ("existing at all times") and the aesthetic notion of time ("a given moment") that govern Enlighten-ment assumptions in favor of a substantial "process that takes time." The "given moment" is the domain of Leibniz's principle of contradiction; "all times" is the domain of "sufficient reason." In *Mysticism and Logic*, using the sun as his example, Russell describes "*matter* ... what is 'really real' in the physical world" as "a whole assemblage of particulars, existing at different times, spreading out from a centre" (1917: 131–32), a "process that takes time." The "assembly" he describes is a version of Benjamin's "constellation" – in *Introduction to Mathematical Philosophy* he even uses "the starry heavens" as his example in explaining the mathematical "arrange-ment"of set theory (1919: 30) – and it offers, as Benjamin does, a fully *temporalized* conception of phenomena as an alternative to "given moments" and "all times."

The constitutive, rather than formal, nature of time distinguishes the formal and atemporal periods of both Mendeleyev's Periodic Table and Saussure's synchronic linguistics – existing, respectively, "at all times" and at "a given moment" – from the temporal periods of subatomic physics. Constitutive time is captured in Russell's presentation of the technical term "action." "In the physics of the atom, as it has become in modern times, everything is atomic, and there are sudden jumps from one condition to another ... According to the quantum theory there are also atomic quantities, not of energy as was thought when the theory was first suggested, but of what is called 'action.' The word 'action,' in physics, has a precise technical meaning; it may be regarded as the result of energy operating for a certain time" (1923: 145). "The theory of relativity," he says later, "would lead us to expect that action would be more important than energy. The reason for this is derived from the fact that relativity diminishes the gulf between space and time which exists in popular thought and in traditional physics" (1923: 161); "action thus turns out to be fundamental both in relativity theory and in the theory of quanta" (1923: 165). An important development in quantum physics in the early century is the reconception of Planck's constant, $h$ – which relates the frequency of light to the amount of energy it contains (Crease and Mann 1986: 24)[4] – in terms of "the nature of action" (1923: 146).

With this term, we can see how "notation" or what Russell calls "mathematical symbolism" – like the "language structure" of Stravinsky which helps to delineate the working of analogy – functions by *formalizing* semantics (or creating what I call in the following chapter "semantic formalism") to allow for the complexities and difficulties Russell mentions. "The dimensions of a number," Robert Crease and Charles Mann explain,

are the units it is written in; for instance, the dimensions of velocity are distance divided by time, miles per hour. Erg-seconds, the dimensions of Planck's constant, are energy multiplied by time, which is identical to those of a quantity scientists call *action*. For this reason, $h$ is often termed a quantum of action. The idea of action was elaborated by eighteenth-century astronomers, who found that they could simplify complicated problems of planetary orbits by introducing a new variable related to energy: action. For example, the action of the earth going about the sun is calculated by dividing the orbit into a series of points, multiplying the earth's momentum at each point by the change in radius from the point before, and adding up the result: engineers have to do this kind of arithmetic today to tell astronauts in the space shuttle when to deploy weather satellites ... Physicists use them to calculate orbits, trajectories, and the like because objects naturally follow the path of least action. (1986: 27–28)

The work that formalism accomplishes is precisely, as Crease and Mann say here, "to simplify complicated problems." Paradoxically, this is what Russell means when he says that mathematical "symbolism is useful because it makes things difficult" (1917: 73).

By "difficult" he means no longer self-evidently obvious, and he also means, more radically, "unnatural" or "irrational." "The theory of relativity," he writes,

has shown that most of traditional dynamics, which was supposed to contain scientific laws, really consisted of conventions as to measurement, and was strictly analogous to the "great law" that there are always three feet to a yard. In particular, this applies to the conservation of energy. This makes it plausible to suppose that every apparent law of nature which strikes us as reasonable is not really a law of nature, but a concealed convention, plastered on to nature by our love of what we, in our arrogance, choose to consider rational. Eddington hints that a real law of nature is likely to stand out by the fact that it appears to us irrational, since in that case it is less likely that we have invented it to satisfy our intellectual taste. (1923: 170)

Russell here, like his contemporary Saussure, is describing the arbitrary nature of the sign, which suggests the difficulties of discontinuity, of the erasure of the opposition between the subject and object of experience, and of the constitutive nature of time – the difficulty of an understanding of time that is neither formal nor substantial, but, as in an operational definition, is itself temporal and finite. Such an operational definition is different from the universal reductionism and complex empiricism of Enlightenment knowledge: "for Wittgenstein," as Henry McDonald argues, "as for Heidegger, time is 'finite' in that the forms in which it is uncovered are themselves finite" (245).

If post-Enlightenment time is "finite," the continuity of the Enlightenment is, in important ways, temporally "infinite": it exists at all times and at a given moment. "The definitions of continuity" developed by the mathematicians Richard Dedekind and Georg Cantor, Russell writes,

do not correspond very closely to the vague idea which is associated with the word in the mind of the man in the street or the philosopher. They conceive continuity rather as absence of separateness, the sort of general obliteration of distinctions which characterises a thick fog. A fog gives an impression of vastness without definite multiplicity or division ...

The general idea vaguely indicated by the word "continuity" when so employed, or by the word "flux," is one which is certainly quite different from that which we have been defining. Take, for example, the series of real numbers. Each is what it is, quite definitely and uncompromisingly; it does not pass over by imperceptible degrees into another; it is a hard, separate unit, and its distance from every other unit is finite, though it can be made less than any given finite amount assigned in advance. (1919: 105)[5]

Russell's "fog" is analogous to time: "the one all-embracing time, like the one all-embracing space, is a construction" (1917: 135). In both *Mysticism and Logic* and *Mathematical Philosophy* – more generally, in his understanding of mathematics in relation to logic – he is attempting to define "continuity" in terms other than the "infinitesimals" of Newton's and Leibniz's calculus. "The banishment of the infinitesimal," he writes, "has all sorts of odd consequences, to which one has to become gradually accustomed. For example, there is no such thing as the next moment" (1917: 78). Infinitesimals, like "force" or "action at a distance" or even Augustine's understanding of "time," which is vaguely felt, but not susceptible to precise definition, allow for the conflation of universal reduction and empirical complication: the conflation of "at all times" and "the given moment" of Enlightenment knowledge is realized within the abstract formalism of infinitesimals.

The technical term "action" that Russell defines in *The ABC of Atoms* asks us to reconsider the self-evident but unarticulable nature of Enlightenment time. Eighteenth-century astronomers simply sought to simplify their calculations, and they invented a formal category that allowed them to do so. But when this formal category found application in areas of study for which it had not been developed, the self-evident (and therefore unarticulated) "meaning" and "function" of time implicit in it changed, even while its formulation didn't. By "finding application" I mean what Russell means by "interpretation": "arrangements" or "constellations" are apprehended at definite particular moments to form new comprehensions. The power of formalism is its ability to be inscribed in seemingly simple "notations" that, apparently contentless, can be used ("interpreted") in different contexts. The power of formalism makes it central to the Enlightenment project of complexification and reduction: in its seeming contentless method – what Russell calls the "mechanical" nature and application of mathematical symbolism (1917: 73) – it allows us to use and discover concepts that make no obvious sense. More specifically, it allows for the Enlightenment project Cassirer describes: the "method of reason," "starting with solid facts based on observation, but not in remaining within the bounds of bare facts" (1951: 21). It is based upon the separation between appearance and reality that conditions, as Ermarth notes, canons of Enlightenment realism.

The "bounds" of bare facts is time, and abstract formalism allows for the apprehension of atemporal (or "universal") truths within time: this is its impulse toward reduction, which can even be found in Einstein (whom Russell calls "the crown of the old dynamics, not the beginning of the new" [1923: 66; this is Latour's global argument in 1988]). Such reduction is central to the principle of contradiction. But equally important to Enlightenment understanding is the principle of sufficient reason, which attempted to master an abundant and complex empiricism. Thus, basic to the "method of reason" is the problematic formalism of time itself as a general framework for understanding both temporal facts and atemporal truths. Formalism allows the easy traffic between a temporal "first" and an atemporal "basic," the empirical complexities and the abstract reductions of Enlightenment understanding. The transformation of energy into "action" in quantum physics, like the transformation of being into "event" in relativity, disrupts the complex reductiveness of time conceived and seemingly experienced simply as a formal framework comprehending the "given moment" and "all times" by reintroducing time as something different from simply a formal category in terms of the complex category of " semantic formalism" that I am describing as an operational definition of analogy. We have learned, Latour says – though he also suggests that we have always known – that "time is not a general framework but a provisional result of the connection among entities" (1993: 74). This is the lesson, in any case, of *The ABC of Atoms*.

The lesson is that of *discontinuities* – precisely what Leibniz, and even Wordsworth – hated. "The discontinuity in the motion of an electron," Russell writes,

is an instance of a more general fact which has been discovered by the extraordinary minuteness of which physical measurements have become capable. It used always to be supposed that the energy in a body could be diminished or increased continuously, but it now appears that it can only be increased or diminished by jumps of a finite amount. This strange discontinuity would be impossible if the changes in the atom were continuous; it is possible because the atom changes from one state to another by revolution, not by evolution. Evolution in biology and relativity in physics seemed to have established the continuity of natural processes more firmly than ever before; Newton's action at a distance, which was always considered something of a scandal, was explained away by Einstein's theory of gravitation. But just when the triumph of continuity seemed complete, and when Bergson's philosophy had enshrined it in popular thought, this inconvenient discovery about energy came and upset everything ... Perhaps it is merely habit and prejudice that makes us suppose space to be continuous. Poincaré ... suggested that we should even have to give up thinking of time as continuous, and that we should have to think of a minute, for instance, as a finite number of jerks with nothing between them. (1923: 63–65)

The continuous time of Enlightenment modernity was understood in terms of the line between the past and the future, what Latour calls "the moderns' flight into the future" (1993: 73). "Modernization," he writes, "consists in continually exiting from an obscure age that mingled the needs of society with scientific truth, in order to enter into a new age that will finally distinguish clearly what belongs to atemporal nature and what comes from humans, what depends on things and what belongs to signs. Modern temporality arises from a superposition of the difference between past and future with another difference, so much more important, between mediation and purification" (1993: 71). For Latour, Enlightenment modernity distinguishes absolutely between things and signs – reality and the formal "notation" of reality – between atemporal nature and historical culture; between a temporality of repetition and a temporality of progress. These things are opposed but compatible and continuous: notation is part and subordinate to "reality"; historical culture is part of and subordinate to atemporal nature; repetition is part of and subordinate to progress. The absolute distinction between things and signs is enshrined in the theoretical and categoreal modes of explanation Ricoeur describes.

The culture of abundance I described in part I of this book – the great historical, experiential, and intellectual crisis of the Enlightenment – disrupts this order by both confusing its elements and marking them as temporally finite and therefore discontinuous. Ricoeur's configurational mode, like the "constellations" of Benjamin and Lawrence's "momentaneous" interruptions, paradoxically presents kinds of *discontinuity* in its reliance on analogical comprehension that I describe in greater length in the following chapter. When geometry "becomes" physic and physics "becomes" geometry; when mathematical formalism finds itself semanticized and narrativized in Einstein; when symbolic formalism (what I am calling "notation" and what Russell opposes to "interpretation") finds itself functioning conceptually as "symbolic fictions"; then time no longer simply functions as a formal and empty category but has become a finite constitutive element in "action" and "events."

All of these phenomena are breaches in the order of the governing continuity of things that is anchored in the strict – the abstractly *formal* and self-evident – opposition between atemporal nature and the consistent temporality of human experience that governed Enlightenment modernity. When Russell argues that "the solution of the problems concerning infinity has enabled Cantor to solve also the problems of continuity" (1917: 86), the solution he describes *requires* the abandonment of traditional conceptions of continuity governing the comprehensions of the man in the street or the philosopher – Ricoeur's conflated theoretical and categoreal modes – across the separate realms of "atemporal" nature and historical culture. That is, the "method of reason," for the Enlightenment, seemed universal across phenomena precisely because it was (formally) separated from phenomena. When the theoretical/categoreal method of reason is found to *alternate* with configuring phenomena in the face of abundance, then first and foremost time explodes into the discontinuous finiteness Wittgenstein describes. "The moderns' flight into the future," Latour writes,

ground to a halt perhaps twenty years ago, perhaps ten, perhaps last year, with the multiplication of exceptions that nobody could situate in the regular flow of time. First there were the skyscrapers of postmodern architecture – (architecture is at the origin of this unfortunate expression); then Khomeini's Islamic revolution, which no one managed to peg as revolutionary or reactionary. From then on, the exceptions have popped up without cease. No one can now categorize actors that belong to the 'same time' in a single coherent group. No one knows any longer whether the reintroduction of the bear in Pyrenees, kolkhozes, aerosols, the Green Revolution, the anti-smallpox vaccine, Star Wars, the Muslim religion, partridge hunting, the French Revolution, service industries, labour unions, cold fusion, Bolshevism, relativity, Slovak nationalism, commercial sailboats, and so on, are outmoded, up to date, futuristic, atemporal, nonexistent, or permanent. (1993: 73–74)

"Every contemporary assembly," Latour concludes, "is polytemporal" (1993: 74).

Russell describes such "polytemporality" in *The ABC of Atoms* under the categories of "discontinuity," "action," and "event." All these things respond to abundance: they respond, as Russell himself says, to "the extraordinary minuteness of which physical measurements have become capable" (1923: 63–64). The minuteness is a result of the "difficulties" to which mathematical symbolism gives rise, to the point that the "basic" atomic units Russell describes – namely, the hydrogen nucleus and the electron – have themselves, since Russell's time, been exploded into a vast abundance of subatomic particles.

### ORDER AND INFINITY: ABSTRACT ABUNDANCES AND SYMBOLIC CONSTELLATIONS

Einstein's great conceptual achievement was to remove infinity from space and time by recognizing in the finite speed of light a limit of velocity. This is, as Latour argues (1988) and Russell suggests, the way that he "crowned" the old dynamics. In mathematics, however, as Russell sees it, the opposite is true. "The solution of the difficulties which formerly surrounded the mathematical infinite," he writes in *Mysticism and Logic*, "is probably the greatest achievement of which our own age has to boast" (1917: 60). This solution, he claims, "conquered for the intellect a new and vast province which had been given over to Chaos and old Night" and created "an exact science of the infinite" (1917: 61). The science of the infinite is appropriate, I am suggesting, to the historical moment of the second Industrial Revolution when abundance along with scarcity became a problem. In chapter 5 I examine Heisenberg's rethinking of negation – the principle of contradiction – in terms of the problem of abundance; in chapter 6 I examine Bakhtin's rethinking of aesthetics – the "given moment" – in terms of this problem. Here, I am examining the rethinking of sufficient reason in the supplementation of mathematical formalism in Einstein and Russell.

Russell examines this achievement in mathematics by reimagining mathematics as the science of order and arrangement instead of the science of quantity and sufficiency. Einstein's operational definition of time, involving clocks, trains, and narratives, is a concrete example of this kind of reimagining. "In former days," Russell writes, "it was supposed (and philosophers are still apt to suppose) that quantity was the fundamental notion of mathematics. But nowadays, quantity is banished altogether, except from one little corner of Geometry, while order more and more reigns supreme"

(1917: 87; in addition, in *Mathematical Philosophy*, he contrasts quantity with logic, 1919: 195–96). "When there are only a finite number of terms," he writes earlier in *Mysticism and Logic*,

we can count them in any order we like; but when there are an infinite number, what corresponds to counting will give us quite different results according to the way in which we carry out the operation. Thus the ordinal number, which results from what, in a general sense may be called counting, depends not only upon how many terms we have, but also (where the number of terms is infinite) upon the way in which the terms are arranged. (1917: 82)

Such "arrangements" are directly related to Benjamin's notion of "constellation," and both are ways of dealing with – or, as Wallace Stevens says, "arranging, deepening, enchanting" – phenomena.

That is, Russell is arguing that in relation to the mathematical infinite the common-sensical mathematical law of commutation (a + b = b + a) does not always hold. The law of commutation is particularly important because it assumes Newton's conception of absolute time: moments are formally interchangeable so that temporal ordering of quantities in addition does not affect the operation of addition itself. But other seeming "self-evident" and common-sensical truths about mathematical operations are called into question as well so that the arrangement of infinite quantities gives rise to qualities that are anti-intuitive. "For instance," Russell writes, "nothing can be plainer than that a whole always has more terms than a part, or that a number is increased by adding one to it. But these propositions are now known to be usually false. Most numbers are infinite, and if a number is infinite you may add ones to it as long as you like without disturbing it in the least" (1917: 73–74).

Later in *Mysticism and Logic* Russell gives a powerful definition – what he calls "the precise definition" – of infinity. "A collection of terms," he writes,

is infinite when it contains as parts other collections which have just as many terms as it has. If you can take away some of the terms of a collection, without diminishing the number of terms, then there are an infinite number of terms in the collection. For example, there are just as many even numbers as there are numbers altogether, since every number can be doubled. This may be seen by putting odd and even numbers together in one row, and even numbers alone in a row below:

1, 2, 3, 4, 5,  *ad infinitum.*
2, 4, 6, 8, 10, *ad infinitum.*

There are obviously just as many numbers in the row below as in the row above, because there is one below for each one above. This property, which was formerly thought to be a contradiction, is now transformed into a harmless definition of infinity... (1917: 81–82)

In *Mathematical Philosophy*, Russell says that "the difficulties that so long delayed the theory of infinite numbers were largely due to the fact that some, at least, of the inductive properties were wrongly judged to be such as *must* belong to all numbers; indeed it was thought that they could not be denied without contradiction. The first step in understanding infinite numbers consists in realising the mistakenness of this view" (1919: 79). The "mistakenness," as Russell calls it, is a function of imagining that the combination of empiricism and universalized reductions governing Enlightenment understanding – the Laplacean theoretical mode and the Platonic categoreal mode of understanding Ricoeur describes – governed *all* understanding. In a world of phenomenal abundance, I am arguing, comprehensions of the mathematical infinite, of explosive multiplications of commodities, ideas, and – as in Joyce and others – "experiences," call for Benjamin's "constellations" and the "arrangements" and "order" of set theory Russell sets forth in *Mysticism and Logic* and *Introduction to Mathematical Philosophy*[6] along with Leibniz's necessary and sufficient truths. In the following chapter I return to this issue of dealing with things that were "formerly" thought to be contradictory. As Heisenberg says, Bohr's work encourages physicists "to apply alternatively different classical concepts which would lead to contradictions if used simultaneously" (1958: 179). Russell wants to envelop the dust of contradiction within the pearl of purely formal and logical "definition" and "interpretation" while Heisenberg *temporalizes* knowledge within alternating applications.

The supplementation of Enlightenment assumptions in cultural Modernism is clearer in Russell's elaboration of the definition of infinity in *Mathematical Philosophy*. The fact that the parts of an infinite collection, such as the even-numbered integers, have the same number of terms as the (whole) collection of which it is a part – the fact, as he says, that "the total number of inductive numbers is the same as the number of even inductive numbers" –

was used by Leibniz (and many others) as a proof that infinite numbers are impossible; it was thought self-contradictory that "the part should be equal to the whole." But this is one of those phrases that depend for the plausibility upon an unperceived vagueness: the word "equal" has many meanings, but if it is taken to mean what we have called "similar," there is no contradiction, since an infinite collection can perfectly well have parts similar to itself. Those who regard this as impossible have, unconsciously as a rule, attributed to numbers in general properties which can only be proved by mathematical induction, and which only their familiarity makes us regard, mistakenly, as true beyond the region of the finite. (1919: 80–81)

The mathematical term "similar"can be understood as an "analogical paraphrase" of Benjamin's term "constellation" examined in chapter 2. (Russell also discusses the term "idea" in *Mathematical Philosophy* in ways that are interestingly parallel to Benjamin's definition of idea examined in chapter 2; see 1919: 138–40.) In fact, it can be understood as a paraphrase of "analogy" altogether. In this passage, Russell suggests the larger argument of *Modernism and Time*: namely, that changes in scales of abundance require and produce new modes of comprehension and modifications of old modes of comprehension.[7]

Specifically, he reinterprets the reductive operation of "equals" – the very operation of identification or equation that *allowed* the great Enlightenment combinations of empirical complexity and abstract reduction – as an operation of complexification, multiplications of abundances of "likeness," the "similar," and "correspondence." He reinterprets the reductive operation of "equals" as an operation that enlarges rather than narrows understanding by linking it to order rather than quantity. "In seeking a definition of order," he says, "the first thing to realise is that no set of terms has just *one* order to the exclusion of others" (1919: 29).[8] Thus, the operation of "similarity" as a category becomes clear in relation to the infinite; more generally for my purposes, it becomes clear in relation to abundance rather than dearth. As opposed to identification, it apprehends relationship: it recognizes correspondences where identities were thought to be. Attempting to define irrational numbers within his logical exposition of mathematics, Russell argues that "just as ratios whose denominator is 1 are not identical with integers, so those rational numbers which can be greater or less than irrationals ... must not be identified with ratios. We have to define a new kind of numbers called 'real numbers' ... Those that are rational 'correspond' to ratios, in the same kind of way in which the ratio $n/1$ corresponds to the integer $n$; but they are not the same as ratios" (1919: 71–72). Russell also describes "structure" this way: "Two relations have the same 'structure,'" he writes, "when the same map will do for both – or what comes to the same thing, when either can be a map for the other (since every relation can be its own map). And that, as a moment's reflection shows, is the very same thing as what we have called 'likeness' " (1919: 61). ("Likeness," he says, describes "similarity of relations" as opposed to the "similarity of classes," for which he uses the term "similar" [1919: 52].) All of Russell's terms – "correspond," "structure," "likeness," "similar" – which seem continually to multiply themselves, participate, at least "analogically," in Greimas and Courtés second definition of "interpretation"; they underline Stravinsky's suggestion that the language structure of art can "map" – his term is "discover a reflective system" of (1982: 147) – the structure of the phenomenal world. Just as order, as Russell says in *Mysticism and Logic*, "more and more reigns supreme" over quantity ( 1917: 87), so Russell multiplies the general terms ("correspond," "structure," etc.) of which "equals" is the particular case.

This multiplication of terms and conceptions, as with the multiplications of infinities of differing sizes Russell describes in *Mathematical Philosophy*, proliferates terms that are like one another but not quite equal. Moreover, these terms are closely tied with the changing phenomenology of time in the early twentieth century. That is, Russell's definitions both of an infinite collection of terms and of rational numbers, like Einstein's definition of time, are operational definitions that replace the "equation" of items or the "simultaneity" of events with "correspondences" of arranged items. Russell "arranges" integers in series; Einstein "arranges" watch hands and trains; even Joyce arranges, as Hugh Kenner has argued and the catechism of this chapter's epigraph suggests, narrative strategies and characters' available voices and vocabularies. In fact, operational definition itself functions through species of "likeness," or "correspondence," or even "structure." It might well be that Roman Jakobson's 1929 definition of "structuralism" is itself an operational definition. "Any set of phenomena examined by contemporary science," he wrote, "is treated not as a mechanical agglomeration but as a structural whole, and the basic task is to reveal the inner, whether static or developmental, laws of this system ... [so that] the mechanical conception of processes yields to the question of their function" (1971: 711).[9]

All these terms – "structures," "correspondences," "similarities," and "likenesses" – oppose themselves to the understanding of "equation" that is absolute and mechanical and help comprehend

Russell's sense of time in the new century. "There has been a great deal of speculation in traditional philosophy," he writes,

which might have been avoided if the importance of structure, and the difficulty of getting behind it, had been realised. For example, it is often said that space and time are subjective, but they have objective counter-parts; or that phenomena are subjective, but are caused by things in themselves ... Where such hypotheses are made, it is generally supposed that we can know very little about the objective counterparts. In actual fact, however, if the hypotheses as stated were correct, the objective counterparts would form a world having the same structure as the phenomenal world, and allowing us to infer from phenomena the truth of all propositions that can be stated in abstract terms and are known to be true of phenomena. If the phenomenal world has three dimensions, so must the world behind phenomena; if the phenomenal world is Euclidean, so must the other be; and so on. In short, every proposition having a communicable significance must be true of both worlds or of neither: the only difference must lie in just that essence of individuality which always eludes words and baffles description, but which, for that very reason, is irrelevant to science. Now the only purpose that philosophers have in view in condemning phenomena is in order to persuade themselves and others that the real world is very different from the world of appearance. We can all sympathise with their wish to prove such a very desirable proposition, but we cannot congratulate them on their success. (1919: 61–62)

The "subjectivity" of time and space, just as their absolute relati-vism, is precisely what the "correspondences" of operational defini-tions and the "correspondences" between appearance and reality Russell is describing in this passage aim to avoid in their semantic formalism. But the semantic formalism of such correspondences avoids other things as well. Above all, it avoids – or "supplement" as Derrida says (1976) – the absolute opposition between appearance and reality that governs the abstract formalism at the heart of Enlightenment understanding and Newtonian time. Leibniz de-scribes this opposition as that between "two kinds of *truths*: those of *reason* ... and those of *facts*" (1902: 259), while Latour describes it as that between "imminence" and "transcendence," and argues that Enlightenment modernity "alternates" between these modes of understanding while maintaining their strict exclusiveness (1993: 34). In both cases, Newtonian time is the condition for the strict opposition between appearance and reality: it allows the "finite" time of appearance and fact always to be "translated" or "absorbed" or "subsumed" (nomologically, in the modes of theoretical or categoreal understanding) into the *formal* ("atemporal") time of reality and reason; it allows the absolute opposition between the narrator and characters of literary realism.

The "mathematical infinity" that Russell claims is the crowning achievement of his age does the opposite. Its processes and elements are both finite and infinite, depending on the order – both temporal and relational – of their arrangement. For this reason in Russell, as in Einstein, there is even a "similarity" between the formality of mathematical abstraction and physical reality. "Just as geometry has become physics, [and], in a sense, physics has become geometry" (1925: 129), as Russell says, and just as mathematics has become logic and logic has become mathematics, so the finite elements and the multiple definitions of classes and the finite particularities and infinite repetitions of "events" and of time itself are "similar," "alike," and "corresponding" in the finite multiple orderings – the analogues – of "interpretations," "arrangements," and "constellations" within comprehension and narrative. These things, as Russell says in another context, are "essentially a one-by-one process" (1919: 116), governed by a comprehension of time not as "flowing," but as finite, whose endless "repetitions" are not of the "same," but of similarities, likenesses, and the analogues of understanding.

Let me return, for a moment, to cultural Modernism by quoting again Stravinsky's assertion of the possibility of breaching the opposition between appearance and reality in his thoughts about Beethoven I mentioned in the Introduction, his assertion that it is "possible," as he said, "to discover a reflective system between the language structure of the music and the structure of the phenomenal world" (1982: 147).[10] Russell makes a similar assertion in the long passage I just quoted, more precisely and formally in his description of the *structural* correspondences between the phenomenal and objective "worlds" as existing on the level of "abstract terms" (e.g., "dimensions," "Euclidean" geometry). But like Stravinsky, who goes on to "interpret" Beethoven's late quartets as "a charter of human rights [and] a perpetually seditious one in the Platonic sense of the subversiveness of art" by asserting this interpretation in relation to the music's *formal semantic correspondence* to the "abstract term" of "a high concept of freedom [that] *is* embodied in the quartets" (1982: 147), so Russell is creating a "reflective system" between formal structure and phenomenal meaning by developing a correspondence with a different level of *semantic* – not logical – abstraction. By "pursuing different levels of meaning in its examination of one single object," as Benjamin says of his treatise on the origin of German tragic drama, the "method" of Russell's exposition – and, for that matter, Einstein's as well – "receives both the incentive to begin again and the justification for its irregular rhythm" (Benjamin, 1977: 28), which I am describing as the rhythm and the timeliness of "corresponding" analogies. Like the "renewals" of the "language structure" of Beethoven, which Stravinsky imagines are a way that art adds something to the world, so Russell, in "crowning" the abstract formalism of mathematics in his exposition of Cantorian infinities and his own "logical" mathematics, is also interpreting and renewing science in a way that allows him a "reflective system" for what he calls his "own age" (1917: 60).

This reflective system between the "language structure" of experience or knowledge and the structure of the phenomenal world is a version of what Bakhtin calls – in *his* Modernist aesthetics – the "answerability" of art to culture. That is, "answerability" describes the ways in which aesthetic phenomena such as the novels, essays and even "pure" mathematics allow the political/economic/technological culture in which they emerge to be grasped as a living event in a series, as Joyce says, "originating in and repeated to infinity." Both Russell's infinity and Bakhtin's answerability are predicated on the (aesthetic) possibility of grasping phenomena whole, momentarily, in order to comprehend them and, as Benjamin says, by means of their enlarged wholeness to "redeem" them. Even T. S. Eliot – whose attention to order rivals that of Russell – calls for such redemption: "Redeem / the time. Redeem / the unread vision in the higher dream" (1964: 88), though Eliot's "redemption" hardly *equals* Benjamin's. Still, what both are doing, along with Russell – in ways that are similar, corresponding, structurally congruent but not quite equal – are attempting to create a sense of order in the abundance and futility of the early twentieth century.

Specifically, the mathematical infinite that Russell describes and the relativity that Einstein formulates "crown" Enlightenment understanding at the price of disrupting time and reorienting experience and understanding. As Bruno Latour notes, Einstein was willing to "jettison what common sense cherishes" (1988: 22), namely "absolute space and time" (1988: 24) – just as Russell was willing to jettison the absolute continuities of space and time – in order to allow the laws of nature to maintain themselves across

different frames of reference. Yet both, in Latour's words, "rework
... the meaning of abstraction" (1988: 33). Each develops a semantic
formalism that disrupts atemporal formalism with the timeliness of
meaning: "the special and the general theories of relativity," Latour
writes, "are various ways of giving back *meanings* to descriptions"
(1988: 26). Thus, in their corresponding tasks and accomplishments,
Einstein and Russell present a distant formal similarity to historical
events and literary experience: the re-apprehension of the definition
of time as operational reflects or shares the "structure" of the non-
transcendental disembodiment of the power of electricity; and the
re-apprehension of mathematics as the science of order rather than
the science of quantities reflects or shares the organization of
understanding in which the position from which narrators speak – a
"margin" which is not "nowhere," since something else always can
happen – matters. The reorientations in Einstein's physics, Russell's
mathematics, Woolf's narrative, and marginal economics – above
all, the reorientation of the understanding and experience of temporality in each of these Modernist comprehensions – are functions of
the fulfillment and success of Newtonian dynamics, Euclidian
geometry, the Enlightenment individualism of the traditional novel,
and entrepreneurial capitalism. They participate in and organize
logics of abundance.

# CHAPTER 5

# Analogy and example: Heisenberg, linguistic negation, and the language of quantum physics

> ... there is no "being" behind doing, effecting, becoming; "the doer" is merely a fiction added to the deed – the deed is everything. The popular mind in fact doubles the deed; when it sees the lightning flash ... it posits the same event first as cause and then a second time as its effect. Scientists do no better when they say "force moves," "force causes," and the like – all its coolness, its freedom from emotion notwithstanding, our entire science still lies under the misleading influence of language and has not disposed of that little changeling, the "subject" (the atom, for example, is such a changeling, as is the Kantian "thing-in-itself") ...
>
> Friedrich Nietzsche, *On the Genealogy of Morals* (1969: 45)

When Nietzsche speaks of "the misleading influence of language" in *The Genealogy of Morals*, he is opposing both positivist materialism and idealist subjectivism of the late nineteenth century, the "double deed" – or, in Bruno Latour's terms, "double task of domination and emancipation" (1993: 10) – of Enlightenment understanding examined in part I. He does so through the reconception of time, which Russell describes in relation to post-Newtonian physics, in relation to the eternal recurrence of the same. Nietzsche's method of transforming the settled self-evidence of received opinion does not simply offer other understandings of "force," "subject," "atom," and even the "same" (*das Gleiche*). Rather, he *temporalizes* understanding, meaning, and value by bringing together and confronting alternative and alternating discourses. (Russell does this as well, in his narrativizing of "force" in *The ABC of Relativity* examined in chapter 4, but without Nietzsche's focus on time itself.) In this "method," Nietzsche is articulating what Werner Heisenberg called a generation later the "new lines of thought" occasioned by the revolution in physics in the early twentieth century (1952: 19) –

which, I am suggesting, take their place among the phenomenal abundances of the second Industrial Revolution that included the explosions of data and knowledge in post-Newtonian science. As Nietzsche did in philosophy, these lines of thought transformed the classical relationship between principle and example – a relationship of cause and effect in science and chronological systematization in philosophy – to the multi-valanced relationships between configuration and analogy, as in Russell's descriptions of "discontinuous time" in subatomic physics (1923: 64–66) or in Wittgenstein's "family resemblances" (1958: §§ 66, 67), relationships that can only be discerned retrospectively and as functions of the questions brought to experience. "In classical statistical mechanics," Heisenberg notes, "uncertainty about the result of a future experiment can be taken to indicate an as yet unsolved problem. But this does not apply to quantum theory since quantum theory always enables us to give full reasons for the occurrence of an event after it has actually taken place" (1952: 56–57). In this retrospective analysis, quantum theory examines phenomena, in Perry Anderson's negative assessment of poststructuralism, "no longer in terms of cause and effect, but [in terms of] the serial and the unpredictable" (1984: 51).

I want to suggest also that the "new lines of thought" pervading Modernist articulations of experience are, in rhetorical terms, metonymic rather than synecdochic, in the very complexity that inhabits the conception of metonymy. Synecdoche is the rhetorical figure that articulates the whole by means of the part or the part by means of the whole: to describe a person by his or her head ("I will have his head for that!") is an example of the first sense; to describe a collection of short stories examining a few citizens of Dublin as *Dubliners* is an example of the second. Metonymy, on the other hand, presents something by articulating something else that is contiguous with it, "crown" used to describe the king, or "White House" to describe the President. In an important way, synecdoche describes necessary and essentializing features, necessary and sufficient attributes: it is impossible to imagine a person without a head, and Joyce's intention is to describe the lives people lead in Dublin that make them *essentially* Dubliners. Metonymy, however, traffics in accidents: the White House could easily have been blue or grey (is it in fact grey?) and while the title *Dubliners* presents, synecdochically, the whole of the citizenry of Dublin (i.e., "Dubliners") for the parts of that citizenry presented in Joyce's stories, alternatively "Dubliners" itself is a metonym, describing people (instead of "citizens") in terms of the accident of where they live. (I develop this opposition at great length in *Rhetoric and Death*, especially chapter 1.)

The complexity of "metonymy" is present in Roman Jakobson's famous essay on aphasia in which the opposition between metaphor and metonymy is articulated by conflating synecdoche and metonymy under the name "metonymy" and opposing it to metaphor (1956). Such a conflation isolates the contiguous temporality of "metonymy" in opposition to the total and atemporal substitutions of "metaphor," but it does so by making the term "metonymy" stand, nontemporally, for what the contiguous figures of synecdoche and metonymy share. In other words, it leaves out the difference between metonymy and synecdoche as *nonessential*. This process encompasses the "nature" of linguistic meaning, which, Jakobson has argued, is synecdochical because the "whole" of meaning is greater than the sum of its parts (1987: 459). Yet metonymy, alternatively, opposes this definition by asserting the *accidental* nature of "meaning" where the "part" cannot be reduced to its place within an ordered whole. It is precisely this "alternating difference" within metonymy – where the difference does not hold "once and for all" – that I am describing as its complexity. To use a phrase describing narration in A. J. Greimas's *Structural Semantics*, metonymy differs from the meaningful reductions of synecdoche precisely insofar as it is "neither pure contiguity nor a logical implication" (1983: 244) – neither the "pure" opposite of synecdoche nor a moment or step within its logically coherent whole.

Such an articulation, like that of structural linguistics more generally which I examine in this chapter, has at least a distant formal similarity to the "uncertainty principle" associated with Heisenberg's name. This principle asserts the impossibility of measuring (or knowing with certainty) both the position and the momentum of subatomic particles at the same time. In *Physics and Philosophy*, Heisenberg presents a version of this "principle" by describing Bohr's contention that wave and particle descriptions of subatomic entities "complement" one another. The "two pictures," Heisenberg writes, "are of course mutually exclusive, because a certain thing cannot at the same time be a particle (i.e., substance confined to a very small volume) and a wave (i.e., a field spread out over a large space), but the two complement each other"(1958: 49).[1] As we have already seen, such a conception of complementarity,

Heisenberg asserts, encourages physicists "to apply alternatively different classical concepts which would lead to contradictions if used simultaneously" (1958: 179). Synecdoches are figures for simultaneity: as Jakobson says, the nature of language is "synecdochic" insofar as the nature of language produces wholes which subsume its parts. Metonymies are alternatively simultaneous (a species of synecdoche as in Joyce's *Dubliners*) and non-simultaneous where, as Jacques Derrida says (and Heisenberg might say) "the part is always greater than the whole" (1979: 96). That is, metonymies – like Heisenberg's "alternation" – import temporality into understanding, the technical "action" of post-Newtonian physics Russell describes. Temporality becomes a *constitutive* attribute of phenomena: as Russell says, in the "quantum principle" "nothing is said, in the first instance, about what is going on at a given moment, or about atoms of energy existing at all times, but only about the total result of a process that takes time" (1923: 151). Neither subjective idealism's "given moment" nor materialism's "at all times" takes precedence in a world of understanding in which parsimony only "occasionally" – or "alternatively" – governs. Instead, modes of understanding alternate in processes that take time and are marked by time in a world of abundances and the principled uncertainties to which they give rise.

## THE INELUCTABLE MODALITY OF TIME

In discussing types of statement in scientific discourse in *Laboratory Life*, Bruno Latour and Steve Woolgar examine the modalities of language. Modalities, they say, are statements that "contain statements about other statements" (1986: 77). Statements, they continue, "are characterised by the presence or absence of modalities. A statement clearly takes on a different form when modalities drop. Thus to state, 'the structure of GH.RH was *reported to be* X' is not the same as saying 'The structure of GH.RH *is* X.'" (1986: 78). In this discussion of modalities, they are following both traditional and contemporary definitions of linguistic modality. As they mention in a footnote to this analysis, "in its traditional Aristotelian meaning a 'modality' is 'a proposition in which the predicate is affirmed or denied of the subject with any kind of qualification' (Oxford Dictionary). In a more modern sense, a modality is any statement about another statement (Ducrot and Todorov, 1972)" (1986: 90).

Such a description of the relationship between linguistic modalities and scientific discourse is important and useful: Heisenberg even describes the problem of speaking about quantum mechanics and the uncertainty principle in terms of the modalities of discourse. His description, moreover, marks the intersection of linguistic modality, the mechanisms of negation in language and cognition, and the temporalities of quantum physics. Such an intersection, I am suggesting, is historically specific, and it takes its place, metonymically, within the larger cultural configurations of European Modernism I have described. The difficulty of articulating subatomic physics in a "plain language, understandable to anybody" as opposed to the formal and technical language of mathematics (1958: 168), Heisenberg says, is a function of the impossibility of *visualizing* the "descriptions" of nature postulated by quantum theory: as Ervin Schroedinger said of Heisenberg's mathematical description of quantum mechanics, the impossibility of picturing them was "disgusting, even repugnant" (cited in Crease and Mann 1986: 57). What prevents the visualization of the explanations that quantum theory presents is the fact that quantum theory questions precisely what seems simply and self-evidently true – what is true for the given moment and for all times – about the world: "in Newtonian mechanics," Heisenberg notes, "the gravitational force had been considered as given, not as an object for further theoretical studies" it becomes in quantum theory (1958: 95). In the revolution in literary studies Northop Frye hoped to initiate in the "Polemical Introduction" to *Anatomy of Criticism* he says the same thing about literary criticism and, indeed, about any intellectual discipline: it must transform the "naive induction" of taking "immediate sensations of experience" as simply given into an attempt to "explain" those immediate experiences "in terms of a conceptual framework different in shape from them" (1969: 24). For this reason, quantum theory attempts to comprehend immediate experience in terms of analyses mediated by a conception of time that functions constitutively in relation to both the analysis and the objects of analysis.

Specifically, it attempts to "comprehend" phenomena by focusing on the basic entities that comprise "matter" or "substance" or "facts" themselves. Such "matter," however, has always, commonsensibly, been understood in terms of its attributes – in terms of synecdoches. This is what sentences do when they attribute predicates to subjects (modally and non-modally). "In our [immediate and direct] experience," Heisenberg writes, "qualities like colour, smell and taste are as much immediate and direct realities as shape and movement. In depriving atoms of these qualities – and the very strength of atomic theory lies in this abstraction – one sacrifices immediately the possibility of 'understanding' the qualities of things in the true sense of the word" (1952: 32). This, in Heisenberg's judgment, is the great achievement of science in general and the specific achievement of ancient Greek "atomic" theory. "According to Democritus," he notes, "atoms had lost the qualities like colour, taste, etc., they only occupied space, but geometrical assertions about atoms were admissible and required no further analysis. In modern physics," he goes on,

atoms lose this last property, they possess geometrical qualities in no higher degree than colour, taste, etc. The atom of modern physics can only be symbolized by a partial differential equation in an abstract multidimensional space. Only the experiment of an observer forces the atom to indicate a position, a colour and a quantity of heat. *All* the qualities of the atom of modern physics are derived, it has no *immediate and direct* physical properties at all, i.e. every type of visual conception we might wish to design is, *eo ipso*, faulty. (1952: 42)

For this reason, the very terms like "substance," "matter," even "mass" are problems in modern physics; they are alternatively true and false descriptions of the world. "The terms 'substance' and 'matter' in ancient or medieval philosophy," Heisenberg writes, "cannot simply be identified with the term 'mass' in modern physics" (1958: 119). "The smallest parts of matter," he says earlier in *Physics and Philosophy*, "are not the fundamental Beings, as in the philosophy of Democritus, but are mathematical forms. Here it is quite evident that the form is more important than the substance of which it is the form" (1958: 69). Such "entities" – again, words fail – are without qualities (1958: 70).

The problem of description in modern physics as Heisenberg describes it, like the necessity and failure of "plain" concepts, revolves around the simultaneous (or rather, the "alternating") compatibility and incompatibility of classical physics and logic and quantum theory – the alternative necessity for and problem with terms like "matter" and "substance." The seeming contradiction between the compatibility and incompatibility of classical physics and quantum theory – what Heisenberg calls a "dualism alien to classical and earlier physics" (1952: 15)[2] – stems from an "inevitable" schism in studying atomic processes. "The validity of Euclidian geometry," Heisenberg writes, "is presupposed in the very instruments – used for the measurement of the deviation of sunlight – which are to show the variations from this same Euclidian geometry" (1952: 49; see also pp. 15–16; and 1958: 44, 53, 56). For this reason, Heisenberg argues in *Physics and Philosophy* that recent work suggests that "the mathematical scheme of quantum theory can be interpreted as an extension or modification of classical logic." Heisenberg isolates "one fundamental principle of classical logic" requiring modification, Leibniz's principle of Contradiction. "In classical logic," he writes, "it is assumed that, if a statement has any meaning at all, either the statement or the negation of the statement must be correct. Of 'here is a table' or 'here is not a table,' either the first or the second statement must be correct" (1958: 181). In quantum theory, however, the (parsimonious) necessity of *either* the first or second statement being correct is not in force.

Heisenberg explains this by citing the discussion of the relationship between quantum theory and discourse proposed by his student, Carl Weizsächer. In this analysis, Weizsächer distinguishes between levels of discourse. One level refers to objects, while a second level of discourse refers to statements about objects (1958: 182). In other words – these are neither Weizsächer's nor Heisenberg's words – "levels" of discourse are a function of linguistic modality and distinguished by means of whether or not statements "contain statements about other statements" (these are Latour's and Woolgar's words). "It is true," Heisenberg notes, "that finally we have to go back to the natural language and thereby to the classical logical patterns [in using natural language to describe physical phenomena] ... Classical logic would then be contained as a kind of limiting case in quantum logic, but the latter would constitute the more general logical pattern" (1958: 182). The concept and metaphor of "limit," which is crucial to Heisenberg's articulation of the uncertainty principle in *Physics and Philosophy* and other non-technical presentations, is especially important in relation to contemporaneous articulations of the limiting cases of linguistic articulation in the work of Louis Hjelmslev among others. It is also striking, especially in the figures of "border" and "borderline," recurring throughout Heisenberg's wartime lectures; and it is crucially important to Bakhtin's development of a Modernist aesthetics described in the following chapter. In all these cases the focus on the limit rather than the essence – the difference, to use an example repeated in structural linguistics, between the "border" between red and orange rather than the "reddest" red (see Hjelmslev 1961: 52–53; Sampson 1980: 94–102) – directs attention to abundances of relationship and interface between various elements rather than the parsimony of identity and essence of a single element.

The nature of limitations of classical logic in quantum logic, as Heisenberg suggests, is the limitation of the concept of simultaneity that, as I discussed in the preceding chapter, Einstein redefined functionally. As we have seen, Heisenberg's description of Bohr's concept of complementarity opposes alternating to simultaneous applications of classical concepts of physics. In this opposition the analogy between the relationship of linguistic "levels" to one another and the relationship between classical conceptions of physical reality and quantum conceptions can be seen. In fact, Heisenberg makes this analogy. Following his discussion of linguistic levels, he describes a situation in which an atom is in a box that is divided by a partition. In measuring the position of the atom (in the left half of the box, the right half, or moving freely throughout the box), quantum theory suggests that "the question whether the atom is left or right is not decided." Heisenberg goes on to note that "the term 'not decided' is by no means equivalent to the term 'not known.' 'Not known' would mean that the atom is 'really' left or right, only we do not know where it is. But 'not decided' indicates a different situation, expressible only by a complementary statement" (1958: 183–84). This "situation" is precisely the assertion that the measurement of subatomic physical reality is susceptible to temporally unique rather than general accountings, to alternating rather than simultaneous and generalizable proofs. "This general logical pattern," Heisenberg concludes, "the details of which cannot be described here, corresponds precisely to the mathematical formalism of quantum theory" (1958: 184).

This situation also corresponds, more or less precisely, to the semantic formalism of the modalities of language. "Semantic formalism" seems a contradiction in terms, though as I suggested in the preceding chapter it was precisely Einstein's "semanticization" of mathematical formalism in the Special Theory of Relativity – especially in the *temporalization* of meaning accomplished in his operational definitions – that was of such moment in his work. Semantic formalism is also central to a "poststructural" literary critic like Paul de Man, whose articulations of the "undecidability" of reading repeatedly offer local, "operational definitions" of meaning. De Man's "undecidability" corresponds to the "undecidability" of the uncertainty principle (as opposed to the "accidental" state of ignorance Heisenberg also describes). For de Man, it is not a question of not *knowing* a particular semantic reading, but rather the *theoretical* impossibility of finding criteria for choosing one reading over another once and for all. The classic example occurs in the opening essay of *Allegories of Reading* where de Man quotes Archie Bunker's response to his wife's question concerning whether he wants his bowling shoes laced over or under. Bunker responds "What's the difference?", and his wife begins to patiently explain the difference. De Man's point is that Bunker's answer – the "grammatical pattern" of his question – alternatively exists on the levels of atemporal grammar and time-specific rhetoric. It is a situation where the "literal meaning" of the grammatical level, as de Man calls it, "asks for a concept (difference) whose existence is denied by the figurative meaning" existing on the different "level" of Bunker's rhetorical question (1979: 9).

In this analysis, de Man distinguishes between grammar and rhetoric as incomparably different yet, like classical physics and quantum theory, still connected to one another. "The grammatical model of the question," he writes,

becomes rhetorical not when we have, on the one hand, a literal meaning and on the other hand a figural meaning, but when it is impossible to decide by grammatical or other linguistic devices which of the two meanings (that can be entirely incompatible) prevails. Rhetoric radically suspends logic and opens up vertiginous possibilities of referential aberration. (1979: 10)

De Man's last sentence here is an apt description of quantum theory as Heisenberg describes it: "quantum theory," he might say, "radically suspends classical logic and opens up vertiginous possibilities of referential aberration – possibilities producing vertigo precisely because they cannot be 'visualized.'" Like Heisenberg's description of quantum theory, this passage captures the need to both use and supersede "classical" logic.

Equally important, de Man's distinction between grammar and rhetoric describes two levels of linguistic activity that, since the work of J. L. Austin, have been described as constative and performative aspects of discourse. A constative statement is one that *describes* the world and is subject to judgments of truth value; a performative statement is an *act* of discourse, something that is done and takes place in time. This opposition articulates the difference between Bunker's question when his wife takes it *literally* and explains the different ways of lacing shoes and its *performed* force as a response to her question which, as de Man says, "did not ask for difference but means instead 'I don't give a damn what the difference is'" (1979: 9). It also marks the difference Latour and Woolgar describe between the "presence" and "absence" of modalities. Here, I am putting these terms in quotation marks because the opposition between presence and absence is a "false" opposition: statements are *alternatively* (and "complementarily") modal and nonmodal rather than either one or the other.

In *How to do Things with Words*, Austin presents but then undoes the distinction between constative and performative language. In this he uses the opposition for his analysis but in so doing shows that it is a "false" opposition. He does so by demonstrating that constative statements – so-called literal descriptions of the world – are special and limiting cases of the more general linguistic pattern of performative utterances, just as Heisenberg notes that classical logic is "a kind of limiting case in quantum logic, [so that] the latter would constitute the more general logical pattern" (1958: 182), and as Russell notes that "quantity" is a small corner of the general mathematics of "order" (1917: 87). Austin does this by arguing that all constative statements imply their own performance: "Benjamin played ball" can always be rewritten to say "I believe [or "I know" or "It is reported that" or "It is true that"] Benjamin played ball." In another example – Latour's and Woolgar's example – "The structure of GH.RH is X." can always be rewritten to say "The structure of GH.RH is *reported to be* X." In other words, the opposition between constative and performative statements is another description of the opposition between the absence and presence of modal articulation, and such "absence" and "presence" is not an absolute opposition but *alternative* apprehensions or "interpretations" of the "same" sentences.

In this understanding, the constative is a special case of modalities in that constative statements *are not marked*. They do not articulate the situation of their expression. As John Lyons notes in *Introduction to Theoretical Linguistics*, modality (or "mood") "is best defined in relation to an 'unmarked' class of sentences which express simple statements of fact, unqualified with respect to the attitude of the speaker toward what he is saying. Simple declarative sentences of this kind are, strictly speaking, non-modal ('unmarked' for mood)" (1968: 307). Linguistics refer to the simple, modally unmarked, statement of fact as the "dictum" which is modified by the modal articulation of the speaking subject's attitude toward that "dictum." A. J. Greimas and J. Courtés describe the unmarked dictum as "informative (or non-modalized) utterances" (1983: 10).

Still, an utterance cannot be simply "non-modalized"; an unmarked feature is not the simple absence of that feature. Rather, the opposition between a marked and unmarked feature (which exists at all linguistic levels, from the basic phonemic level of sound production to the level of semantic articulation) is a special case of negation: the marked or unmarked feature corresponds to the presence or absence of the feature, but the "absence" is always noted within the context of the *categorical* presence of the feature. In phonology, for instance, the opposition between /d/ and /t/ in English is a function of the presence or absence of the phonological feature of /voicing/, but the fact that /t/ is unmarked for voice only makes phonological sense – only carries phonological information – in the context of the category of /voicing/ altogether. In this context, moreover, the very *absence* of a feature signifies: as Saussure notes, "a material sign is not necessary for the expression of an idea; language is satisfied with the opposition between something and nothing" (1959: 86).

A marked element of language, however, always conveys more information than an unmarked element. In phonology the engagement of the vocal cords takes more energy and produces a sounded ("voiced") articulation. In Latour's and Woolgar's example of modal marking, "reported to be" specifies more closely the situation of articulation than does "is." Other forms of semantic marking are also noteworthy. "In comparison to the unmarked term," Elmar Holenstein has written,

the marked term provides more information. This is best illustrated by the example of polar adjectives and nouns. The statement "Peter is as young as Paul" is more informative than the statement "Peter is as old as Paul." Someone unfamiliar with Paul's age knows, after the first statement, that he is relatively young while the second statement reveals nothing about his age. *Young* is the marked term, *old* the unmarked term. Two oppositions overlap in the relation marked/unmarked – the opposition between a positive and negative term and between an indefinite and a definite one. (1976: 131)

The two kinds of opposition Holenstein describes in marking are two forms of negation articulated in discourse. The opposition between a positive and negative term is the special case of opposition I have been describing in marking: for instance, the presence and absence in phonological voicing or the (semantic) fact that /not young/ (the negation of /young/) can be equated with /old/.

But, as Holenstein notes, a second form of opposition inhabits linguistic marking, that between the definite and indefinite terms. Here, the very fact that the unmarked term conveys *less* information opposes it to the marked terms as an indefinite situation opposes a definite one. Such "indefiniteness" creates the semantic effect of *universalizing* understanding: in Holenstein's example, /old/ doesn't simply signify /not young/. It also signifies, in the "dualism alien to classical and earlier physics" Heisenberg describes (1952: 15), the general, indefinite meaning of /agedness/, that remains the same at the given moment and at all times. The universal of the unmarked category is the universal of Enlightenment understanding. When "young" is used in the statement "Peter is as young as Paul," we understand both are relatively young; when "old" is used in the statement "Peter is as old as Paul," we simply understand that their age, young or old, is the same. Both of these oppositions are inscribed in what Greimas calls "the elementary structure of signification." Greimas, following Jakobson, calls the first opposition "contrary" and the second "contradictory." Any semantic signification, he argues, can be articulated into a four-term homology governed by these oppositions (1987: esp. 49). This is, of course, Greimas's "semiotic square," and above all what the semiotic square does is bring together, as alternatives, parsimonious universals and time-specific instances.[3] It accomplishes this by "doubling" the deed through the operation of negation that is both the negation of atemporal logic and the negation of temporally-specific semantics.

That is, two alternative versions of negation are implicit in the elementary structure of signification Greimas outlines in the semiotic square. Negation itself, like other aspects of language, can be modally marked or unmarked. The negation of something can be a constative negation: "The structure of GH.RH is *not X*." (Such negation can also take place in the context of a modally articulated sentence: e.g., "The structure of GH.RH is reported to be *not X*.") But, negation can also modify a sentence whose modality is marked: "The structure of GH.RH *is not reported to be* X." The first two sentences present a logically "contrary" opposition between positive and negative terms (X and not X): there the predicate is negated and its negation positively affirmed. The third sentence presents a "contradictory" opposition between definite and indefinite terms: the definite statement, "GH.RH is (reported to be) X," is not affirmed, but neither is its negation, "GH.RH is (reported to be) not X," affirmed. Rather, the definite statement, "GH.RH is X," is opposed by the absence of any definite conclusion: the affirmation has not been reported, but still remains potential. (For the inscription of such a modal relationship on a semiotic square, see Greimas 1987: esp. 130.)

Holenstein's analysis allows us to understand these two alternative versions of negation in terms of modal activity (or "performance"). On the level of semantics, "young" vs. "old" exist as positive and negative terms – they are the extreme ends of the spectrum of "agedness." But, at the same time, within particular *performances* of language, such as the sentence "Paul is 25 years old," "old" signifies the indefinite quality of agedness in general. In this way, the conception of "unmarked" is not as univocal as Lyons and others suggest. Rather, the unmarked term – again on all levels of linguistics – is alternatively the definite negation of the predicate (e.g., "GH.RH is reported to be *not X*") and the indefinite negation of the modally marked term (e.g., "GH.RH *is not reported to be* X"). Such an indefinite opposition temporalizes meaning. It constitutes the "denial" of the marked term: rather than opposing the definite meaning of "young" with the definite meaning of "old," it opposes it with the indefinite meaning – the apparently *simultaneous* meaning – of "agedness." In the case of the mark of modality, rather than opposing the definite meaning of "X" with the definite meaning "not X" (or some positive term such as "Y" or, in Latour's and Woolgar's example, GFS), it opposes it with the indefinite meaning "not reported" (which still allows X or not X). What is important is that whether or not it is X or not X can only be determined retrospectively, after the fact. As Russell says, it is "a process that takes time" (1923: 151).

In linguistics, the complex relationship between marked and unmarked features and the two forms of negation they produce – such complexity being precisely a "dualism alien to classical and earlier physics" – exist in a relationship of complementarity in the sense that Neils Bohr defines it. Like an optical illusion such as an outlined cube in which one of two sides can be seen as closest to the observer, but never both at the same time,[4] the opposition between *alternative* and *simultaneous* explanations presents the complex relationship of definite and indefinite opposition of markedness (Greimas's "contradictory"). But the category of marking *also* presents the opposition between positive and negative terms in ways, as Holenstein says, that "overlap." The figure of "overlapping" offers, again, an analogy for metonymy which both is and is not a species of synecdoche.

Such a complex conception of negation presents the complexity of the opposition between performative and constative statements – the relationship between rhetoric and grammar de Man describes – and the opposition between modality and dictum. Performative statements are the logical opposite to constative statements, but constative statements are all *performed* no matter how much effort is made to erase their situation of articulation. In other words, they are *alternatively* apprehensible as performatives and constatives. In the same way, the "simple declarative sentences ... [which] are, strictly speaking, non-modal ('unmarked' for mood)" that Lyons describes (1968: 307) can also, in fact, be understood ("alternatively") as existing at the extreme, "unmarked" pole of modality. Here are the alternative interpretations: declarative (constative) sentences can be seen as general (indefinite) non-modalized *affirmations*, universally true (or at least subject to evaluation in terms of truth value), and, alternatively, complementarily, they can be seen as definite *assertions* of their universality in the modality of "dictum." For instance, Nietzsche's statement, "There is no 'being' behind doing," is alternately an *affirmative* statement of universal truth, once and for all; and an *assertive* statement, offered in response to statements affirmed by "the popular mind" and "scientists" – assertions of Kantian metaphysics clothed in the language of simple affirmations. In the second alternative, as Latour and Woolgar suggest, the temporally specific circumstances and conditions of their assertion are legitimate areas of inquiry. In the same alternating apprehension, modally marked sentences (e.g., "it was reported," "he wishes to go to the store," "I bet") can be taken to be constative statements about the world (it *really was* reported, his activity of wishing *did* take place, I *am* betting).

LANGUAGE AND REALITY IN MODERN PHYSICS

In this discussion of quantum physics I have brought together, in a small space, Latour's analysis of the modalities of scientific discourse, Austin's analysis of the performative and constative aspects of language, the structural linguistic category of marking, poststructuralism's penchant for complex alternative descriptions of difference, Bohr's description of complementarity, and Heisenberg's narration of modern physics in terms of the rigorous, principled conception of uncertainty. I have done so in order to articulate a particular conception of negation – strictly speaking, a conception which is neither materialist nor nonmaterialist, a conception of "negative materiality" that I develop in *Rhetoric and Death* (chapters. 1–4) that has a distant formal similarity to "semantic formalism" – and also, more generally, to describe what Heisenberg calls "the spirit of a time" (1958: 109), the remarkable time of the second Industrial Revolution in central and eastern Europe. All of these analyses present analogical attempts to articulate a logic of abundance, to deal with irreducible complexities that, in the early years of the twentieth century, seemed to inhabit understanding, economic and political realities, and the experience of everyday life.

Many of the strategies of these "logics," I think, come together in Heisenberg's description of the relationship between language and reality in modern physics – the complex relationship between dictum and modality. "In classical logic," Heisenberg writes,

the relation between the different levels of language is a one-to-one correspondence. The two statements, "The atom is in the left half [of the box]" and "It is true that the atom is in the left half," belong logically to different levels. In classical logic these statements are completely equivalent, i.e., they are either both true or both false. It is not possible that the one is true and the other false. But in the logical pattern of complementarity this relation is more complicated. The correctness or incorrectness of the first statement still implies the correctness or incorrectness of the second statement. But the incorrectness of the second statement does not imply the incorrectness of the first statement. If the second statement is incorrect, it may be undecided whether the atom is in the left half; the atom need not necessarily be in the right half. There is still complete equivalence between the two levels of language with respect to the correctness of a statement, but not with respect to the incorrectness. (1958: 184)

In this narration, Heisenberg presents quantum theory as analogous to the complexity of language where statements alternatively – that is, non-coincidentally – can be taken to be statements about the world and statements about other statements.

He also presents a mathematical analogy for quantum theory in which the same complexity can be seen. "The atom of modern physics," he writes,

shows a distant formal similarity to the $\sqrt{-1}$ in mathematics. Though elementary mathematics maintains that among the ordinary numbers no such square root exists, yet the most important mathematical propositions only achieve their simplest form on the introduction of this square root as a new symbol. Its justification thus rests in the propositions themselves. In a similar way the experiences of present-day physics show us that atoms do not exist as simple material objects. (1952: 62)

Neither do they exist, of course, as *nonmaterial* objects. Rather, in the microphysics of quantum mechanics, they exist *outside the alternative* between material and nonmaterial just as $\sqrt{-1}$ is neither positive nor negative, is neither a number nor not a number. As an abstract form, $i$ is a number like any other number (not outside the category /number/): it is modally and semantically unmarked in the abstract formalism of mathematics. But as $\sqrt{-1}$, it is marked semantically (literally spelled out, "the square root of minus one") and, in the context of elementary mathematics, it is marked modally as well. In this, $\sqrt{-1}$ is a scandal to Enlightenment parsimony as expressed by Leibniz, Samuel Johnson, and others. However, in its achievement of mathematical simplicity, as Heisenberg says, it is, alternatively, the fulfillment of Enlightenment parsimony.

This scandal to common sense is clearer in another aspect of Heisenberg's development of quantum mechanics. In articulating the quantum matrices that he developed to describe subatomic particles, Heisenberg found – as Russell found in relation to infinite numbers – that the mathematical computations were not commutative. That is, unlike ordinary multiplication, the results of their multiplication changes when the order of their multiplication changes so that a × b does not equal b × a. The breach in the law of commutation was a breach in the universality of unmarked dicta and of abstract formalism more generally. Literally, matrices could not be formally described as a number (like $i$, for instance), but rather behaved, as modally marked sentences do, in relation to their ordered enunciation. (As Lyons notes, modally marked sentences are qualified "with respect to the attitude of the speaker toward what he is saying" [1968: 307].) And in this, the mathematics of quantum mechanics shows a distant formal similarity in Heisenberg sentences in the analogy he presents between linguistic modalities and quantum theory. In other words, the semantic equation of the sentences "The atom is not in the left half [of the box]" and "It is not true that the atom is in the left half" depends on the order in which they are presented.[5]

In this presentation – as in "The structure of GH.RH *was not reported to be* X." – the negation of modality is neither negative nor positive. Rather, such negation is complex. It is what Shoshana Felman describes in a much different context as a form of "radical negativity (or 'saying no') [which] belongs neither to *negation*, nor to *opposition*, nor to *correction* ('normalization'), nor to *contradiction* (of the positive and the negative, the normal and the abnormal, the 'serious' and the 'unserious,' 'clarity' and 'obscurity') – it belongs precisely to *scandal*: to the scandal of their nonopposition. This scandal of the *outside of the alternative*, of a negativity that is neither negative nor positive" (1983: 141–42). In this discussion Felman *is* talking about modality: "saying no" is precisely a negative statement about another statement. As such, it participates in the logic of discourse which is different from the referential logic of truth value. The opposition which I am trying to articulate is that between modality and dictum. Yet insofar as any dictum can *alternatively* be apprehended as a modally unmarked statement – insofar as the (negative) "unmarking" of modality is both its absence and also a "mode" or "state" of its presence – we are faced, again, with the scandal of nonopposition of a negativity that is neither negative nor positive.[6]

ANALOGY AND EXAMPLE

The third alternative spelled out here ("neither positive nor negative") enjoins us, as quantum theory does, to reconceive what we mean by a fact or state of an object and to reconfigure the nature of reference in discourse and science. It is precisely Heisenberg's point that this distinction is only *alternatively* operable in quantum theory. (It is clearly *alternatively* operable in semiotics where "elements" are alternatively defined as relationships and entities.) What alternates are the "two very different" conceptions of "interpretation" itself that Greimas and Courtés describe I mentioned in the preceding chapter. According to the "classical" concept of interpretation, "every system of signs may be described in a formal way that does not take into account the content and is independent of possible 'interpretations' of these signs" (1983: 159). In this conception – which governs the "classical" logic of "the mathematical forms of atomic theory" (1952: 120) – "semantic interpretation" comes after and follows from abstract formalism, which, like the propositional "dictum," is general and unmarked. In this understanding of interpretation, an interpretation is always an example of more general preexisting truths, an exemplary part for the whole of truth. Moreover, this conception preserves the common-sense, parsimonious idea of the referential function of interpretation and sign systems more generally: the world to which language refers *preexists* ("objectively," "substantially," as a kind of "base") the language that describes it just as the necessities of formal logic preexist the phenomena that exemplify those logical necessities and basic human needs – food, clothing, shelter – preexist more or less desirable fulfillments of those needs. Interpretation, in this understanding, consists of finding a language which *conforms* to preexisting *forms*.

The second concept of interpretation, as Greimas and Courtés argue, "is completely different." Within this perspective (which they identify with Saussurian linguistics, Husserlian phenomenology and Freudian psychoanalysis – all intellectual movements contemporaneous with quantum theory and which, I am suggesting, participated in and responded to the abundances of the second Industrial Revolution), "interpretation is no longer a matter of attributing a given content to a form which would otherwise lack one; rather, it is a paraphrase which formulates in another fashion the equivalent content of a signifying element within a given semiotic system" (1983: 159). In this second understanding of "interpretation," form and content are not distinct, but rather every "form" is, alternatively, a semantic "content" as well, a "signifying form," so that interpretation offers an analogical paraphrase of something which *already* "signifies within a system of signification." In this *semantic formalism* such paraphrases are alternatively the "same" and "different" from their "model," and as such raise serious questions about the referential truth value that seems to govern linguistic dicta and classical science. That is, the *alternativeness* of paraphrase offers what Derrida calls "seriality without paradigm ... [in which elements are] at once analogous (hence the series) and utterly different, offering no guarantee of analogy" (1979: 130). "Seriality without paradigm" might well offer an abstract definition of "abundance" altogether in the mode of semantic abstraction I discussed in relation to Russell and Stravinsky in the preceding chapter. In any case, the opposition between modality and dictum presents just such seriality without paradigm. This is especially clear in the extreme case of the negation of modal articulations: the negation of a statement *taken to be* modally inflected – e.g., "It is not true that the atom is in the left half of the box" or "It is not true that the multiplication of two negative numbers equals a positive number" – presents *metonymic* iteration without paradigm, paraphrase as interpretation.

Like Heisenberg's analogy between quantum theory and the levels of language, this understanding of interpretation presents the *form* of an example, yet, by virtue of the fact that the abstraction it exemplifies is necessarily *semanticized*, it offers an analogy rather than an example. Even the abstract formalism of mathematics, which from the vantage of classical logic is form without content, carries meanings that can be translated and paraphrased. (In fact, as we saw in the preceding chapter, it is precisely the transformation of mathematical formalism into more or less narrativized semantics that characterized Einstein's "natural history" of time; and it is precisely the repeated assertion of the formal, and "contentless" nature of mathematics in Russell that functions as a signifier for his meanings.) Although the number $i$ operates like any "ordinary number" within the abstract formalism of mathematical operations, when it is apprehended modally – when it is understood as a paraphrase of $\sqrt{-1}$ – it alternatively seems to be no number at all. All these "difficult definitions and distinctions," Heisenberg writes, "can be avoided if one confines the language to the description of facts, i.e., experimental results" (1958: 185). In this, Heisenberg is suggesting that as soon as one *interprets* "facts" – and elsewhere he defines the "facts" of quantum mechanics positivistically as "the black spots on a photographic plate or the water droplets in a cloud chamber" (1958: 179) – one enters the realm of the "dualism" of alternation and paraphrase. Positivism – in which "facts" are assumed to be simple positive entities like the water droplets in a cloud chamber – does not admit negation. The droplets are either present or absent, there or not there, and when they are not there nothing signifies. As Jacques Lacan says, "the real, whatever upheaval we subject it to, is always in its place" (1989: 309) precisely because, unlike symbolic systems (to which Lacan opposes the "real"), it does not admit negation. The absence of droplets only signifies in the logic of semantics in which absence takes on complex positive meaning within a symbolic system just as the unmarked absence of the engagement of vocal chords takes on positive meaning in the phonological system of English in which the absence of voicing distinguishes the phoneme /t/ from /d/. Absences signify only when the given moment is not for all times but is one moment within temporal contexts. Those contexts are always the result of a process that takes time and, for this reason, they can only be discerned retrospectively.

These two traditions of interpretation – one classical, the other post-Enlightenment – themselves present a *complex* double articulation in the same way that twentieth-century linguistics and Bohr's description of complementarity do. In this complexity, the distinction between these traditions is not absolute, but rather alternates as a function of the questions asked so that interpretation itself remains undecided. Interpretation and understanding, in Emile Benveniste's terms, are cultural phenomena "which have the characteristic that they can never be taken as simple data or defined in the order of their own nature but must always be understood as double from the fact that they are connected to something else, whatever their 'referent' may be" (1971: 38). In an analogical way, the nature of the data of physics, at least at subatomic scales, cannot simply be defined in the order of their own nature. Instead, in the same way that even the most straight-forward, self-evident *literal* propositions of a sentence – even the pure "informative (or non-modalized) utterances" Greimas and Courtés describe (1983: 10) – can always also be taken to be a *figure* or an analogue for something metonymically outside of them (such as the "being" behind doing, the "force" behind events, the very "subject" articulating propositions that Nietzsche describes), so the data of quantum physics also can always be taken to be connected to something else outside that data: the subject of (modally inflected) knowledge, the quality of spatial and temporal position, the semiotic system that governs interpretation.

## THE ONTOLOGICAL ARGUMENT

The problem, I think, is the semantic problem of *qualities* that Heisenberg repeatedly brings up. Thus, as we have seen, he speaks of "the quality of taking up space" in terms that equate this "quality" with those of "other properties, say colour and strength of material" (1958: 62). Elsewhere, also, he talks of the "geometrical properties" of atoms. "Anything that can be imagined and visualized," he writes,

cannot be indivisible. The indivisibility and homogeneity, in principle, of elementary particles makes it quite understandable that the mathematical forms of atomic theory can hardly be visualized. It would even seem unnatural if atoms lacked all the general qualities of matter like colour, smell, taste, tensile strength, and had yet retained geometrical properties. It is much more plausible to think that all these properties can be attributed to an atom only with the same reservations, and such reservations may also later enable us to relate space and matter more closely. The two concepts, atom and empty space, would then no longer stand side by side yet be completely independent of one another... (1952: 120)

Usually, in the common-sense of secular and parsimonious Enlightenment thinking, the geometrical properties of location in time and space are not equated with the other properties Heisenberg lists here. Color, smell, taste, strength – the *"immediate and direct* physical properties" Heisenberg speaks of elsewhere (1952: 42), the "sense-properties" of matter (1952: 81) – are understood as attributes, detachable "parts," of some (positive) underlying whole.

But to speak of atoms "retaining" geometrical properties is to equate them with something seemingly outside of them, not a part at all. Democritus, Heisenberg notes, deprived the atom of the qualities of color, smell and taste, "and his atom is thus a rather abstract piece of matter." But, Heisenberg goes on, he "has left to the atom the quality of 'being,' of extension in space, of shape and motion," of existence within abstract Newtonian time. He has left these qualities because "it would have been difficult to speak about the atom at all if such qualities had been taken away from it" (1958: 69–70). In other words, quantum mechanics reintroduces "being" as a quality or attribute rather than a positive physical substance to which other qualities can be attributed: it reintroduces the premises of Saint Anselm's ontological argument for the existence of God that Kant had seemingly demolished in the *Critique of Pure Reason* when he argued that existence is not a predicate or an attribute of an entity in the same way that its color or taste is. To put this in rhetorical terms, quantum theory, unlike Jakobson, erases the opposition between synecdoche and metonymy – the opposition between part and whole – without erasing difference, multiplicity, plurality; without ignoring abundance or time. It presents a *non-reductive* logic of comprehension. When geometrical extensions of shape and motion are considered properties, like the negation I have been discussing, those properties become unthinkably – unvisualizably – complex. In this complexity, the outside and inside of matter and being are alternatively (and, in Felman's words, scandalously) opposed and nonopposed.

In other words, quantum theory limits the common-sense Enlightenment understanding of reference as a *special case* of retrospective interpretation in which, as Nietzsche points out, the seeming preexistent "cause" of reference is taken to be a function of the subject of knowledge. As in Russell's description of the mathematical term "equal" in which identification becomes a special case of relationship (1919: 71–72), parsimonious simplicity is comprehended as a species of abundant complexity. In this process negation has a special place. Negation, after all, *only* exists retrospectively, in relation to what is negated. For the same reason, then, that Heisenberg turns to the linguistic negative for his analogy, Umberto Eco has argued that "semiotics is in principle the discipline studying everything which can be used in order to lie" (1976: 7). George Steiner has similarly argued that negation – and "the more general framework of non- and counter-factuality" – is the genius of language (1975: 160). In these complex descriptions, negation "means" both something and nothing alternatively, and the alternatives, as we saw in modal negation, are not quite or not completely ("at all times") compatible. This complex conception of negation creates the possibility of conceiving of phenomena in *alternative* rather than *simultaneous* frameworks (or levels) of understanding, where understanding itself is analogical rather than exemplary, and the abundances of understanding and experience are not too-quickly reduced. As Heisenberg notes, in one framework a problem is "sensible," in another it is "false" (1952: 57). In the same way, in one framework, Edith Bunker's response to her husband is sensible, in another it is nonsense. Moreover, the difference between the frameworks are functions of what is being examined – they are functions, that is, of observation, an action that takes time. The emphasis on observation, however, does not simply mean subjectivity replaces objectivity. "The introduction of the observer," Heisenberg writes, "must not be misunderstood to imply that some kind of subjective features are to be brought into the description of nature. The observer has, rather, only the function of registering decisions, i.e., processes in space and time, and it does not matter whether the observer is an apparatus or a human being" (1958: 137).

Discursive negation is a pronounced case of such registration because it is a function of discourse and interpretation: as we have seen, concepts such as "false" or "lack" or even "out of place" – like "scarcity" and "abundance" themselves – do not make sense in relation to the real world. Moreover, this case suggests that interpretation itself must be seen as different from the forces of cause and effect posited by Newtonian mechanics and nineteenth-century positive science. The importance of this, finally, is that with his modal analogy, Heisenberg situates quantum theory within the wider cultural phenomenon of post-Enlightenment Modernism. A central aspect of Modernism – in economics, linguistics, rhetoric, art, and even unreflective experience itself – is what Heisenberg describes as a "new method of thought" (1952: 53) that supplements the old method of causal explanation: post-Enlightenment Modernism itself is marked by logics of abundance that, from time to time, transform causal explanations (understanding phenomena, both in a given moment and for all time, in terms of their causes) to functional explanations (understanding phenomena in terms of the ends they serve within a matrix of beginning, middle, and end). Such logics, in one analogical expression, replace simple synecdoche with complex metonymy. Moreover, they are pragmatic and operational, answering particular needs for explanation, just as Bunker's performative utterance answers the situation rather than an abstract grammatical question – a situation that, like Wittgenstein's "family resemblances," can only be discerned *retrospectively.*

To ask why this should be, what factor is common to the disparate phenomena of post-Enlightenment Modernism is to return to classical modes of explanation (which, to some degree I have done with my repeated attention to historical "abundances"). Alternatively, Modernism understood in terms of metonymic configurations, Benjamin's "constellations," Russell's "arrangements," Heisenberg's "alternatives," and even Yeats's phenomenology of holding "in a single thought reality and justice" (1965: 25), rather than synecdochic descriptions of cause and effect, offers the possibility of discerning what Raymond Williams calls the historically determined "structure of feeling" that pervades any particular cultural moment.[7] In this alternative, the relationship between post-Enlightenment Modernism and the classical approaches to experience that preceded it is analogous to the relationship between particle and wave descriptions of subatomic particles. That is, it is a function of what one is looking for. Such an alternative understanding places Heisenberg and quantum mechanics within the ambiguously metonymic cultural configuration of Modernism I have described by assuming that the abundances of goods, understandings, and experiences at the turn of the twentieth century are not simply historical accidents. It situates Heisenberg's post-Newtonian physics within a constellation of various attempts to articulate representations of a world in which the parsimony of atemporal truth no longer fully or simply or always makes sense nor corresponds to the phenomenologies of over-whelming experience. With his contemporaries, Heisenberg attempted to create a logic to describe this experience using the seeming curiosity of modal articulations to describe a kind of definite uncertainty at the limits of understanding.

CHAPTER 6

# The global aesthetics of genre: Mikhail Bakhtin and the borders of modernity

But they were not alone, nor had they been from the start, from the start of love. Their time sat in the third place at their table. They were the creatures of history, whose coming together was of a nature possible in no other day – the day was inherent in the nature. Which must have been always true of lovers, if it had taken till now to be seen. The relation of people to one another is subject to the relation of each to time, to what is happening. If this has not been always felt – and as to that who is to know? – it has begun to be felt, irrevocably.

Elizabeth Bowen, *The Heat of the Day* (1962: 194–95)

In this chapter, I examine Mikhail Bakhtin's early neo-Kantian analysis of aesthetics in relation to cognition and ethics in order to examine his conceptions of genre as central to ordinary discourse and verbal art. Bakhtin's conception of genre, like Russell's conception of order and Heisenberg's articulation of the meaning of quantum mechanics, is a response to the abundances of knowledge, materiality, and experience in the new century – a third logic of abundance, joining Russell's and Einstein's temporalization of sufficient reason and Heisenberg's temporalization of the law of contradiction. Just as Russell develops an understanding of interpretation and Heisenberg develops a mode of analogical thinking in order to come to terms with the phenomenal abundances of the new century, so Bakhtin attempts to create the possibility of aesthetics – a phenomenology of the "given moment" – that does not ignore or reduce temporality to infinitesimal moments. In this chapter I will examine Bakhtin's aesthetics in relation to Roman Jakobson's understanding of the science of linguistics and Walter Benjamin's sense of culture and history. In this way, I hope to create a configuration of experience, understanding, and history in this discussion of Bakhtin's aesthetics that is parallel to the larger discussions of understanding, history, and experience I have pursued in *Modernism and Time*. If, as I have argued, the criteria for secular Enlightenment comprehension are the atemporal generalizability, accuracy, and simplicity of explanation, then the sciences of Einstein and Russell, the representational discourse of Heisenberg, and the generic aesthetics of Bakhtin in Part II of this book all modify – they all "temporalize" – received notions of the logic of explanation. They assume that what is to be explained – the self-evidence of apparently self-contained objects of knowledge, self-standing events, and instantaneous experiences – all exist within and by means of configurations of time that cannot be ignored. What precedes and succeeds objects, events, and experiences – abundances of time – are constituent elements of these phenomena.

Bakhtin presents two conceptions of genre: the primary conception of "speech genre" he describes in his late work, which encompasses, in my understanding, the "genres" of cognition and ethical judgment; and his secondary conception of "literary genre," which embodies the larger, global category of aesthetics in verbal art.[1] Against the Kantian definition of disinterested aesthetics – and particularly the "overall aesthetic concept" of *simple wholeness* – Bakhtin attempts to recover a sense of the always-interested nature of semantics, its complexity within multiple contexts. That is, Bakhtin wants to recover the interested nature or moment in art – its ethical moment – but he wants to do so without abandoning the simplicity and wholeness of aesthetics as categories of understanding. His early assertion of a neo-Kantian reading of aesthetics in the contexts of knowledge and value recovers a sense of a contextualized "interest" for understanding that is less narrow than the sense of interest contained in literary formalism, whether it be the Russian Formalism of the 1920s or the American New Critical formalism of the 1940s.

That is, throughout his career, Bakhtin repeatedly is trying to make sense of his early dictum drawn up in the wake of the post-World War I crisis in culture, which I examined in the Introduction, that art and life are separate, but must be "answerable" to each other (1990: 1–2) without reducing either the "aesthetics" of art or the "responsibilities" of life to a secondary status – without reducing the one or the other to an "example" of a principle, a "superstructure" of a base, or an "instance" of an atemporal condition. Important to my argument, of course, is the larger question con-

cerning the historical conditions, which I examined in part I, that
gave rise to need to integrate interest with understanding in the early
decades of the twentieth century in formalism, structuralism, or
Bakhtinian dialogics. But my overall aim is to examine the ways that
art and poetry were important places in which Bakhtin could
recover the aesthetic value of "wholeness" in the early twentieth
century just as Benjamin attempts to recover the wholeness of
historical events and the modernist sciences of Russell, Heisenberg,
and Jakobson attempt to recover a conception of wholeness within
their studies of phenomena that seems to explode received conceptions of self-contained objects. To this end, I will examine the
scientific-structuralist analysis of "poeticalness" in Jakobson and the
social and ethical analysis of "aura" in Walter Benjamin in relation
to Bakhtin's analysis of the aesthetics of genre. I have chosen these
two figures because about the same time Bakhtin was developing his
*aesthetics* of culture – in the decades between the great wars of the
early twentieth century – Jakobson was pursuing the *cognitive* analysis
of art and culture, his attempt to create a method of scientific study
of cultural objects and values, while Benjamin was developing an
*ethics* of cultural analysis.[2] Examined in relation to Bakhtin, these
writers can help us understand the purpose and function of Bakhtin's
Modernist aesthetics.

### THE AESTHETICS OF WHOLENESS

In one of his various attempts to define poetry, Roman Jakobson
offers the following narrative. "A missionary blamed his African
flock for walking around with no clothes on. 'And what about
yourself?' they pointed to his visage, 'are not you, too, somewhere
naked?' 'Well, but this is my face.' 'Yet in us,' retorted the natives,
'everywhere it is face.' So in poetry any verbal element is converted
into a figure of poetic speech" (1987: 93). With this story, Jakobson is
attempting to develop a definition of poetry and literature that
avoids both idealism and vulgar materialism. Another way to say
this is that Jakobson reads poetry from the position of what one
might call a "literary scientist": the structuralism that he named in
1929 aimed at the generalizations, simplicity, and accuracy that
allow phenomena to be grasped globally, as simple wholes that
science – and philosophy more generally – since the Enlightenment
has pursued. Jakobson and the Prague structural linguistics he

helped to establish emphasized the "generalizing" function of science, just as Noam Chomsky emphasizes its "simplicity" and Leonard Bloomfield emphasized its "accuracy."[3] This is the significance, I think, of his narrative describing faces "everywhere." The truth is, from the vantage of a global perspective, faces *are* everywhere. In this story, Jakobson is trying to define what I call a global sense of things and what both Walter Benjamin and Mikhail Bakhtin call their "aura" (Benjamin 1969: 221; Bakhtin 1986: 88): a sense of the whole of something that is not quite reducible to the sum of its parts. He is trying to develop a way of holding and trusting intuition without mysticism. It may well be a way of holding, trusting, and preserving value – the "reality" of what we most value – without know-nothing mysticism or the desert-reality of cynicism, the "idealism and psychologism," on the one hand, that Vološinov contrasts to the positivism of the "facts" linguistic science isolates and studies (1986: 11, 53). As citizens, teachers, and readers – as subjects of experience, knowledge, and goods in the late twentieth century – we all know that things of value are real and true and worthy of our devotion, and that a large part of our jobs is to find ways to talk about them with neither cynicism nor otherworldly dream.

One way of talking about them is to find a vocabulary for the global sense of things I have mentioned. Such global entities are wholes in which we intuit significance and value that are not locatable so that we cannot simply say *here* is the mark of value, *there* is the combination in which the intention and import of a discourse, its purpose that inhabits each of its parts yet is not quite any single one of its parts, resides. Bakhtin examines such global entities aesthetically, in the context and vocabulary of art, and calls them the "genres" of discourse. When he talks of the "aura" of an utterance, he says "this aura belongs not to the word of language as such but to that genre in which the given word usually functions. It is an echo of the generic whole that resounds in the word" (1986: 88). This definition makes genre itself distinct from language and discourse, a whole greater than the sum of its parts. In *Kinds of Literature*, a book describing the history and purposes of literary genre very different from what Bakhtin might have written, Alastair Fowler also begins by distinguishing literary genres from language and discourse. Taking exception with Northrop Frye's famous affirmation – "Literature is not a piled aggregate of 'works,'" Frye wrote, "but an order of words" – Fowler notes that this "dictum is not a very happy

one. When we read literature, what we read are groups of works, or
works, or parts of works: not words." In fact, he says, "if we think
mainly of works ... we shall probably adopt a broader art concept
taking other elements besides language into account; or a concept
based on fiction; or a value concept. It is mainly in works, not in
words, that literature embodies values" (1982: 4). Both Fowler's
descriptions of literature and genre and Bakhtin's distinguish themselves from the scientific analytics of structuralism and the functionalism of constructivism[4] insofar as these sciences seek to define
phenomena in relation to – as aggregates of – simple, basic elements.

For Bakhtin the concept of genre is parallel to what Fowler calls
the concept of the "work": as Bakhtin/Medvedev note in *The Formal
Method in Literary Scholarship*, genres are "the forms of the whole"
(1985: 132; see 129). "It is not the sentence, the period, or their
aggregate that implement the theme [of an utterance], but the
novella, the novel, the lyric, the fairy tale – and these genre forms do
not lend themselves to any syntactic definition" (1985: 132; see also
Vološinov 1986: 102). Still, Bakhtin's generic forms, unlike the
"works" Fowler describes, are situated on and realize the "border"
between aesthetic signification – what Bakhtin/Medvedev call the
"theme" of discourse and art which "always transcends language"
(1985: 132) – and historical experience: "the thematic unity of the
work and its real place in life organically grow together in genre"
(1985: 133). His conception of aesthetic wholeness is not quite as
"disinterested" as Fowler's more traditional senses of "work" and
"value." This is why, later in his career Bakhtin could write that
generic tradition exists, but it "is reborn and renewed in each
[particular author] in its own way, that is, in a unique and
unrepeatable way" (1984: 159).

Such a "rebirth," as I argue in *Rhetoric and Death*, is not resurrection but transmission (1990: 108), neither the mysticism of coming
back to life miraculously nor the cynicism of random, unrelated
"facts." The theme of transmission is central to Benjamin's writing,
contemporaneous with that of Bakhtin and of much of Jakobson,
and it can help us to understand, I think, the ways Bakhtin's
conceptions of genre and, earlier, his concept of aesthetics, participate in the cultural moment of twentieth-century Modernism. Each
of these writers, I am suggesting, avoids both the cynical explanation
of empirical accident ("it's simply what happened") and the mystical
explanation of *zeitgeist*. Instead, they "answer" the sense of over-

whelming change, everywhere felt in educated experience during the second Industrial Revolution, with particular "language structures," as Stravinsky describes them: as attempts to define and comprehend versions of wholeness in terms of descriptions as vague – that is, as insusceptible to analysis into parts and wholes – as "literariness," "aura," or even "utterance." It is clear, in Jakobson's need for a structural analysis of "poeticalness," Benjamin's socio-cultural analysis of the "aura" of a work of art, and Bakhtin's aesthetic analysis of "genre," that some comprehension of phenomena conceived *globally* answered the experience of the early twentieth century in ways that received versions of idealism and empiricism did not. Later, I describe this experience in terms of difference, strangeness, and otherness – terms, like those followed by Bakhtin, that comprehend this experience phenomenally and aesthetically. But this experience might equally be understood as effects of historical events militating against any everyday sense of "wholeness": the vast commodification of European life, the development of fantastic new technologies, and the transformations of class and nation-state in the new century.

### FORMS OF THE WHOLE

Bakhtin, more than Jakobson or Benjamin, pursues an aesthetics of wholeness, an interested global aesthetics. He follows a vocabulary borrowed from Kantian metaphysics in his early analysis of aesthetics as a category of global apprehension that he later described, in verbal art, in terms of genre. In an early fragment, published under the title *Toward a Philosophy of the Act*, Bakhtin attempts to describe aesthetic experience in opposition to intellectual or "cognitive" understanding and "ethical" judgment. Aesthetic contemplation is "what remains" when "intellectual elements are subtracted from intuition" (1993: 13). These "aesthetic moments," he writes, consist in "unity, wholeness, self-sufficiency, distinctiveness" (14) – the very "finalization" that *The Formal Method* argues exists only in art. "Outside of art," Bakhtin/Medvedev write,

all finalization, every end, is conditional, superficial, and is most often defined by external factors rather than factors intrinsic to the object itself. The end of a scientific work is an illustration of such conditional finalization. In essence, a scientific work never ends: one work takes up where the other leaves off. Science is an endless unity. It cannot be broken down into a series of finished and self-sufficient works. The same is true of other spheres of ideology. There are really no finished works there. (1985: 129–30)

"Finalization," Bakhtin makes clear in his earlier essay, "The Problem of Content, Material, and Form in Verbal Art" (1924), is above all "aesthetic," and such aesthetics transcends both the materials of art and the formal techniques or devices that shape and compose that material. Thus he writes, "*The form of self-sufficiency, of self-containment,* belonging to everything consummated aesthetically, is the purely architectonic form least of all capable of being transferred to the work as organized material" (1990: 269). Above all, "architectonic" is a phenomenological category, a mode of apprehension in which the whole is greater than the sum of the parts.[5] As a phenomenological category, as we will see, it calls attention to difference, to what Bakhtin calls the "border" or "ultimate limit" and to what contemporaneous economics called the "margin." Architectonics mark the confrontation of significance or purport and historical or social events.

In verbal art, aesthetic architectonics realize themselves the generic forms. "The *novel*," Bakhtin writes, "is a purely compositional form of the organization of verbal masses; through it, the architectonic form of the artistic consummation of a historical or social event is realized. It is a variety of the form of *epic consummation*." Similarly, "*drama* is a compositional form (dialogue, division into acts, etc.), but the *tragic* and *comic* are architectonic forms of consummation" (1990: 269). Later in the essay, speaking about poetry, Bakhtin makes even clearer the global nature of generic forms. "Language," he writes,

> reveals all of its possibilities only in poetry since here maximal demands are placed upon it: all its aspects are strained to the extreme, and reach their ultimate limits ... But in placing such demands on language, poetry nevertheless *overcomes it as language, as a linguistically determinate entity.* Poetry is no exception to the general proposition concerning all the arts: *artistic creation, determined in relation to its material, constitutes an overcoming of that material.* (1990: 294)

Bakhtin's description of poetry in particular and aesthetics ("artistic creation") in general comes very close to Jakobson's description of poetry with which I began. "Poeticalness," Jakobson writes, "is not a supplementation of discourse with rhetorical adornment but a total reevaluation of the discourse and of all its components whatsoever."

This is why poetry, as he says, converts "any verbal element ... into a figure of poetic speech" (1987: 93). (The comprehensions of experience and thought and time itself in relation to the problems of abundance – the problems of organizing experience, constellating ideas, and experiencing and understanding time as alternatively continuous and discontinuous – are each also a "total reevaluation.")

Poetry creates a conversion of any verbal element into poetic speech for Jakobson because it is a mode of apprehension: for this reason Elmar Holenstein can describe its analysis in Jakobson as a mode of "phenomenological structuralism" (1976: 1–5). In Jakobson, as in phenomenology in general (in Jacques Derrida's words), "all experience is the experience of meaning ... Meaning is the phenomenality of phenomenon" (1981: 30). Moreover, the story of the African missionary with which I began implicitly suggests that the "meanings" of poetry are tied up with the encounter and apprehension of difference, strangeness, and otherness.[6] In narrating an encounter with otherness, Jakobson is true to the Russian Formalism of his youth, just as Bakhtin comprehends the insight of Formalism in his insistence, from his earliest work, that dialogism encompasses otherness, that "to contemplate aesthetically means to refer an object to the valuative plane of the *other*" (1993: 75). Unlike Bakhtin, however, Jakobson assumes that the understanding of poetry can be accomplished fully within the science of linguistics, just as he assumes the historical and political content and context of his narrative – what Bakhtin calls its "uniqueness" – can be completely ignored. That is, he assumes that, as in the *cognitive* project of science, time is simply accidental so that a unique event can always be understood as a repeatable event and that the other can always be reduced to the same. Thus, he claims boldly that "meaning" can be simply defined as "the translation of a sign into another system of signs" (1977: 1029), and he develops a thoroughgoing method of *binarism* that allows, on all levels of language and discourse, for an "unbiased, attentive, exhaustive, total description of the selection, distribution and interrelation of the diverse morphological classes and syntactic constructions in a given poem" (1987: 127). Above all, Jakobson is pursuing the Cartesian dream of repeatable, anonymous method.

The various conceptions of translation in Jakobson, Benjamin, and Bakhtin can help describe what Bakhtin means in defining genres as "the forms of the whole" and the ways in which that definition participates in a more general Modernist understanding of wholeness as marginal value. The method of binarism governing Jakobson's conception of translation marks it as the extreme opposite to Benjamin's conception of translation. Benjamin claims that both translation and original text signify some greater language: "a translation," he writes, "instead of resembling the meaning of the original, must lovingly and in detail incorporate the original's mode of signification, thus making both the original and the translation recognizable as fragments of a greater language" (1969: 78). Bakhtin, in his aesthetic analysis of translation, marks the difference between Jakobson's cognitive approach and Benjamin's sense of the larger purposes of signification, the *ethical* task of translation which he describes earlier in this essay, "The Task of the Translator," as articulating "the relationship between life and purposefulness, see-mingly obvious yet almost beyond the grasp of the intellect" (Benjamin 1969: 72). Bakhtin opposes both the easiness and frag-mented ordinariness of Jakobson's sense of translation as a kind of methodical cognitive empiricism and Benjamin's almost mystical ethics of translation in relation to some "greater language," his vision of discourse as a kind of extraordinary fragmentation. Instead, he asserts that "the text (as distinct from the language as a system of means) can never be completely translated, for there is no potential single text of texts" (1986: 106). That is, while Bakhtin, Benjamin and even Jakobson all share a sense of the strangeness of otherness that art captures – the "defamiliarization" of Russian Formalism and the always-pressing *need* for translation – Bakhtin acknowledges in ways that Jakobson does not the plural abundances of art and meaning, and he acknowledges in ways that Benjamin does not the unique *self-contained* wholenesses of art. Both of these acknowledg-ments can be seen in the plurality – the "extreme heterogeneity" (1986: 61) – of genres in Bakhtin.

In his cognitive, scientific project, his sense of the ultimate *simplicity* of understanding, Jakobson takes his place among the three neo-Kantian modes of apprehension Bakhtin describes in "The Problem of Content, Material, and Form in Verbal Art," cognition, ethics, and aesthetics, corresponding to the material, content, and purposive form of the essay's title. (Kant's categories also correspond to the generalizability, accuracy, and simplicity of Enlightenment science.) In fact, near the end of his life, in "The Problem of the Text

in Linguistics, Philology and the Human Sciences," Bakhtin specifically distinguishes between "explanation," which is the mode of
cognition, and "comprehension," which is the mode of aesthetics:
"To see and comprehend the author of a work means to see and
comprehend another, alien consciousness and its world, another
subject ('Du'). With *explanation* there is only one consciousness, one
subject; with *comprehension* there are two consciousnesses and two
subjects" (1986: 111). Benjamin makes a similar distinction in "The
Storyteller," where he distinguishes between the novel, whose aim
(in his reading) is above all to convey "information" and "explanation," and the oral story, whose aim is to convey "wisdom" and
"experience."

With his political and cultural project, Benjamin also takes his
place within Bakhtin's scheme. That is, if Jakobson occupies the
place of cognition, then Benjamin offers an ethics of culture. In the
cognitive information conveyed by the novel, everything is "shot
through with explanation" (1969: 89). The "birthplace of the novel,"
Benjamin argues, "is the solitary individual, who is no longer able to
express himself by giving examples of his most important concerns
[and] is himself uncounseled, and cannot counsel others" (1969: 87).
Storytelling, on the other hand, is above all a social and *ethical*
activity: it is "passed on from mouth to mouth" (84); it is the source
of "tradition" (98); and above all it is dialogical, an encounter with
an other that creates the possibility of recovering value – the
disembodied but non-transcendental *aura* of value – in the world.
"After all," Benjamin writes defining his version of "answerability,"
"counsel is less an answer to a question than a proposal concerning
the continuation of a story which is just unfolding. To seek this
counsel one would first have to be able to tell the story ... Counsel
woven into the fabric of real life is wisdom. The art of storytelling is
reaching its end because the epic side of truth, wisdom, is dying out"
(1969: 86–87). In his emphasis on social and, more importantly,
generational contexts for value Benjamin is recovering the sacred
within the Marxist critique of Enlightenment individualism – the
war of all against all – by remembering the temporality of human life
that encompasses the global values of epic and wisdom existing
beyond self-standing events.

Bakhtin occupies the third position, that of aesthetics. For
Bakhtin, the nature of aesthetic experience, of the "aesthetic event,"
is the creation of a relationship between – above all, a relationship

on the border between – cognition and ethics, knowledge and wisdom, and reality and understanding. "Aesthetic activity," he writes, "does not create a reality that is wholly new. Unlike cognition and performed action, which create nature and social humanity, art celebrates, adorns, and recollects this preveniently encountered reality of cognition and action (nature and social humanity). It enriches and completes them"; the aesthetic event is "the intuitive unification of the cognitive and the ethical" (1990: 278–79; 283; compare this to Latour's analysis of the distinction between nature and society governing Enlightenment modernity, 1993). Central to Bakhtin is the *simple wholeness* of a work of art: self-sufficiency *and* self-containment distinguishes aesthetic experience from the "pure reason" of scientific cognition (such as the "self-containment" of Jakobson's simple definition of translation) and the temporal and, above all, future orientation of ethical judgments (the "self-sufficiency" of Benjamin's transcendental definition of translation). That is, Jakobson deals with repeated scientific reductions, simplicity without wholeness; Benjamin deals with the ethics of culture, non-simple wholes. Bakhtin answers both of these positions with aesthetics. For him, "the content of a work [of art] is, as it were, a segment of the unitary open event of being that has been isolated and freed by form from responsibility to the future event, and that is why it is as a whole self-sufficiently calm, consummated, having absorbed isolated nature as well into its calm and self-containment" (1990: 307). By "nature," Bakhtin means the objects of cognition. In this description he is presenting a version of his thesis that aesthetic experience brings together the unending reasoning of cognition and the constantly repeated judgments of ethics in an isolated – a "finalized" – whole. In verbal art, such "wholes" are defined by genre.

Such wholeness is also defined by the necessary separation between the subject of contemplation and its object. In his early fragment, "Author and Hero in Aesthetic Activity," Bakhtin describes this in terms that later will develop into his "dialogics." "If there is only one unitary and unique participant," he writes,

there can be no *aesthetic* event. An absolute consciousness, a consciousness that has nothing transgredient to itself, nothing situated outside itself and capable of delimiting it from outside – such a consciousness cannot be "aestheticized"; one can commune in it, but it cannot be seen as a *whole* that is capable of being consummated. An aesthetic event can take place only when there are two participants present; it presupposes two noncoinciding consciousnesses. When the hero and the author coincide or when they find themselves standing either next to one another in the face of a value they share or against one another as antagonists, the aesthetic event ends and an *ethical* event begins (polemical tract, manifesto, speech of accusation or of praise and gratitude, invective, confession as a self-accounting, etc.). When there is no hero at all, not even in a potential form, then we have to do with an event that is *cognitive* (treatise, article, lecture). And, finally, when the other consciousness is the encompassing consciousness of God, a *religious* event takes place (prayer, worship, ritual). (1990: 22)

In this long description Bakhtin reverts, in his parentheses, to what he later came to call the "speech genres" of social language. Speech genres are above all matters of habit and of ongoing life: they are, as Bakhtin says, "typical forms of utterances" that are more or less independent of conscious intention (1986: 63). Habit, as Benjamin mentions (1969: 240), is the opposite of aesthetic contemplation, and the relationship between speech genres and aesthetic genres is an important one for Bakhtin, especially in the context of his repeated assertion that "the reality of the genre and the reality accessible to the genre are organically interrelated." "Genre," Bakhtin/Medvedev go on, "is the aggregate of the means of collective orientation in reality, with the orientation toward finalization. This orientation is capable of mastering new aspects of reality" (1985: 135). Speech genres are tools for living, and the relation between speech genres and aesthetic genres is subtle but important: the former are oriented toward negotiating repeated relationships between cognition and ethics while the latter create repeated aesthetic moments, the phenomenality of simple wholeness.

In both cases genre locates, aesthetically, the intersection of signification and reality, and it functions insofar as signification itself – the active signification of utterances and themes (as opposed to lexical meanings) – can only take the form of bounded wholes. It is to create such an intersection that Benjamin, in what Bakhtin might call his ethics of art and culture, defines the "aura" of a work of art precisely in terms of the "distancing" of the object of contemplation from its observer. "The aura," he says, is "the unique phenomenon of a distance, however close it may be" (1969: 222). For Benjamin the aesthetic event is most importantly conceived as a unique social event: "an ancient statue of Venus, for example," he writes, "stood in a different traditional context with the Greeks, who made it an object of veneration, than with the clerics of the Middle Ages, who viewed it as an ominous idol. Both of them, however, were equally confronted with its uniqueness, that is its aura" (1969: 223). Still, for Benjamin, as this last sentence suggests, the work of art's "uniqueness" is transcendental, an irruption in time, sublime rather than aesthetic.

For Bakhtin, on the other hand, aesthetic events, embodied in verbal art as genre, are temporally unique, a plurality of repeated wholenesses since, as we have seen, "the text ... can never be completely translated, for there is no potential single text of texts" (1986: 106). To the uniqueness of utterances – including the utterances of speech genres and literary genres – Bakhtin opposes the cognitive generality of language studied by linguists (such as Jakobson) cognitively, within the systematics of meaning. Thus in *Toward a Philosophy of the Act* Bakhtin argues that "it is an unfortunate misunderstanding (a legacy of rationalism) to think that truth [*pravda*] can only be the truth [*istina*] that is composed of universal moments; that the truth of a situation is precisely that which is repeatable and constant in it." In fact, Bakhtin goes on, rather than "unity" the word "uniqueness" should be used, describing "the uniqueness of a whole that does not repeat itself anywhere" (1993: 37–38). That is, for Bakhtin utterances exist as *events* of cognition, aesthetics, or ethics. If Jakobson studies such events cognitively, then Benjamin studies them ethically, in relation to transcendental value, the text of texts of which phenomenal events are mere "fragments." In both cases, Jakobson and Benjamin are attempting to discover some comprehension of wholeness in a world that seemed to offer little more than what Benjamin calls a sense of falling into "bottomlessness" (1969: 84). For Bakhtin, that wholeness was best apprehended aesthetically, as the "forms of the whole" he called genres.

## TEMPORALIZED AESTHETICS: MARGINAL VALUE, FLEETING IMAGES, MOMENTARY WHOLES

The multiple attempts to understand and situate discursive arts in the early twentieth century that I have been tracing – Jakobson's pursuit of scientific structuralism in a *cognitive* study of poetry; Benjamin's pursuit of a messianic-Marxian analysis of art and culture in political and ethical studies of culture, narrative, and film; and Bakhtin's pursuit of a neo-Kantian cultural analysis in an *aesthetic* study of verbal art – all arrive at versions of what I have called the "global" aspects of art in attempts to find non-idealistic understandings of cultural artifacts. These projects are various responses to the enormous changes in intellectual, social, and material life occasioned by the second Industrial Revolution, the constellation of seeming unrelated events in the period between 1880 and 1930 that gave rise to what Stephen Kern describes as major changes in the very "foundations of experience" in Western culture (1982: 5). As I argued in chapter 3, these events transformed daily life for most people in the very "feel" of experience. Such changes can be seen in the effects of the telephone or incandescent lighting, in the advent of a consumer society and mass advertising, or even in the subtler effects of the non-convertibility of currency to gold and of the progressive abstraction of the visual and plastic arts. In broader terms, they included the democratization of Europe, huge increases in urban populations, the rearrangement of class structures, enormous changes in literacy, education, and in the relations between men and women; they include the confrontations of cultures following from the vast expansions of European imperialism, the transformation to large-scale economic production, and intellectual revolutions in philosophy, technology, science, and the arts. As I have argued, the experiences of these transformations – often "unconscious" in the sense of being too large to comprehend rather than of being the result of agencies of repression – demanded new ways of making sense out of experience, whose confusions weren't the result of need and dearth, as they were for great Enlightenment figures such as Isaac Newton, Adam Smith, and George Eliot, but whose confusions stemmed from difficulties that arise from abundance and plenty.

The mode of economic analysis developed by the neoclassical or marginalist economists of the last decades of the nineteenth century I described in part I offers one way of comprehending this experience of modernity which sheds light on the understandings of science, ethics, and literature in Jakobson, Benjamin, and Bakhtin. As both Lawrence Birken and Jean-Joseph Goux have argued, the work of these economists focused on the transformation of need to desire in the remarkably changing world of the second Industrial Revolution in a vocabulary of marginal utility which analyzed consumption rather than production. Modernist representation – including the science, ethics, and aesthetics of Jakobson, Benjamin, and Bakhtin – is, I think, usefully comprehended under the category of marginalism because marginal analysis, in Bakhtin's vocabulary, always "doubles" the objects of analysis. In this way, marginal analysis participates in the "crisis of abundance" of the turn of the twentieth century Kern describes (1983: 9). Moreover, the crisis of abundance conditioned other Modernist modes of "doubling" – that is, of understanding phenomena in their plurality rather than singularity – implicit in Jakobson's focus on semantic borders, Benjamin's retrospective interpretation that articulates possibilities of historical "redemption" (which is remarkable in its similarity to retrospective interpretation that Heisenberg articulated), and Bakhtin's notion of dialogism itself. Instead of representation functioning within a hierarchical structure of principle and example where an atemporal essence or invariant is isolated from the seeming accidental or marginal variants of experience – where plural examples are reduced to a simple, necessary and sufficient principle – signification came to be understood as a constellation (in Benjamin's term) or a complex (in Pound's term) of essentially non-simple phenomena.

This can be seen in the static economic analyses of the marginal economists I have already discussed. In economics, marginal analysis *begins* with a world of abundance: it assumes that "a fixed quantity of anything" can be divided "among a number of competing uses" (Blaug 1985: 297). That is, it makes possibility rather than necessity its object of analysis. If classical economics in Adam Smith and Karl Marx attempts to analyze the positive value of a commodity, then marginalist economics attempts to analyze the relational value of that commodity. To do this, as we have seen, it measures the value of the last in a series of commodities. My example in chapter 1 was a last pair of shoes, but the example Marx offers in *Capital* of a single (i.e., "first") commodity is a table. (Both examples take their place among the food, clothing, and housing of the labor theory of value. Food is a weaker example of a commodity, however, because it is less durable. Still, as the example of Conrad's description of hunger suggests, it also lends itself to definitions of parsimonious "need" outside any particular examples.) When we focus on the "first" table, the basic one, without which we would eat on the floor, that commodity possesses, as Marx says in *Capital*, a two-fold nature: it is both empirical and ideal at the same time. A table, for instance, is, as he says, a "common, every-day thing, wood. But so soon as it steps forth as a commodity, it is changed into something transcendent. It not only stands with its feet on the ground, but, in relation to all other commodities, it stands on its head, and evolves out of its wooden brain grotesque ideas, far more wonderful than 'table-turning' ever was" (1967: 71). Thus, in its two-fold nature, Marx's commodity embodies the two-fold atemporal simplicity of the Enlightenment, simple facticity and simple ideality. Along with its everyday usefulness, it possesses the "mystical" grotesqueries of transcendence; as such, it situates us in the position of the individual in the Enlightenment world, *within* positive material reality and atemporal understanding, a kind of "transcendental embodiment" – the positivist materialism and otherworldly idealism that faced Jakobson, Benjamin, and Bakhtin. This paradoxical situation is created by the parsimonious equation of a temporal first and an atemporal basic.

But when we focus on the value of the last table that we have – the marginal table in a situation of (relative) abundance, in which a household already has a half-dozen tables for dining, working, even for playing games – the position of the analyst is no longer *within* the positivities of fact and idea, but on a border, a margin. Yet even the distinction between "margin" and "inner territory" is not atemporally absolute – it is neither necessary nor sufficient for understanding – precisely because in the world of (relative) abundance of the second Industrial Revolution, poverty exists alongside bounty, just as the causal explanations of mechanistic science exist alongside the probabilities of post-Newtonian science, and – in writers like Joyce and Lawrence – the synchronic symbolisms of Modernism coexist with the diachronic metonymies of realism. In fact, such coexistences condition Bakhtin's analyses of Dostoevsky not only in the Dostoevsky book, but in *Marxism and the Philosophy of Language* as well.

In the conception and analysis of value as marginal what is lost above all is the transcendental simplicity of *atemporal* wholeness. Temporality invades everything in a world where what *happens next* is a constitutive aspect of value. Writers such as Jakobson, Benjamin, and Bakhtin – in their very different ways (like Lawrence, Russell, and Heisenberg in *their* different ways) – are both responding to and organizing a world that no longer lends itself absolutely to the received modes of parsimonious value, the atemporal simplicities of facticity and ideality. If a key operation in this tradition is the opposition between materialism and idealism – the reduction of experience and explanation to one or the other of these assumptions about the world and the choice between what I called at the beginning of this chapter the desert-reality of cynicism and know-nothing mysticism and what I called in chapter 1 the "general semiotics" and "subjective idealism" of Enlightenment ideology – then Jakobson, Benjamin, and Bakhtin are all struggling to find modes of explanation that can comprehend wholeness outside these stark alternatives, the "non-simple" wholeness of intellectual, ethical, and aesthetic value.

Thus Bakhtin writes: "There is absolutely no reason to be afraid of the fact that the aesthetic object cannot be found either in the psyche or in the material work of art. It does not become in consequence some sort of mystical or metaphysical essence. The multiform world of action (the being of the ethical) finds itself in the same situation. Where is the state located? In the psyche? In the physicomathematical space? On the pages of constitutional records? And where is the law located?" (1990: 301). Jakobson makes a similar argument for the "poeticalness" of a discourse: in asking "where is a face located?" he is attempting to develop repeatable scientific methods of defining poetry that is neither mystical nor cynical. And Benjamin similarly attempts to describe the global nature of the aura of a work of art, and the global nature of the ethics of social life in his conceptions of tradition and wisdom more generally. All three – like Woolf, Heisenberg, and Lawrence – are attempting to develop comprehensions and understandings beyond the reductions of the necessities and simplicities of positivism.

That is, all three are attempting to realize intuitions of significance in a world of non-simple phenomena by asserting the possibility of apprehending value – including, in Benjamin's case, *negative* value – as a *momentary whole*. Moreover, they each develop a method or semiotics for their apprehensions of value. This method focuses on the "border," to use again Bakhtin's vocabulary – what the neo-classical economists called the margin – that marks abundance, plurality, and strangeness. Speaking of language, Bakhtin notes (in a discussion that nicely comports with the epigraph from Joyce in chapter 4) that "any speaker ... is not, after all, the first speaker, the one who disturbs the eternal silence of the universe"; "the topic of the speaker's speech, regardless of what this topic may be, does not become the object of speech for the first time in any given utterance; a given speaker is not the first to speak about it" (1986: 69, 93). Discourse for Bakhtin, like numbers for Russell, exists in contexts of abundances of discourse – temporally conditioned discourses –

before and after. Speaking of art in a text I had already cited, he says: "aesthetic activity does not create a reality that is wholly new" (1990: 278–79). In the scientific tradition of structural linguistics – the tradition of Jakobson and Saussure – Emile Benveniste has similarly asserted that "we can never get back to man separate from language and we shall never see him inventing it. We shall never get back to man reduced to himself and exercising his wits to conceive of the existence of another" (1971: 224). Finally, in the tradition of ethics and cultural studies, Benjamin similarly asserts that "the uniqueness of a work of art is inseparable from its being imbedded in the fabric of tradition" (1969: 223).

In all these instances, the beginning point of analysis – the semiotics of genre, meaning, and value – is abundance and fullness rather than a blank slate of dearth. Moreover, for all three writers, in aesthetics, science, and ethics, it is the focus on the *borders* of phenomena that allows the possibility of analysis that is neither positivistic materialism nor the dream of pure intellectual analysis. Jakobson does this with his insistence on binary oppositions as the *structure* of cognitive apprehensions. His beginning point is the material base of binary structures, the physiology of the mouth and of speech organ that conditions the distinctive features of language and allows his great student, Lévi-Strauss, to assert that structure is "content itself, and the logical organization in which it is arrested is conceived as a property of the real" (1984: 167). Yet more than Jakobson – probably because Jakobson's scientific project seeks "the universal equality of things" – Benjamin and Bakhtin emphasize the otherness inhabiting borders. Benjamin does this with his insistence on the constellations of meaning in which the idea "belongs to a fundamentally different world from that which it apprehends" and what he calls in *The Origin of German Tragic Drama*, as we have seen, "the jagged line of demarcation between physical nature and significance" (1977: 34, 166).

The function of borders in Bakhtin is even more striking and constitutes the aesthetics of genre: it is precisely the limits of utterances, what Bakhtin calls their "clear-cut boundaries," that are "essential and fundamental" to utterances altogether (1986: 71). It is the boundaries or margins of utterances – their difference from other utterances they respond to and provoke – that is the *mark* of their uniqueness and their "aura." The boundaries of utterances create that "finalized wholeness" which guarantees "the possibility of a response (or of responsive understanding)" (1986: 76). "Any word," he writes, "exists for us in three aspects: as a neutral word of a language, belonging to nobody; as an *other's* word, which belongs to another person and is filled with echoes of the other's utterance; and, finally as *my* word ... In both of the latter aspects, the word is expressive, but, we repeat, this expression does not inhere in the word itself. It originates at the point of contact between the word and actual reality" (1986: 88). In "Toward a Reworking of the Dostoevsky Book," Bakhtin even describes self-consciousness as "not that which takes place within, but that which takes place on the boundary between one's own and someone else's consciousness, on the threshold. And everything internal gravitates not toward itself but is turned to the outside and dialogized, every internal experience ends up on the boundary, encounters another, and in this tension-filled encounter lies its entire essence" (1984: 287). The mark of border, like the "markedness" of structural linguistics or the jagged edges of Benjamin's Modernist definition of allegory, allows the possibility that "science can deal with such absolutely unrepeatable individualities as utterances" (1986: 108).

More than utterances, borders and margins define the nature of genre and aesthetics as well. "The artist's enormous labor over the word has the ultimate goal of overcoming the word," Bakhtin writes, "because the aesthetic object arises on the boundaries of words, on the boundaries of language as such" (1990: 297). This "overcoming" in verbal art, as we have seen in the case of poetry, is a function of literary genres. Moreover, it is the borders of phenomena that is the work of aesthetics in general. "Aesthetic creation," Bakhtin writes, "overcomes the infinite and yet-to-be-achieved character of cognition and ethical action by referring all constituents of being and of yet-to-be-achieved meaning to a human being in his concrete givenness – as the event of his life, as his fate. A given human being constitutes the center of value in the architectonics of an aesthetic object; it is around him that the uniqueness of every object, its integral concrete diversity, is actualized" (1990: 230). Finally, such boundedness defines culture altogether. "The domain of culture," he writes, "should not be thought of as some kind of spatial whole, possessing not only boundaries but an inner territory. A cultural domain has no inner territory. It is located entirely upon boundaries, boundaries intersect it everywhere, passing through each of its constituent features" (1990: 274). Here, then, Bakhtin is describing a global sense of meaning and value – an interested, global aesthetics – by focusing on the border and the margin. Time is a constituent feature of this sense insofar as temporality cannot be bracketed from experiences and knowledges that seem to propel toward the future in the purposiveness of ethical judgment and recover the past in constellations of comprehension – the infinite and yet-to-be achieved character of cognition and ethics Bakhtin describes. The very temporal restlessness of Enlightenment modernity seems to have exploded in the time of Bakhtin, Benjamin, and Jakobson – the time of the second Industrial Revolution – so that it no longer could be ignored as simply an unnecessary accident in a world of secular, atemporal truths.

In fact, with Bakhtin's description of the boundary nature of culture we have returned to the Jakobson's global sense of "face" and, as I am arguing, to twentieth-century Modernism more generally. Like Jakobson's analogy with face, the figure Benjamin uses for the uniqueness of a work of art, especially in his discussion of photography, is the human face. If the mechanical reproduction of art works destroys the aura of an object – "To pry an object from its shell, to destroy its aura," he writes, "is the mark of a perception whose 'sense of the universal equality of things' has increased to such a degree that it extracts it even from a unique object by means of reproduction" (1969: 223) – then the photograph of a face resists this perception. The "universal equality of things" Benjamin is describing is the unintelligible flux and terror of the borderless abundance and otherness of Modernity he figures, somewhat ambivalently, in his conception of the "mechanical reproduction" not only of art, but of ethical judgment as well. The photographed face resists this in its uniqueness and its circumscription; like less "mechanical" art works, the photograph of a face embodies the unique moment of its creation and its perception.

What "aesthetics" does for Bakhtin, what the "aura" does for Benjamin, what "poeticalness" does for Jakobson, is allow for a unique whole embedded in the world in which it finds itself – the world of the enormous changes of the second Industrial Revolution where no "wholes" are apparent. This is the "bottomlessness" of experience that Benjamin described in 1936 – the contradictions of "strategic experience by tactical warfare, economic experience by inflation, bodily experience by mechanical warfare, moral experience by those in power" (1969: 84) – in which the events of knowledge, judgment, and art are overwhelmingly at odds with one another, unintelligible, incomprehensible, and irreducible to basic simplicity. In photographed faces of people we love Benjamin describes a similar sense of the apocalyptic in the "aura" of photographs: "for the last time," he says, "the aura emanates from the early photographs in the fleeting expression of a human face" (1969: 226). The global sense of such faces – a significance neither reducible to particular elements or their interplay nor expandable to a "fleeting expression" that is, as Benjamin says, "almost beyond the grasp of the intellect" (1969: 72) – offers the "uniqueness" of a particular moment. It signifies the abundance and the otherness that characterizes the experience many felt in the early twentieth century – marginal abundance and marginal otherness, like the description of "family resemblances" Wittgenstein offers – woven into the fabric of phenomenal experience.

Unlike Benjamin – or even Jakobson, whose story of the missionary contains, almost unconsciously, the hint of apocalyptic imperialism – Bakhtin describes the faces of art under the more general term of "image," and it is precisely as an image that the artistic category of genre functions in verbal art. (Benjamin also uses the term image to describe "dialectics at a standstill," yet Benjamin's use of the term is political and ethical: above all, it attempts to gather together – or constellate – *historical* significance rather than *aesthetic* significance. And Jakobson characteristically examines imagery rather than the image.) For Bakhtin, speech genres, the primary modes of utterance, are the typical forms of the meaningful wholes in the life of social discourse, describing nature and embodying the future-oriented judgments of ethics. They embody ordinary human life and return us from the extraordinary sublimity that Benjamin is describing, his apocalyptic notions of "Messianic time" and "dialectics at a standstill" (1969: 263). When the activities of description and judgment of speech genres become the objects of aesthetic activity – when the aesthetic event brings together nature and value – they take the form, in verbal art, of the complex secondary genres of literary art. In these forms, the abundance and strangeness of the image join together the knowledge, judgment, and comprehension of an aesthetics that gathers together cognition, ethics, and art; they join together the recognition, love, and beauty we find in one another's faces. Benjamin describes such abundance and strangeness in terms of the authority and aura, the power and the distance of the work of art; Jakobson embodies them in the abundant structures and the curious phenomenologies – what Holenstein calls the "phenomenological structuralism" – of his analyses.

Unlike Benjamin (or even Jakobson), Bakhtin eschews the sublime in aesthetics, the great power of European Modernism, for the sake of what he calls art's "kindness": in the "acceptance of the ethical and the cognitive into its proper object," he writes, "resides the distinctive *kindness* of the aesthetic, its *mercifulness*" (1990: 279). "Almost all of the kind, accepting and enriching, optimistic categories of human thinking about the world and man," he says, "are aesthetic in character" (1990: 279). "Isolation," he says, is "the first gift bestowed by form upon content, making possible for the first time all the subsequent, purely positive, enriching gifts bestowed by form" (1990: 315). Such isolation is what he came to call later the "finalization" of genre: "the image," he wrote in 1972, "is in the work as a whole" (1986: 110); in verbal art it is the accomplishment of genre.

Above all, I believe, Bakhtin seeks to recover both understanding and ethics within aesthetics – the knowledge and power of Yeats's high Modernism, but also the ordinary experience of sympathy and affection in Thomas Hardy's love poetry, to suggest literary parallels for Jakobson and Benjamin. Above all, he seeks to recover the ethical for art, which is missing or "unconscious" in Jakobson, without Benjamin's apocalyptic judgments. To this end he replaces Jakobson's "universal" face and Benjamin's "fleeting" face with the image, as he calls it in "The Problem of Content, Material, and Form in Verbal Art," and what he later calls the genres of verbal art, the momentary realization of an event of value. "The components [of the aesthetic object]," he writes, "are joined together to form the unity of an axiologically valid event of life, aesthetically shaped and consummated ... The ethical-aesthetic event is completely determinate and artistically unambiguous: we could call its components – images, understanding by this term not visual representations, but fully shaped moments of content" (1990: 299–300). The "moment" of content is the ethical and historical *situation* of aesthetics; the "content" is its cognitive universalization. Bakhtin's aesthetics of genre *answers* and *shapes* such moments of content.

In other words, Bakhtin's project creates what I am calling "temporalized aesthetics," a post-Enlightenment aesthetics that doesn't reduce art to transcendental experience or atemporal ideas.

Jakobson pursued the disinterestedness of science in order to comprehend the possibility of art for the modern world, and Benjamin pursued the interests of history and ethics in his political and messianic apocalyptics.[7] In these pursuits, Jakobson attempted to describe the structures of phenomenology, a science of the experience of global meaning, and Benjamin attempted to constellate a global ethics of tradition in which activities and events can be seen to exist within the context of their future history. Like this work in cognition and ethics, Bakhtin attempted to comprehend an aesthetics of borders, inhabited by the ordinary virtues of kindness and mercy, which would allow room for both abundance and otherness in momentary, comprehending wholes. Such wholes above all are *aesthetic*; they are an aesthetics of genre that comprehends knowledge, judgment, and the apprehension of unified, unique wholes. Throughout his career, Bakhtin attempts to make a global aesthetics of verbal art possible within a post-Enlightenment culture of abundance.

ENVOI

Bakhtin, Jakobson, and Benjamin – like the others I have examined throughout *Modernism and Time*, Stravinsky, Joyce, Woolf, Lawrence, late nineteenth-century economists, Einstein and Russell, Heisenberg, and the whole contemporary enterprise of articulating the meaning and ethos of postmodernism – are attempting to find vocabularies of understanding in a world of post-Enlightenment abundance. The most troubling aspect of the abundances of goods, understanding, and experience that arose in the apotheosis of Enlightenment values I have described as the second Industrial Revolution – "the climax of the Enlightenment" as Carleton Hayes described it many years ago (1941: 328) – was the ways in which abundance disrupted settled notions and experience of time. The simplicity and consistency of time conditioned the necessary and sufficient truths of understanding and ethics in a world of limited choices of action, consumption, and reason. This is the lesson of literary realism, economic individualism, and scientific positivism.

The lessons of post-Enlightenment values, as I have tried to show, are more difficult and complicated. They replace (but not altogether) the principle of contradiction with temporal alternations, the economics of sufficient reason with overdeterminations, and the aesthetics of given moments with repeated, momentary global comprehensions of time. In other words, twentieth-century Modernism at its best – in science, quotidian experience, and aesthetics – can be understood as struggling with the ambiguous success of secular Enlightenment values in order that it might articulate logics of abundance which comprehend the highest values of Enlightenment ideology without ignoring their costs. These logics all include time as a constituent feature, which means neither science, nor history, nor aesthetics can avoid what Bakhtin calls the "infinite" character of cognition, the "yet-to-be-achieved" character of ethical action (1990:230), and, as he suggests, the multiplication of the seemingly singular moments of aesthetics. Russell, I have argued, articulates the logic of infinities just as Benjamin articulates the logic of redemption implicit in the yet-to-be-achieved character of ethical action and Lawrence multiplies seemingly overwhelming singular moments across time and across subjects.

But even these strict equations are subject to revision – and, perhaps, redemption – in the ways in which Woolf (but also Stravinsky, Wiener and Marshall) traffic in infinities, Joyce (but also Einstein and Heisenberg) traffic in events that are never quite complete, and Bakhtin (but also Lawrence, Joyce, Heisenberg, Einstein and a host of figures – Picasso, Planck, or even Cole Porter – whom I did not include in this book) traffic in given moments which are not and no longer can be conceived as the only moment or the representative moment, once and for all. The figures left out – like commodities such as advertising and radios that could supplement the electricity of chapter 3, or post-Enlightenment information science that could supplement post-Newtonian physics in chapter 4 and 5, or figures such as Thomas Jefferson and John Stuart Mill who could supplement George Eliot in chapter 1 and 2 – are analogous to the temporalities that were left out by the ideology of Enlightenment secularism, reason, and universalism. The alternative to this ideology encompasses a notion of time that is neither infinite nor atemporal and therefore beyond the opposition of secular and sacred; of temporal events that are susceptible to recurrence and redemptive transformation and therefore always comprehensible as incomplete; and of moments of experience that are alternatively singular and multiple and therefore manifest themselves as instances of non-transcendental disembodiment. That is, by the early twentieth century, scientific, cultural, and artistic timeliness could no longer be left out, once and for all, in the pure isolations of reason, ethics, and aesthetics. Instead, they called for a logic of abundance – or multiple logics of abundance – that comprehended the experience of time without rendering understanding, wealth, and experience simply what Paul Ricoeur describes as "radically dissimilar particulars" (1984: 124). This is the task, I believe, of post-Enlightenment science, ethics, and aesthetics: to discover and articulate truth, value, and meaning in a world that offers, along with dearth, abundances of choice. It is a task that is both momentary and global. It is never realized, once and for all, but always yet-to-be-achieved; it is one to which others can always and repeatedly be added, on to "infinity"; and, finally, it is a task whose achievements – whose given moments of truth, wealth, and pleasure – must be given back and passed on, time and again.

# Notes

1  As I argue in chapter 3, this period has come to be described as the "second Industrial Revolution," the transformation of the relatively small-scale industrialism of entrepreneurial or "industrial" capitalism to large-scale "finance" capitalism, what Carleton Hayes describes as "the climax of the Enlightenment" (1941: 328). For a historical survey of the vast wealth created by the second Industrial Revolution, see Frank Tipton and Robert Albrich (1987), especially chapters 1–3 (1987). In *The Culture of Time and Space,* Stephen Kern offers a wide-ranging phcnom-enology of intellectual and quotidian life in this period. For a discussion of the relationship between the second Industrial Revolution and the sociology of postmodernism, see David Harvey (1990), especially part II. Harvey argues the continuity of early and late twentieth-century capitalism in terms of economic growth in the context of a larger argument that the distinction between "modernism" and "postmo-dernism" should be abandoned (or at least modified) in relation to a Marxist reading of the economic "base" of these phenomena. In a very different register, Norbert Wiener traces the social transformations occasioned by the replacement of steam energy with electricity at the end of the nineteenth century (1967: 185–222), technologies he associ-ates with the first and second Industrial Revolutions respectively. The critique of "the logic of general equivalents" in the work of Jean-Joseph Goux (1990: 6; see also 1994) can easily be assimilated to the argument I am pursuing that the remarkable abundance of material, intellectual, and human resources associated with the second Industrial Revolution occasioned transformations in the modes of explanation inherited from the Enlightenment. See also the specialized studies of Banta, Birkin, and Lears. I examine some historical, economic, and aesthetic implications of the second Industrial Revolution at greater length in chapter 3.

2  Ermarth argues that "when quattrocento painters began to use the single vanishing point to organize their pictures, they made their chief formal principle the point of view of a single, fixed spectator: a graphic

illustration long before Descartes of that primacy of individual experience over received truths that characterizes realism and that has its philosophical analogues in Cartesian epistemology" (1983: 5).

3 Bruno Latour develops a strong sense of the double-mindedness of the Enlightenment towards secularization in his book, *We Have Never Been Modern*. Among other things, he argues that Enlightenment comprehensions have never been as "pure" and self-consistent as many – including the exposition here – have suggested. For a detailed examination of the complicated relationship between religiosity and secularism in the emerging sciences at the turn of the eighteenth century, see Markley (1993). For an examination of the relationship between the universalism of Enlightenment thought and the particular historical moment out of which it emerged, see Stephen Toulmin, *Cosmopolis*.

4 In *Consuming Desire* Lawrence Birken offers an important discussion of psychoanalysis particularly and sexology more generally in the context of late nineteenth-century intellectual and economic life. Birkin's assumption, like my own, is that experience, value, and understanding form what Benjamin describes as a "constellation" of phenomena and forces which condition one another outside of conceptions of "base" and "superstructure" or – in a more intellectual framework – "principle" and "example." In chapter 5 I discuss these last categories in terms of Modernist science, but throughout *Modernism and Time* – indeed, throughout the second Industrial Revolution – the "simple" relationship between atemporal principle and temporal example is complicated. Brown's discussion of Swift, I think, remains "anachronistic" insofar as he, like Freud, brings concepts based upon the assumptions of Enlightenment modernity to pre-Enlightenment phenomena. But, as I argue later in this chapter and in chapter 3 – and as I demonstrate, without argument, in the reading of George Eliot and Walter Benjamin in chapter 2 – the very procedures of anachronism and "retrospection" help distinguish post-Enlightenment modes of understanding, evaluation, and experience from received modalities of Enlightenment apprehension.

5 See Davis and Schleifer (1991: ch. 1; esp. pp. 3–6) for a discussion of "right reason" in relation to reason as critique as it developed in the Enlightenment. As opposed to this tradition, in *Reason and Culture* Ernest Gellner traces the history of "reason" as a concept arising with Descartes and Leibniz (among others) in the late seventeenth-century. He argues forcefully the intimate connection between Enlightenment reason and individualism (see esp. Gellner 1992: ch. 1). Similarly, Heidegger elaborately argues for the connection between modern subjectivity and the will to power in volume 4 of *Nietzsche*; see especially chapter 15, "The Subject in the Modern Age." In *What is a Thing?*, he argues that "what was natural to a man of the eighteenth century, the rationality of reason as such in general, set free from any other

limitation, would have seemed very unnatural to the medieval man"
(1967: 39). Jacques Derrida (1994) presents a capsule "history" of reason
arising in the Enlightenment and a critique of that history in relation to
the institutionalization of reason in the university. The subject of
reason, like the more general atemporal subject of knowledge, was
almost universally gendered male as the "unmarked" general category
of "humanity." For a short discussion of linguistic markedness and its
political implications, see Schleifer (1987: 51–55).

6 Descartes' conception of "clear and distinct ideas" is analogous to
Leibniz's necessary and sufficient truth. Descartes' formulation, moreover, corresponds to the parsimonious simplicity (= clear), accuracy (=
distinct), and generalizability (= ideas) that govern Enlightenment
science. These criteria for scientific "truth" – simplicity, accuracy, and
generalizability – are examined in detail in Schleifer et al. (1992:
Introduction). Similarly, Thomas Kuhn describes five "characteristics of
good scientific theory": namely, simplicity and self-consistency; accuracy; and broad scope and fruitfulness (1977: 321–22), which, as I
arrange them here, comport with the three criteria mentioned above I
repeatedly discuss throughout this book.

Descartes' overriding assumption, as Stephen Gaukroger argues, is
that "the corporeal world can be characterized exhaustively in geometrical terms, and that such a characterization provides one with a clear
and distinct grasp of its constituents and their behaviour." The key to
this undertaking, Gaukroger continues, "is the doctrine of clear and
distinct ideas, and the general aim is to use the criterion to generate
indubitable veridical notions of God and the mind, and then to show
that the same criterion, when applied to the corporeal world, yields a
mechanist model of the corporeal world" (1995: 338). At the heart of
this description is the parsimony of applying "the same criterion" – that
of clear and distinct ideas – to spirit and matter. In the *Meditations* while
Descartes concedes that "corporeal things exist," he adds that "they
may not all exist in a way that exactly corresponds with my sensory
grasp of them, for in many cases the grasp of the senses is very obscure
and confused. But at least they possess all the properties which I clearly
and distinctly understand, that is, all those which, viewed in general
terms, are comprised within the subject-matter of pure mathematics"
(1984:55). Descartes' reconception of mathematics at a level of abstraction that allows him to equate algebra and geometry forms the basis of
mathematical physics. Ernst Cassirer describes this project towards the
end of *The Philosophy of the Enlightenment*:

Descartes' outline of physics, as he sketches it in his treatise *The World*, illustrates
the motto: "Give me matter, and I will build you a world." The physicist and
natural philosopher can risk such a construction, for the plan of the universe lies
clearly before him in the general laws of motion. He does not have to take these
laws from experience; they are of a mathematical nature and, accordingly, are

contained in the fundamental rules of "universal knowledge" (*mathesis universalis*) whose necessary truth the mind recognizes within itself. (1951: 335)

Stephen Toulmin also describes Descartes' clear and distinct ideas in terms of the combination of semiotics and idealism described later in this chapter. "The method of basing theories on 'clear and distinct' concepts thus appealed to Descartes for two distinct kinds of reasons," he writes; " – *instrumental*, as solving problems in the empirical sciences, and *intrinsic*, as a source of 'certainty' in a world where skepticism was unchecked" (1992: 73). "Given the *Meditations* alone," Toulmin concludes, "we may read Descartes as a pure 'foundationalist'; but, in the *Principles* [*of Philosophy*], he is clearly working more as a code breaker, or 'cryptanalyst' ... [in an attempt] to decipher natural phenomena in terms that apply generally to phenomena he has not yet had the chance to consider" (1992: 73–74).

7  As these terms suggest and as I have already suggested, the subject of knowledge in the Enlightenment was consistently male. Lawrence Birken argues persuasively that the transformation of the pre-Enlightenment "caste" system into an Enlightenment "class" system failed to apply to gender distinctions. "As numerous scholars have recognized," he writes, "bourgeois individualism rigorously excluded the family from its domain ... For between men and women, an eternal *difference* appeared to block the inclusion of the latter in the political economic world of the former. A male/female caste system founded on the perceived natural difference between the sexes thus replaced the older three-function caste system of the aristocratic epoch" (1988: 6).

In *Cosmopolis*, Toulmin complicates the Cartesian quest for certainty by historicizing it. "The 17th-century philosophers' 'Quest for Certainty,'" he writes,

was no mere proposal to construct abstract and timeless intellectual schemas, dreamed up as objects of pure, detached intellectual study. Instead, it was a timely response to a specific historical challenge – the political, social, and theological chaos embodied in the Thirty Years' War. Read in this way, the projects of Descartes and his successors are no longer arbitrary creations of lonely individuals in separate ivory towers, as the orthodox texts in the history of philosophy suggest. The standard picture of Descartes' philosophical development ... gives way to what is surely a more lifelike and flattering alternative: that of a young intellectual whose reflections opened up for people in his generation a real hope of *reasoning* their way out of political and theological chaos, at a time when no one else saw anything to do but continue fighting an interminable war. (1992: 70–71)

8  Latour's rereading of the Enlightenment in *We Have Never Been Modern*, like that of Toulmin, can be seen, in this context, as a retrospective comprehension of Enlightenment ideals that underlines the "worldliness" and "timeliness" of their work. Cornel West makes an argument similar to Said's when he argues that "the approach appropriate for the new cultural politics of difference" "is partisan, partial, engaged, and

crisis-centered, yet always keeps open a sceptical eye to avoid dogmatic traps, premature closures, formulaic formulations, or rigid conclusions" (1993: 213). Both Said and West engage in temporalized responsibilities, calling for repeated and temporal choices and judgments that I hope this chapter and *Modernism and Time* more generally describe and participate in. Latour does not identify the post-Enlightenment ethos I am describing in this book as fully with "postmodernism" as I do in this chapter. Rather, he defines the postmodern as simply "despair," but I hope to show that such simplicities are not adequate to post-Enlightenment experience and sense of value.

9 The complexity of the intellectual history of Enlightenment reason – Leibniz's necessary and sufficient reason and Descartes' clear and distinct ideas – beyond the argument I am presenting here can be seen in the great debate between Leibniz and Newton concerning volunteerism. Newton argued throughout his career that God could disrupt history, messianically – or, in the terms of Foucault in this paragraph, "revolutionarily" – at any time, that his "voluntary" power took precedence over his omniscient knowledge. This idea, as Robert Markley amply demonstrates, is an important source of Newton's empiricism as opposed to Descartes' rationalism. But it is important in other ways as well. In the heart of the Enlightenment Newton held a position that combined the simplicities of Enlightenment reason with a sense of the "mysterious" abundance of God's power that significantly modified the Cartesian ideology of clear and distinct ideas. As Markley has argued, Newton's

> commitment to a voluntaristic conception of God's dominion ... is also a commitment to viewing the physical and spiritual universe as irreducibly complex. The universe, in other words, is noisy: the noise of history, like the complexity of the physical universe, is paradoxically a sign of God's dominion, of his continuing intervention in his creation. Newton's paradox, then, is that although the "remnant" [of God's people] may be called to seek for "truth," its duty is not to systematize the universe, as Leibniz tries to do, nor to systematize history, as the trinitarians do, but to preserve as well as to interpret the ways in which noise and meaning are dialectically interrelated. Every suppression of noise is, in effect, a suppression of God's manifestation in creation ... (1993: 177)

Leibniz, as Markley suggests, held the opposite view, that God's omniscience took precedence over omnipotence and that the universe was a "system" governed by the simplicities of necessary and sufficient reason – and, implicit within this reason, the simplicities of rational and continuous development. (The distinction between Newton and the Newtonian tradition of Enlightenment science I have maintained embodies, as Markley shows, this debate between Newton and Leibniz.) By the end of the eighteenth century it was clear that Leibniz's position that God's reasonable consciousness was the supreme heavenly faculty had won the day in the very offhanded way Samuel Johnson simply assumes the simplicities of Leibnizian Reason when he has Imlac say in

*Rasselas* (1759) that "it is no limitation on omnipotence ... to suppose that one thing is not consistent with another, that the same proposition cannot be at once true and false, that the same number cannot be even and odd, that cogitation cannot be conferred on that which is created incapable of cogitation" (1958: 609–10). The triumph of Leibniz's position leads to the clock-work simplicities of Deism at the end of the century.

10 Note here that Marx's reasoning, in a world of need, possesses the sequential structure ("primary ... secondary") of the absolute sequence of Newtonian time. Max Horkheimer and Theodor Adorno in *Dialectic of the Enlightenment* describe the importance of quantification for Enlightenment thinking, which is implicit in the ability to equate "first" and "basic." "The mythologizing equation of Ideas with numbers in Plato's last writings," they write, "expresses the longing of all demythologization: number became the canon of the Enlightenment. The same equations dominate bourgeois justice and commodity exchange ... Bourgeois society is ruled by equivalence. It makes the dissimilar comparable by reducing it to abstract quantities. To the Enlightenment, that which does not reduce to numbers, and ultimately to the one, becomes illusion; modern positivism writes it off as literature. Unity is the slogan from Parmenides to Russell. The destruction of gods and qualities alike is insisted upon" (1972: 7). Such quantification is closely related to the continuity as well as the absolute ongoingness of Newtonian time. Horkheimer and Adorno are expressing, of course, another version of Rorty's description of the transformation in Enlightenment philosophy of the quest for wisdom to the quest for certainty. Thus, despite the reference by Horkheimer and Adorno, when Bertrand Russell argued early in the twentieth century (as I discuss in chapter 4) that "quantity is banished altogether [from mathematics], except from one little corner of Geometry, while order more and more reigns supreme" ( 1917: 87), he is participating in a post-Enlightenment ethos. For a further discussion of the functioning of number in the "money-exchange system" of Capitalism in relation to the senses of abundance and scarcity, see Xenos (1989: 74–75, 81).

11 Thus, Lawrence Birken, whom I have been quoting, is not an economist but a social historian tracing the emergence of the science of "sexology" in Freud and his contemporaries at the turn of the twentieth century. His book is called *Consuming Desire: Sexual Science and the Emergence of a Culture of Abundance, 1881–1914*. His study as a whole traces the transformation of need into desire in conceptions and practices of sexuality during the second Industrial Revolution. More generally, in *Fables of Abundance* Jackson Lears traces the history of advertising in America that created "the broad redefinition of abundance that was occurring during the early twentieth century under the auspices of managerial thought" (1994: 117). Specifically, he describes the uses of

"longing" and desire in "eroticizing" consumption. Such eroticization, he writes, arose in part "from a self-defeating pattern of human desire – a pattern that may have been virtually universal and timeless but that resonated especially with the emergent market cultures of the modern West" (1994: 47). The whole of part I of Lears's book is relevant to my argument in providing a social-historical description of the second Industrial Revolution. His uses of methods from art history, photography, semiotics, Foucauldian poststructuralism, and other disciplines in his work also underline my point about the breakdown of disciplinary "simplicities" in a world of abundance. For a survey of historical treatments of Western consumerism, see McCraken 1988.

12 I also pursue Taylor's distinction at greater length in *Analogical Thinking*, especially chapter 4. For a strong "post-Enlightenment" (though she doesn't use that word) refutation of the charge of "subjectivity," see Katherine Hayles, "Boundary Disputes: Homeostasis, Reflexivity, and the Foundations of Cybernetics." Hayles describes how Donald MacKay rescued "information affecting the receiver's mindset from the 'subjective' label" by proposing that the founder of mathematical "information theory," Claude Shannon, was "concerned with what he called 'selective information' – that is, information calculated by considering the selection of message elements from a set" while he, MacKay, was arguing "for another kind of information that he called 'structural' ... [which] has the capacity to 'increase the number of dimensions in the information space' by acting as a metacommunication" (1994: 449). "Structural information," as this description suggests, replaces the reductive simplicities of mathematic encoding with a "structure" of abundance, increasing dimensions of information space. Both MacKay's and Hayle's use of "structure" in this way has a distant formal similarity to Stravinsky's description of the connection between the "language structure" of art and the structures of the phenomenal world.

Moreover, the term "structural information" obviates the opposition between subject and object – a founding constituent of Enlightenment modernity, as I have argued. Similarly, in *Cybernetics* Wiener writes of the opposition between matter and energy in ways that can help us to grasp a post-Enlightenment understanding of the opposition between "objective" and "subjective": "Whether we should call the new point of view materialistic," he writes, "is largely a question of words: the ascendancy of matter characterizes a phase of nineteenth-century physics far more than the present age, and 'materialism' has come to be but little more than a loose synonym for 'mechanism.' In fact, the whole mechanist-vitalist controversy has been relegated to the limbo of badly posed questions" (1961: 44).

Finally, I should add that the "problem" of information created by material, intellectual, and phenomenological abundances gave rise to the "new" lower middle class of clerks, commercial travelers, and teachers I discuss in chapter 3: at the end of the century there was an explosion of non-manual labor associated with information. Joyce's characters inhabit this class – Leopold Bloom is a commercial traveler, Stephen Dedalus a grade-school teacher, and little Chandler, Farrington, and Mr. James Duffy are clerks – and the sense of panic associated with them (different from the metaphysical panic associated with Clarissa Dalloway and her circle) is a function of the newness and precariousness of this class of "information workers."

## 2 TEMPORAL ALLEGORIES: GEORGE ELIOT, WALTER BENJAMIN, AND THE REDEMPTION OF TIME

1 "Each metaphor," Derrida has written, "can always be deciphered simultaneously as a particular figure and as a paradigm of the very process of metaphorization: *idealization* and *appropriation*. Everything in the discussion on metaphor that passes through the sign *eidos*, with its entire system [of metaphysics], is articulated with the analogy between the vision of the *nous* and sensory vision, between the intelligible sun and the visible sun" (1982: 253–54).

Any metaphor is both an elemental whole and a metonymic part of a hierarchically distinct process; it is an observation and an action. When Derrida distinguishes between "the vision of the *nous* and sensory vision" (1982: 253) – what an earlier translation of "White Mythology" rendered as "*our* looking and sensible looking" (1974: 55) – he is marking the difference between modes of attention. Derrida's opposition of modes of apprehension is more clearly seen in the pun on "looking" in the earlier translation, in which the first phrase emphasizes the verbal aspect of the gerund, the second the nominal. In this discussion he sugests that the identification of the human act of looking ("sensory vision") and the look of being itself ("the vision of the *nous*") effectively erases temporality as a determination of comprehension, transforming time, as Heidegger notes in the epigraph to this chapter, into something that can be represented like a "thing."

2 Ermarth writes: "The narrator is 'nobody' in two ways ... : it is not individual, and it is not corporeal. First, the narrator is a collective result, a specifier of consensus, and as such it is really not intelligible as an individual. Second, since the general consensus thus specified exists only through a dissociation, at a distance from the concrete, the narrator-specifier is also not intelligible as a corporeal existence" (1983: 65–66). George Eliot complicates this by naming and seemingly situating the narrator of her novels in time, but the "time" of the narrator is never specified beyond a vague futurity. Such futurity guarantees the continuity of Enlightenment thinking. "Futurity," Ermarth writes,

provides that horizon and that vanishing-point which at once mark the (arbitrary) limits of our perception and guarantee the extension beyond those limits of the order visible in the field. Futurity insures that, in a different time and place, the same familiar system will operate. Continuous with past and present, the future, like the narrator, exists beyond the arbitrarily limited horizon and it insures that, in moving toward it, we will run along the same rails that brought us from past to present. (1983: 42)

3  Colin MacCabe makes a similar argument concerning the privileged discourse of the narrator – discourse *outside* quotation marks – in George Eliot. This language, he writes, is "transparent" and, like visible reality itself, in no need of interpretation and in no reciprocal relationship with the narrative's characters. "The text outside the area of inverted commas," MacCabe writes, "claims to be the product of no articulation, it claims to be unwritten ... Whereas other discourses within the text are considered as materials which are open to reinterpretation, the narrative discourse functions simply as a window on reality. This relationship between discourses can be taken as the defining feature of the *classic realist text*" (1979: 15). If the characters exist in time, MacCabe argues, the narrator – and narration itself – does not. Existence in time makes the characters' actions and discourse interpretable: in fact, such existence in time makes discourse a form of action, an *event* in time! But it is only the characters' discourse that is equivalent to action. The narrator is privileged and does not need to act, but simply to observe. "To transform language into pure communicative absence," MacCabe writes, with *Middlemarch* as his example, "is to transform the world into a self-evident reality where, in order to discover truth, we have only to use our eyes" (1979: 18). The beginning of *The Mill on the Floss*, therefore, betrays the spirit of classic realism by characterizing the narrator in terms of action: telling a story and falling asleep. Yet never again in *The Mill on the Floss* will the narrator characterize "himself" beyond the realm of observation and transparent discourse. Never again will the narrator's language be "modalized," as I discuss the modalization of experience in chapter 5, so that the subject of discourse can be seen to affect that discourse.

4  Robert Markley argues persuasively that Newton himself understood the atemporality of mathematics to be a kind of code to access the divine, outside of time. The followers of Newton, who attempted to supplement "Newton's 'authoritative' texts in the forms of lectures, demonstrations, coffee-table folios, [etc.]" (1993: 180) radically recontextualized his work so that the theocratic basis of Newton's work was displaced into political, social, and disciplinary agendas. "Newtonianism," Markley concludes, "thus seeks to legitimate both a hierarchical, theocentric economy of absolute value and an exchange economy that fetishized mathematical and scientific knowledge as commodities. The development of Newtonianism, then, can be described not as a

simple 'rise' of modern science but as the contested and internally divisive processes of reinscribing a metaphysics of order into the economies of nature and culture, processes that both exacerbate and repress the contradictions and tensions within Newton's work" (1993: 181). Markley is describing, *retrospectively*, the temporal complications of cultural history. What he calls the fetishization of "mathematical and scientific knowledge as commodities" is the desacralization of natural philosophy into the "secular" and parsimonious mechanics that became the official doctrine of educated opinion by the late nineteenth century. This doctrine, I am arguing, manifests itself as far afield as George Eliot's humanist realism.

5 As Lowe argues in the *History of Bourgeois Perception*, "development-in-time" forms "the epistemic order of bourgeois society." "Development," he writes, "was a new connection which posited dynamics (as opposed to stasis); transformation (as opposed to unrelated, specific change); structure (as opposed to taxonomy); and totality (as a spatio-temporal whole) ... The new spatio-temporal order defined, as well as validated new knowledges of history, society, language, philosophy, and even the human psyche" (1982: 11). It is what William Everdell calls "ontological continuity" (1997: 11): "the heart of Modernism," he asserts, "is the postulate of ontological discontinuity" (1997: 351).

6 The unmarked case, as Barthes' description suggests, is the general or "normal" case against which the marked case distinguishes itself. The unmarked case thus subsumes the marked case: accented language is a special case of language in general; "woman" is apprehended as a special case of man(kind). I pursue this distinction in chapter 5. For a linguistic description of markedness, see Schleifer (1987: pp. 50–55; and 2000: ch. 3).

7 Much of what is described as postmodern and what I prefer to call "post-Enlightenment" can be found in attempts to find a new language for describing the experiential, intellectual, and material abundances I described in chapter 1 and which I will examine more closely in chapter 3. Bruno Latour's argument in *We Have Never Been Modern* is one instance of developing the language of "hybrids" and "networks" in response to abundance. Other recent attempts to articulate a "postpositivist" objectivity also take their place within this constellation of terms (see Monhanty 1995), as do Derrida's neologisms, Foucault's "genealogies," the convoluted metalanguages of structuralism and the non-visualizable mathematics of quantum mechanics, and even the term "negative materialism" I describe in *Rhetoric and Death* – all are attempting to "rescue" the achievements of Enlightenment modernity where the very abundance of their successes – the very *worldliness* of their success – has led to crisis. Even the science of information theory, as I noted in chapter 1, develops the language of "redundancy" to comprehend abundance.

### 3 THE SECOND INDUSTRIAL REVOLUTION: HISTORY, KNOWLEDGE, AND SUBJECTIVITY

1  The articulation of "non-transcendental disembodiment" is an aim, as I suggested earlier, of the analogies that are presented throughout this book – as a theme and a procedure – and that govern its organization as a whole. It is the *semantic formalism* of such analogies – what Stravinsky describes as the "reflective system between the language structure of the music and the structure of the phenomenal world" (1982: 147) and what Benjamin describes as its "nonsensuous similarity" (1978: 334) or, in Buck-Morss's translation, its "non-representational similarity" (1977: 90) – that allows them to encompass the contradiction of disembodiment without transcendence. This is why Benjamin uses the literary and discursive figure of the tragic hero, whose "life, indeed, unfolds from death, which is not its end but its form" (1977: 144), as an image of his understanding; it is why the "answerability" of art – and of other intellectual formations examined throughout this book – do not simply reflect a logic of abundance but in fact *inform* it. Such "material disembodiment," as I might also call it, is characteristic of the semiotics of finance capital, the non-absolute usurpation of positive "real" estate by monied estates (see Baudrillard 1988 for repeated analyses of this situation), and even the dialectic of abundance and poverty in art I examined in the Introduction. It is certainly a image in which many of the most striking technical innovations of the second Industrial Revolution examined in this chapter can be gathered together. For a more extended discussion, see my *Analogical Thinking*.

2  It is measured in the universal standard – the general equivalent – of money conceived as semiotic. For an important discussion of the relationship between semiotics and economics, see Jean-Joseph Goux (1990).

3  In *Capital* Marx notes that it is the nature of the commodity to transform any "definite social relation between men" into "the fantastic form of a relation between things" (1967: 72). This is why Richard Terdiman, following the analyses of Lukács, Adorno, and Benjamin, argues that "*the enigma of the commodity is a memory disorder*" (1993: 12). "The experience of commodification and the process of reification," he writes, "cut entities off from their own history. They veil the memory of their production from their consumers, as from the very people who produced them. The process, in Theodor Adorno's terms, created an unprecedented and uncanny field of 'hollowed-out' objects, available for investment by any meaning whatsoever, but organically connected with none at all" (1993: 12). This leads, Terdiman argues, to the occultation of memory and the abstraction – to the point of attenuation – of time itself. Thus, he says, "in the same way that under capitalism Marx had claimed that the power and creativity of the worker seem to pass into the tool," so "... in the modern period memory appears to

reside not in perceiving consciousness but *in the material*: in the practices and institutions of social or psychic life, which function within us, but, strangely, do not seem to require either our participation or our explicit allegiance" (1993: 43). If the analogies I pursue in this study can be categorized as non-transcendental disembodiments, then this description of commodified labor is a kind of embodied transcendentalism. "Under capitalism," Terdiman concludes, "the traces of history, of process, of *time*, disappear from the forms of bourgeois thought. The self-confident stability, the apparently untroubled absolutism of ideology in its modern guise, are the rhetorical reflexes of such abstractions" (1993: 53).

4  In *Consuming Desire*, Lawrence Birken describes this abstraction in terms of the Enlightenment transformation of the "caste" system of the three estates of aristocratic Europe to the "class" system of the political economies of Adam Smith, Ricardo, and Marx. "The movement" in the Enlightenment, he writes, "from a transcendental divine to an immanent natural law occurred within the framework of a profound shift from a holistic (or caste) to an individualistic (or class) conception of the social order" (1988: 4). The only caste distinction that remained intact until the second Industrial Revolution, he argues, is that of "the male/female caste system founded on the perceived natural difference between the sexes [that] ... replaced the older three-function caste system of the aristocratic epoch" (1988: 6). In this system, women participated in domestic "nonproductive" labor while men participated in the "productive" labor of capitalism. When women sold their labor-power, just as, in George Eliot, when they faced a spiritual crisis, they were simply universally "human," functionally men. (See Sayer 1991 for repeated discussions of the failure of Marx to analyze gender.)

5  Such a "universal" bourgeois order was both local and short-lived. As Hobsbawn argues, modern conceptions "of nation and nation-state" were closely associated with "the era of triumphant bourgeois liberalism: say from 1830 to 1880" (1990: 38). In important ways, classical nineteenth-century liberalism is the political ideology of Enlightenment assumptions, and the liberal idea of "nation" – which is a thoroughly historical and *timely* idea, "situated," as Hobsbawm notes, "at the point of intersection of politics, technology and social transformation" (1990: 10) – was assumed to be "universal." That is, liberal conceptions of nation and nation-state attempt "to fit historically novel, emerging, changing and, even today, far from universal entities into a framework of permanence and universality" (1990: 6). One form of "abundance," as I suggest later in this chapter, is the emergence, proliferation, and transformation of "nations" and "nation states" at the end of the nineteenth century, "the heyday of bourgeois liberalism, which was also the era when the 'principle of nationality' first became a major issue in international politics" (1990: 40).

6 A second great theme of Anglo-American literary Modernism is that of imperialism. The authors mentioned in this paragraph – Yeats, Forster, Joyce, even Eliot in *The Waste Land* – are writers who focus on imperialism as well as the lower middle class. Even Woolf in *The Years* explores the effects of the British empire in significant ways. Conrad is perhaps the most striking example of this counterpoint: the protagonist of *The Secret Agent* and the narrator of *Under Western Eyes* are a lower-middle-class shop-keeper and a teacher, each dealing with international intrigue as exotic as the scenes of *Lord Jim* or *Nostromo*. Later, I touch upon the relationship between the lower middle class and imperialist nationalism in the context of the abundance of the late nineteenth century.

Edward Said treats the relationship between Western literary culture and imperialism in *Culture and Imperialism* (1993), and – using the same metaphor emphasizing the temporality of music over its "themes" that Adorno uses in describing Benjamin's work – he emphasizes the provisional nature of reading culture against history. (This is also closely related to Heisenberg's figure of "alternating" interpretations, which, in fact, Said also takes up.) "In the counterpoint of Western classical music," he writes, "various themes play off one another, with only a provisional privilege being given to any particular one; yet in the resulting polyphony there is concert and order, an organized interplay that derives from the themes, not from a rigorous melodic or formal principle outside the work. In the same way, I believe, we can read and interpret English novels, for example, whose engagement (usually suppressed for the most part) with the West Indies or India, say, is shaped and perhaps even determined by the specific history of colonization, resistance, and finally native nationalism. At this point alternative or new narratives emerge, and they become institutionalized or discursively stable entities" (1993: 51).

7 Thus, Frank Kermode has argued that Lawrence "will not make up stories which *explain* how one thing leads to another. There are concessions to contingency, for without them we should fail to recognize the book as a novel, but we move with a minimum of formal continuity from one crux to the next" (1968: 36). Kermode is describing a resistance in Lawrence to the "self-evident" continuities of Enlightenment thinking I examined in chapter 1.

8 For a fine analysis of one such way that literary Modernism tutors understanding and apprehension, see Thomas Richards's discussion of the "Nausicaa" Chapter in *Ulysses*, where he traces Joyce's confrontation with "the lived reality of the advertised spectacle" (1990: 207). Quoting Leo Lowenthal, Richards describes the advertizing industry that developed at the turn of the century "psychoanalysis in reverse" (1990: 210).

9 Katherine Hayles describes in great detail the relation between Law-

rence's rhetoric and the ways in which post-Newtonian physics – or what I am calling, more generally, the overwhelming abundance of the second Industrial Revolution – seems to "resist articulation" (1984: 86) in the languages inherited from the Enlightenment. Hayles describes nicely the problem of articulation and subjectivity in Lawrence I describe in the next few paragraphs. "On the one hand, Lawrence feels deeply that reality is essentially mystical and unspeakable, to be experienced rather than understood rationally. On the other hand, he is committed to depicting this ineffable reality with words. The closer he comes to rendering the unconscious in language, the closer he paradoxically comes to destroying its realization, because language is necessarily conscious" (1984: 94–95). Lawrence, like Benjamin, struggles throughout *The Rainbow* to be able to ratify a sense of the sacred within the secularism of the received Enlightenment ideology. In this, he joins Heidegger and many from the lower middle class from which he sprang in turning toward the rituals and absolutism of fascist politics.

## 4 THE NATURAL HISTORY OF TIME: MATHEMATICS AND MEANING IN EINSTEIN AND RUSSELL

1 In "The Philosophy of Logical Atomism" (1918) Russell echoes Augustine's description of the relationship between experience and representation.

That is a rather singular fact that everything you are really sure of, right off, is something that you do not know the meaning of, and the moment you get a precise statement you will not be sure whether it is true or false, at least right off. The process of sound philosophizing, to my mind, consists mainly in passing from those obvious, vague, ambiguous things, that we feel quite sure of, to something precise, clear, definite, which by reflection and analysis we find is involved in the vague thing that we start from, and is, so to speak, the real truth of which the vague thing is a sort of shadow. (1956: 179–80)

Among other things, Russell is describing the complicated relationship between the "language structure" of the arts and of understanding and the seeming indefiniteness of the phenomenal world that Stravinsky is also trying to grasp.

Wittgenstein himself makes Augustine's question and the larger question of the "queerness" of time particularly apposite in understanding thought. "When we are worried about the nature of thinking," he writes in *The Blue Book*,

the puzzlement which we wrongly interpret to be one about the nature of a medium is a puzzlement caused by the mystifying use of our language. This kind of mistake recurs again and again in philosophy; e.g. when we are puzzled about the nature of time, when time seems to us a *queer thing*. We are most strongly tempted to think that here are things hidden, something we can see from the outside but which we can't look into. And yet nothing of the sort is the case. It is not new facts about time which we want to know. All the facts that concern us lie open before us. But it is the use of the substantive "time" which mystifies us. If we look into the grammar of that word, we shall feel that it is no less astounding that man should have conceived of a deity of time than it would be to conceive of a deity of negation or disjunction. (1965: 6)

In a fine discussion of this and other examinations of time in Wittgenstein, Henry McDonald notes that "for Wittgenstein, as for Heidegger, time is 'finite' in that the forms in which it is uncovered are themselves finite" (p. 245).

2 The term "operational definition" was coined by P. W. Bridgman in 1928 (after Russell wrote the descriptions from the *ABC of Atoms* quoted below) in order to understand Einstein's work. It is different from the classical forms of definition, the Aristotelian definition by means of identifying the genus and/or the species of a term (an oboe is a woodwind instrument with a double reed) and definition by example (an oboe is a double-reed instrument with a slender conical body that comes in various sizes, such as the "English horn," the "Bassoon," etc.). An operational definition defines things functionally. Thus, in the *ABC of Atoms*, Russell defines electricity operationally. "Some readers," he writes,

may expect me at this stage to tell them what electricity 'really is.' The fact is that I have already said what it is. It is not a thing, like St. Paul's Cathedral; it is a way in which things behave. When we have told how things behave when they are electrified, and under what circumstances they are electrified, we have told all there is to tell ... When we have enumerated these laws of behaviour, there is nothing more to be said about electricity, unless we can discover further laws, or simplify and unify the statement of the laws already known. When I say that an electron has a certain amount of negative electricity, I mean merely that it behaves in a certain way. Electricity is not like red paint, a substance which can be put on to the electron and taken off again; it is merely a convenient name for certain physical laws. (1923: 31–33)

Later, I will note Rudolph Carnap's discussion of operational definition in terms of "correspondence rules."

These three modes of definition – exemplary, Aristotelian, and operational, which I have called here formal, conceptual, and operational – correspond to Paul Ricoeur's descriptions of modes of explanation cited below in this chapter: theoretical, categoreal, and configurational. The fact that a "new" method of definition *emerged* in the early twentieth century – one opposed to the "necessary" (i.e., Aristotle's "conceptual") and "sufficient" (i.e., empirical "exemplary") truths of Enlightenment parsimony – is of the utmost importance. Operational definitions call into question Leibniz's "second great principle," that of sufficient reason. "It will not be assumed," Russell writes in *Mysticism and Logic*, "that *every* event has some antecedent which is its cause in this sense; we shall only believe in causal sequences where we find them, without any presumption that they always are to be found" (1917: 187).

3 Eve Bannet describes the erasure of the differences inscribed in analogies in the Enlightenment as "a basic principle of [Newton's] new science": "stressing resemblance over difference to make different entities more or less alike transformed analogy into an equivalence" (1997: 658).

4 A striking feature of Planck's constant, like that of the speed of light ($c$), $\sqrt{-1}$, or $g_{ab}$ of Einstein's formula I discussed earlier, is that it "works" – in its mathematical formalism, it conditions interpretations and semantic understandings – in contexts different from those in which it emerged. Thus, as I observe in the following chapter (note 5), Planck's constant, $h$, allows for the mathematical articulation of the limit-point of precision in Heisenberg's uncertainty principle (see Crease and Mann 1986: 50–51).

5 The echoes of Ezra Pound's description of the "image" in Russell's description is striking. For a discussion of the relationships between geometry and modernist poetics, see Michael Levenson, *Genealogy of Modernism*.

6 *Introduction to Mathematical Philosophy* is Russell's attempt to set forth the basic concepts of *Principia Mathematica*, which argued for the identity of logic and mathematics. The basis of this "identity" is, in fact, the transformation of mathematics from the study of quantities to the study of order effected, in large part, by the crisis in geometry and the development of set theory in the late nineteenth century. It is these kinds of crises – in examining the Modernist novels of Lawrence, Woolf, and Mann, Daniel Albright describes their similarities in relation to "some common crisis, a tendency inherent in the structure of the nineteenth-century novel itself" (1978: 2) – that instantiate the "answerability" of intellectual formations and cultural formations I discussed in the Introduction with Stravinsky's observation as my guide. Even the semiotics of finance capitalism – which certainly can be thought of as a tendency inherent in the structure of nineteenth-century industrial capitalism – can also be seen as structurally "similar to" (to use a technical mathematical phrase of Russell's examined later in this chapter) the structural tendencies of narrative subjectivity and intellectual implication in other early twentieth-century phenomena.

7 The place of Russell's discussion of the mathematical infinite within my larger argument might be clearer, perhaps, if we compare Russell's use of "similar" to Nietzsche's conception of the eternal return. In the discussion of "the eternal return of the same," Joan Stambaugh has written, "the greatest difficulty with Nietzsche's word for the Same is that there is no exact equivalent for it in English." "*Das Gleiche*," she goes on, "does *not* express simple identity, and therefore does not, strictly speaking, mean the Same. It lies somewhere between the Same and the Similar, but means neither exactly. For example: If two women have the same hat on, they have, strictly speaking, one hat on at

different times. (One borrowed or stole the other's hat.) If two women have the 'same' (in the sense of *gleich*) hat on at the same time, they have two hats which resemble each other so exactly that one could think that one woman had borrowed the other's hat, if one saw these women at different times. This is more than similarity, but it is not identity" (1972: 31). At the end of her study, Stambaugh returns to this difficulty.

If time is not thought as a form in which things occur (or, here, recur), "what" occurs in eternal return should not be thought as the content of this form. If "what" occurs in eternal return is not a content, the kind of "identity" to be thought in Nietzsche's word "the Same" refers neither to the self-identity of things or persons nor even, strictly speaking, to some kind of "identity" between time and eternity in the sense that individual successive moments of time are subsumed under the simultaneous whole of eternity. At best, the "identity" of time and eternity could be expressed by saying that time is as-*simil*-ated to eternity. The Same is this *process of as-simil-ation*, a manner of occurring which first determines *any* possible "what," any thing or person or whatever. (1972: 127)

The relationship between content and form Stambaugh describes in Nietzsche is congruent with Russell's discussion of the resolution of "a piece of matter . . . into a series of events" in which "the whole series of these events makes up the whole history of the particle, and the particle is regarded as *being* its history, not some metaphysical entity to which the events happen" (1925: 208–09). Moreover, her discussion of assimilation is parallel to Russell's redefinition of the relationship between parts and wholes when dealing with infinities. It is as if the impossibility of the temporal infinity of "eternity" coincides with the possibility of thinking the "exact science" of the *formal* infinity of mathematics. Explicitly in Nietzsche, and implicitly in the mathematics Russell describes, the understanding and experience of time in relation to the atemporal ("eternity") is transformed.

8 Towards the end of *Mathematical Philosophy* Russell restates this in the more formal and technical terms of logic:

We shall come much nearer to a satisfactory theory if we try to identify classes with propositional functions. Every class . . . is defined by some propositional function which is true of the members of the class and false of other things. But if a class can be defined by one propositional function, it can equally well be defined by any other which is true whenever the first is true and false whenever the first is false. For this reason the class cannot be identified with any one such propositional function rather than with any other – and given a propositional function, there are always many others which are true when it is true and false when it is false. (1919: 183)

9 The term "operational definition" has a technical history. As I noted earlier, it was introduced by P. W. Bridgman in *The Logic of Modern Physics* (1928). Charles Taylor examines operational definitions in *The Explanation of Behaviour*, where he traces its uses in the social and well as physical sciences. Specifically, he cites Rudolph Carnap's examination

of operational definitions in terms of "correspondence rules" (Taylor 1964: 78). What I am concerned with is the formal similarity between operational definitions and the "correspondences" Russell describes in set theory, especially in relation to Einstein's more or less "narrative" definition of time in his 1905 paper. The correspondences of set theory, which posit that two sets are "equal" if each element of one set can be "paired" with an element of a second set, allow "equivalence" "without recourse to counting" (Moore 1990: 5), that is, without recourse to the quantification that only makes sense in relation to sets of finite elements and to a world of need, where the "first" and the "basic" can be, atemporally, identified with one another.

For an extended discussion of Jakobson that examines Prague linguistics more generally in terms of its functionalism, see my *A. J. Greimas and the Nature of Meaning* (1987: 46–48).

10 In discussing Claude Lévi-Strauss's description of music (as opposed to painting) at the beginning of *The Raw and the Cooked* (1975: 22), I have offered an alternative to Stravinsky's term "reflective system," what I call "the syncopated opposition between phenomenological 'organization' and semiotic 'representation'" (1999: 22 [note 1]). By emphasizing the temporal "syncopations" of the relationship between the "language structure" of music and the "structure of the phenomenal world" Stravinsky describes, I underline the ways that music foregrounds the temporality and affectiveness of aesthetics, the ways in which it is related to worldly desire. Stravinsky, by contrast, is discussing art more generally, and his emphasis on the systematic "reflection" of language structure and the structure of phenomenal experience underlines what I have been calling the semantic formalism of analogical thinking. His emphasis on the formal, but semantic abstractions I discuss in this paragraph foregrounds the relationship of his Modernist aesthetics to the Modernist sciences of Einstein and Russell.

### 5 ANALOGY AND EXAMPLE: HEISENBERG, LINGUISTIC NEGATION, AND THE LANGUAGE OF QUANTUM PHYSICS

1 In the *ABC of Atoms* Russell quotes J. Jeans to describe this mutual exclusivity.

Thus it appears that there is no hope of reconciling the undulatory theory of light with the quantum-theory by regarding the undulatory theory as being, so to speak, only statistically true when a great number of quanta are present. One theory cannot be the limit of the other in the sense in which the Newtonian mechanics is the limit of the quantum-mechanics, and we are faced with the problem of combining two apparently quite irreconcilable theories. (1923: 148–49)

For a thorough examination of complementarity in relation to the semantics of literary and philosophical theory, see Plotnitsky 1994. For a comprehensive examination of the poetics of high Modernism in terms of the figure of the wave-particle opposition, see Albright 1997.

2 In *We Have Never Been Modern*, Latour argues that this dualism is not "alien" to classical physics, but is ignored (I might say "repressed") in it. The Enlightenment project, he argues, achieved its great successes through the uses of this dualism and its refusal to acknowledge the "hybridity" of its processes, opting instead for a concept of "purity" – and, again I would add, "simplicity." Although he doesn't emphasize this in his argument, the abundances of twentieth-century experience – symbolized in his discussion by the plethora of seemingly "unconnected" phenomena encountered in the daily newspaper – makes the "repression" he describes impossible to avoid. He describes the dualism inhabiting the Enlightenment project in terms of its aim at "domination and liberation" (1993: 10) which I have repeatedly cited as parallel to the dual "atemporalities" of material positivism and subjective idealism.

3 For an elaboration of Greimas's square in relation to the basic criteria of Enlightenment science – simplicity, accuracy, and generalizability – see Schleifer et al. 1992, especially "Introduction: Science, Cognition, and Culture."

4 Fred Alan Wolf uses this figure to describe complementarity in Wolf 1989: 130–33.

5 Such ordering, however, is not simple. Rather, it depends on *negating* the propositions. In a similar way, Heisenberg's reluctant articulation of the violation of the mathematical law of commutation in quantum matrices is not simple. Specifically, when Max Born rewrote Heisenberg's matrix equations,

the first thing he figured out was that the matrix $q$ for position and the matrix $p$ for momentum are noncommutative in a very special way: That is, $pq$ is not only different from $qp$, but the difference between $pq$ and $qp$ is always the same amount, no matter what $p$ or $q$ you chose. Mathematically he wrote this

$$pq - qp = \hbar/i$$

where $\hbar$, as usual, is Planck's constant divided by twice pi, and $i$ is the special symbol mathematicians use for the square root of minus one. (Crease and Mann 1986: 50)

The square root of minus one is, of course, an imaginary number, and later Crease and Mann note that "imaginary numbers, whatever the difficulty one has in picturing them, are a central feature of contemporary physics" (p. 142). The difficulty, of course, like the difficulties in visualizing quantum mechanics more generally that I discussed earlier, is that $\sqrt{-1}$ is neither negative nor positive.

6 In "Toward a Theory of Modalities," Greimas asserts "a difference in treatment between *logic* (which is phrastic in nature and functions only by means of substitutions) and *discoursive semiotics* (whose utterances have, in addition, a *positional* signification)" (1987: 122). See also my *A.J.*

*Greimas and the Nature of Meaning*, p. xx, for a further discussion of the difference between formal and semantic logic.

7 "What we are defining" in the term "structure of feeling," Williams writes in *Marxism and Literature*, "is a particular quality of social experience and relationship, historically distinct from other particular qualities, which gives the sense of a generation or of a period" (1977: 131). This is the "felt sense of the quality of life at a particular place and time," he describes in *The Long Revolution*, "a sense of the ways in which the particular activities [of life] combined into a way of thinking and feeling" (1961: 63). The term "structure of feeling" combines seemingly incompatible elements analogous to those brought together in my term "semantic formalism"; the articulation or circumscription of such a structure of feeling for the early twentieth century is one of the goals of *Modernism and Time*.

## 6 THE GLOBAL AESTHETICS OF GENRE: MIKHAIL BAKHTIN AND THE BORDERS OF MODERNITY

1 The recovery of Bakhtin's conception of aesthetics in early post-World War I fragments published in Russia in the last fifteen years suggests a significant alternative to the conception of literary theory I examined in the preceding chapter in the example of Paul de Man. The concept and term *theory* in Anglo-American literary studies that developed in the twentieth century – like postmodernism in relation to post-Enlightenment cultural formations or Bataille's attempt to provoke a sense of an alternative to idealism and abstract materialism in relation to Benjamin's attempt to recover and redeem such alternatives for comprehension – has repeatedly opposed itself to Enlightenment aesthetics on the level of the personal and the idiosyncratic. W. K. Wimsatt was probably the first to use the term "theory" when he argued in 1949 that "literary theorists of our day have been content to say little about 'beauty' or about any overall aesthetic concept. In his most general formulation the literary theorist is likely to be content with something like 'human interest'" even though "disinterestedness, we remember, is something that Kant made a character of art" (cited in Davis and Schleifer [1994: 83]; see Miller [1992: 140] for a discussion of "theory" and visibility).

2 Roman Jakobson's connection with Bakhtin is clear, especially in relation to his participation in Russian Formalism. In fact, Morson and Emerson suggest that Bakhtin's work in prosaics in the twenties was a response, in large part, to the Jakobsonian concepts of "literariness" and "linguistic poetics" (1990: 86): they even point out, citing Robert Matthews, that "Bakhtin's primary antagonist in the 1920s was not Shklovsky at all ... but the much more powerful Roman Jakobson" (478). Above all, I am arguing that the heart of his disagreement with Jakobson was the latter's sense of the impersonal "cognitive" method of

analyzing literary and cultural texts and the "anti-aesthetics" of Russian Formalism more generally. (Even New Critical formalism, as Wimsatt suggests, is "anti-aesthetic." See note 1 above.)

Walter Benjamin is less closely related to Bakhtin in any historical way. Closely associated with Theodor Adorno, Max Horkheimer, and the Frankfurt School during the 1920s and 1930s, Benjamin (along with Bakhtin) has become in the last decade a major figure for humanistic scholarship in the United States in his articulation of literary and cultural studies for the years between the great European wars of the twentieth century. As I suggest in chapter 2, his combination of Messianic Judaism and revolutionary Marxism while focusing on the cultural impact of modernity from Baudelaire to contemporary film has made his analyses of culture and history crucial in attempts, in literary studies, to find ways of developing what I am calling here an "ethics" of culture. This too, I believe, is a response and a rejection of the provinciality of received practices of aesthetic analysis. By bringing together Jakobson and Benjamin in relation to Bakhtin's "global" aesthetics, I hope to help delineate the crisis in culture that conditioned the work – the cultural "logics" – of all three.

3 For a discussion of the relations among Prague structuralism, transformational grammar, and the mid-century American linguistics of the Bloomfield school, see Schleifer (1987: ch. 2). For a sympathetic treatment of the empiricism of Bloomfield in relation to the other linguistics schools, see Sampson (1980).

4 For one such functionalist conception, see Dubrow (1982), especially pp. 2–4 where genre is described as analogous to "social codes ... [that] differ from culture to culture."

5 For an important discussion of Bakhtin's conception of "architectonics" that describes the ways "architectonics strives to articulate the general aspects of particular acts so that their particularity is nevertheless not compromised," see Morson and Emerson (1990: 70). This definition of architectonics comes close to the problem in ethics more generally of creating a relationship between the general and particular that neither privileges the general, as "cognition" does, not the particular, as traditional notions of "aesthetics" do. Morson and Emerson go on to discuss Bakhtin's "The Problem of Content, Material, and Form" as a critique of Russian Formalism (77–83).

6 Implicit in this description – perhaps "unconscious" in it – is the very fact of European imperialism that is one of the defining features of the turn of the twentieth century through which Jakobson, Benjamin, and Bakhtin lived. For Benjamin this is a clear aspect of his messianic Marxism; and for Jakobson, writing in 1956 after his exiles from Russia, then from Prague, to his final residence in the United States, the sense of displacement and otherness is also easily discerned. For Bakhtin, whose exiles were internal, the "other" never assumed the political

nature it had for Benjamin and Jakobson, both Jews fleeing Hitler; rather, in his work the "other" is a discursive and aesthetic category. It is perhaps for this reason that he can "redeem," as Benjamin might say, the category of aesthetics that seems so bankrupt for other post-Holocaust thinkers.

7 In this pursuit, Benjamin is attempting a transformation of aesthetic analysis into the sublimity of "theory," which is another reason for the importance of Benjamin to literary studies in the age of "theory." For a fine discussion of the relationship between literary theory and the Modernist sublime, see Daniel O'Hara's essay, "Yeats in Theory."

# References

Adorno, Theodor. 1981. "A Portrait of Walter Benjamin." In *Prisms*, trans. Samuel and Shierry Weber. Cambridge, MA: MIT Press, pp. 227–42.

1989. "Progress," trans. Erick Krakauer. In *Benjamin: Philosophy, Aesthetics, History*, ed. Gary Smith. Chicago: University of Chicago Press, pp. 84–101.

1992. "Introduction to Benjamin's *Schriften*." In *Notes to Literature*, Vol. 2, trans. Shierry Weber Nicholsen. New York: Columbia University Press, pp. 220–32.

Albright, Daniel. 1978. *Personality and Impersonality: Lawrence, Woolf, and Mann*. Chicago: University of Chicago Press.

1981. *Representation and the Imagination: Beckett, Kafka, Nabokov, and Schoenberg*. Chicago: University of Chicago Press.

1989. *Stravinsky: The Music Box and the Nightingale*. New York: Gordon and Breach.

1997. *Quantum Poetics: Yeats, Pound, Eliot, and the Science of Modernism*. Cambridge: Cambridge University Press.

Anderson, Perry. 1984. *In the Tracks of Historical Materialism*. Chicago: University of Chicago Press.

1988. "Modernity and Revolution." In *Marxism and the Interpretation of Culture*, ed. Carey Nelson and Lawrence Grossberg. Urbana: University of Illinois Press, pp. 317–39.

Augustine. 1960. *Confessions*, trans. John Ryan. New York: Penguin Books.

Austin, J. L. 1962. *How to do Things with Words*. Cambridge MA: Harvard University Press.

1979. *Philosophical Papers*. New York: Oxford University Press.

Bachelard, Gaston. 1984. *The New Scientific Spirit*, trans. Arthur Goldhammer. Boston: Beacon Press.

Bakhtin, M. M. 1981. *The Dialogic Imagination*, trans. Caryl Emerson and Michael Holquist. Austin: University of Texas Press.

1984. *Problems of Dostoevsky's Poetics*, trans. Caryl Emerson. Minneapolis: University of Minnesota Press.

1986. *Speech Genres and Other Late Essays*, trans. Vern McGee. Austin: University of Texas Press.

1990. *Art and Answerability*, trans. Vadim Liapunov and Kenneth Brostrom. Austin: University of Texas Press.

1993. *Toward a Philosophy of the Act*, trans. Vadim Liapunov. Austin: University of Texas Press.

Bakhtin, M. M. and P. N. Medvedev. 1985. *The Formal Method in Literary Scholarship*, trans. Albert J. Wehrle. Cambridge MA: Harvard University Press.

Bakhtin, M. M. and V. N. Vološinov. 1986. *Marxism and the Philosophy of Language*, trans. Ladislav Matejka and I. R. Titunik. Cambridge MA: Harvard University Press.

Bambach, Charles. 1995. *Heidegger, Dilthey, and the Crisis of Historicism*. Ithaca: Cornell University Press.

Bannet, Eve Tavor. 1997. "Analogy as Translation: Wittgenstein, Derrida, and the Law of Language," *New Literary History*: 28, 655–72.

Banta, Martha. 1993. *Taylored Lives*. Chicago: University of Chicago Press.

Barber, William. 1968. *A History of Economic Thought*. New York: Praeger.

Barthes, Roland. 1968. *Elements of Semiology*, trans. Annette Lavers and Colin Smith. New York: Hill and Wang.

1977. *Roland Barthes by Roland Barthes*, trans. Richard Howard. New York: Hill and Wang.

1981. *Camera Lucida: Reflections on Photography*, trans. Richard Howard. New York: Hill and Wang.

Bataille, Georges. 1985. *Visions of Excess: Selected Writings, 1927–1939*, trans. Allan Stoekl, with Carl R. Vovitt and Donald M. Leslie, Jr. Minneapolis: University of Minnesota Press.

1988. *Inner Experience*, trans. Leslie Anne Boldt. Albany: State University of New York Press.

Badrillard, Jean. 1983. *Simulations*, trans. Paul Foss, Paul Patton, and Philip Beitchman. New York: Semiotext(e).

1988. *Selected Writings*, ed. Mark Poster. Stanford: Stanford University Press.

Beckett, Samuel. 1984. *Disjecta: Miscellaneous Writings and a Dramatic Fragment*, ed. Ruby Cohn. New York: Grove Press.

Bell, Carla Huston. 1984. *Olivier Messiaen*. Boston: Twayne Publishers.

Benjamin, Walter. 1969. *Illuminations*, trans. Harry Zohn. New York: Schocken.

1977. *The Origin of German Tragic Drama*, trans. John Osborne. London: Verso.

1978. *Reflections: Essays, Aphorisms, Autobiographical Writing*, trans. Edmund Jephcott. New York: Schocken Books.

1979. *One-Way Street and Other Writings*, trans. Edmund Jephcott and Kingley Shorter. London: New Left Books.

1989. "N [Re: the Theory of Knowledge, Theory of Progress]," trans. Leigh Hafrey and Richard Sieburth. In *Benjamin: Philosophy, Aesthetics, History*, ed. Gary Smith. Chicago: University of Chicago Press, pp. 43–83.

Benveniste, Emile. 1971. *Problems in General Linguistics*, trans. Mary Elizabeth Meek. Coral Gables: University of Miami Press.

Bergson, Henri. 1960. *Time and Free Will*, trans. F. L. Pogson. New York: Harper Torchbooks.

Berman, Marshall. 1982. *All that is Solid Melts into Air: The Experience of Modernity.* New York: Simon and Schuster.

Birken, Lawrence. 1988. *Consuming Desire: Sexual Science and the Emergence of a Culture of Abundance, 1881–1914.* Ithaca: Cornell University Press.

Blanchot, Maurice. 1986. *The Writing of the Disaster*, trans. Ann Smock. Lincoln: University of Nebraska Pres.

Blaug, Mark. 1985. *Economic Theory in Retrospect.* 4th edition. Cambridge: Cambridge University Press.

Bowen, Elizabeth. 1962. *The Heat of the Day.* London: Penguin Books.

Brantlinger, Patrick. 1996. *Fictions of State: Culture and Credit in Britain 1694–1994.* Ithaca: Cornell University Press.

Brown, Norman O. 1959. *Life Against Death.* New York: Vintage.

Buck-Morss, Susan. 1977. *The Origin of Negative Dialectics: Theodor W. Adorno, Walter Benjamin, and the Frankfurt Institute.* Hassocks, Sussex: Harvester Press.

1989. *The Dialectics of Seeing: Walter Benjamin and the Arcades Project.* Cambridge MA: MIT Press.

Cassirer, Ernst. 1951. *The Philosophy of the Enlightenment*, trans. Fritz Kolln and James Pettegrove. Princeton: Princeton University Press.

Christ, Carol. 1993. "Painting the Dead: Portraiture and Necrophilia in Victorian Art and Poetry." In *Death and Representation*, ed. Sarah Goodwin and Elisabeth Bronfen. Baltimore: Johns Hopkins University Press, pp. 133–51.

Conrad, Joseph. 1971. *Heart of Darkness.* Norton Critical Edition. New York: W. W. Norton and Company.

Coser, Lewis. 1973. "Class." In *Dictionary of the History of Ideas*, Philip Weiner, editor in chief. New York: Charles Scribner's Son's, vol. I, 441–49.

Crease, Robert and Charles Mann. 1986. *The Second Creation: Makers of the Revolution in Twentieth-Century Physics.* New York: Macmillan Publishing Company.

Crossick, Geoffrey. 1977. "The Emergence of the Lower Middle Class in Britain: A Discussion." In *The Lower Middle Class in Britain 1870–1914.* New York: St. Martin's Press, pp. 11–60.

Culler, Jonathan. 1976. *Saussure.* Glasgow: Fontana Books.

Davidson, Donald. 1980. *Essays on Actions and Events.* Clarendon: Oxford University Press.

Davis, Robert Con and Ronald Schleifer. 1991. *Criticism and Culture*, Essex: Longman.

Davis, Robert Con and Ronald Schleifer (eds.). 1994. *Contemporary Literary Criticism: Literary and Cultural Studies*, 3rd edition. New York: Longman.

Deleuze, Gilles. 1983. *Nietzsche and Philosophy*, trans. Hugh Tomlinson. New York: Columbia University Press.

    1984. *Kant's Critical Philosophy*, trans. Hugh Tomlinson and Barbara Habberjam. Minneapolis: University of Minnesota Press.

    1986. *Cinema I: The Movement Image*, trans. Hugh Tomlinson and Barbara Habberjam. Minneapolis: University of Minnesota Press.

De Man, Paul. 1969. "The Rhetoric of Temporality." In *Interpretation: Theory and Practice*, ed. Charles S. Singleton. Baltimore: Johns Hopkins University Press, pp. 173–210.

    1971. *Blindness and Insight*. New York: Oxford University Press.

    1979. *Allegories of Reading*. New Haven: Yale University Press.

    1986. " 'Conclusions': Walter Benjamin's 'The Task of the Translator.' " In *The Resistance to Theory*. Minneapolis: University of Minnesota Press, pp. 73–105.

Derrida, Jacques. 1974. "White Mythology," trans. F. C. T. Moore, *New Literary History*: 6, 5–74.

    1976. *Of Grammatology*, trans. Gayitri Spivak. Baltimore: Johns Hopkins University Press.

    1978. *Writing and Difference*, trans. Alan Bass. Chicago: University of Chicago Press.

    1979. "Living On/Border Lines," trans. James Hulbert. In *Deconstruction and Criticism*, ed. Harold Bloom et al. New York: Continuum Press, pp. 75–176.

    1981. *Positions*, trans. Alan Bass. Chicago: University of Chicago Press.

    1982a. *Margins of Philosophy*, trans. Alan Bass. Chicago: University of Chicago Press.

    1982. "Choreographies," interview with Christie McDonald, *Diacritics*: 12 (no. 2), 66–76.

    1994. "The Principle of Reason: The University in the Eyes of its Pupils." In *Contemporary Literary Criticism*, 3rd edition, ed. Robert Con Davis and Ronald Schleifer. New York: Longman, pp. 320–40.

Descartes, René. 1984. *The Philosophical Writings*, 3 vols., trans. John Cottingham, Robert Stoothoff, and Dugald Murdoch. Cambridge: Cambridge University Press, vol 2.

Dewey, John. 1969. *Outlines of a Critical Theory of Ethics*. In *Early Works, Volume 3, 1889–1892*, ed. Jo Ann Boydston. Carbondale: Southern Illinois University Press, pp. 239–388.

Dubrow, Heather. 1982. *Genre*. New York: Methuen.

Ducrot, Oswald and Tzvetan Todorov. 1979. *Encyclopedic Dictionary of the Sciences of Language*, trans. Catherine Porter. Baltimore: Johns Hopkins University Press.

Eagleton, Terry. 1981. *Walter Benjamin; or, Towards a Revolutionary Criticism*. London: New Left Books.

Eco, Umberto. 1979. *A Theory of Semiotics*. Bloomington: Indiana University Press.

Edwards, George. 1938. *The Evolution of Finance Capitalism*. New York: Longmans.

Einstein, Albert. 1905. "On the Electrodynamics of Moving Bodies," trans. W. Perrett and J. B. Jeffery. In Albert Einstein et al., *The Principle of Relativity*, New York: Dover Press, 1952, pp. 35–65.

1961. *Relativity*, trans. Robert W. Lawson. New York: Crown Publishers.

1982. *Ideas and Opinions*. New York: Crown Publishing Co.

Ekeland, Ivar. 1988. *Mathematics and the Unexpected*, trans. by the author. Chicago: University of Chicago Press.

Eksteins, Modris. 1989. *Rites of Spring: The Great War and the Birth of the Modern Age*. New York: Anchor Books.

Eliot, George. 1961. *The Mill on the Floss*. Boston: Houghton Mifflin Company.

1961a. *Adam Bede*. Boston: Houghton Mifflin Company.

Ermarth, Elizabeth Deeds. 1983. *Realism and Consensus in the English Novel*. Princeton: Princeton University Press.

Everdell, William R. 1988. "The Problem of Continuity and the Origins of Modernism: 1870–1913," *History of European Ideas*: 9, 531–52.

1997. *The First Moderns*. Chicago: University of Chicago Press.

Felman, Shoshana. 1983. *The Literary Speech Act*, trans. Catherine Porter. Ithaca: Cornell University Press.

Foucault, Michel. 1970. *The Order of Things*. New York: Random House.

1972. *The Archaeology of Knowledge*. New York: Harper Colophon.

1977. "A Preface to Transgression." In *Language, Counter-Memory, Practice: Selected Essays and Interviews*, trans. Donald F. Bouchard and Sherry Simon. Ithaca: Cornell University Press, pp. 29–52.

1977(a) "Nietzsche, Genealogy, History." In *Language, Counter-Memory, Practice*, trans. Donald Bouchard and Sherry Simon. Ithaca: Cornell University Press, pp. 139–64.

1984. "What is Enlightenment?" In *The Foucault Reader*, ed. David Rabinow. New York: Pantheon Books, pp. 32–50.

Fowler, Alastair. 1982. *Kinds of Literature: An Introduction to the Theory of Genres and Modes*. Cambridge MA: Harvard University Press.

Fraser, J. T. 1982. *The Genesis and Evolution of Time*. Amherst: University of Massachusetts Press.

1987. *Time: The Familiar Stranger*. Amherst: University of Massachusetts Press.

Freud, Sigmund. 1963. "The Wolf Man." In *Three Case Histories*. New York: Collier Books.

1965. *The Interpretation of Dreams*, trans. James Strachey. New York: Avon.

Frye, Northrop. 1969. *Anatomy of Criticism*. Princeton: Princeton University Press.

Gaukroger, Stephen. 1995. *Descartes: An Intellectual Biography*. New York: Oxford University Press.

Gellner, Ernest. 1992. *Reason and Culture*. Oxford: Blackwell.

Goux, Jean-Joseph. 1990. *Symbolic Economies: After Marx and Freud*, trans. Jennifer Curtiss Gage. Ithaca: Cornell University Press.

1994. *The Coiners of Language*, trans. Jennifer Curtiss Gage. Norman: University of Oklahoma Press.

Greimas, A. J. 1983. *Structural Semantics*, trans. Daniele McDowell, Ronald Schleifer, and Alan Velie. Lincoln: University of Nebraska Press.

1987. *On Meaning*, trans. Paul Perron and Frank Collins. Minneapolis: University of Minnesota Press.

Greimas, A. J. and J. Courtés. 1982. *Semiotics and Language: An Analytical Dictionary*, trans. Larry Crist, Daniel Patte et al. Bloomington: Indiana University Press.

Griffiths, Paul. 1985. *Olivier Messiaen and the Music of Time*. Ithaca: Cornell University Press.

Haberman, Jürgen. 1987. *The Philosophical Discourse of Modernity*, trans. Frederick Lawrence. Cambridge: MIT Press.

Hale, Oron. 1971. *The Great Illusion: 1900–1914*. New York: Harper Torchbooks.

Hansen, F. R. 1985. *The Breakdown of Capitalism*. London: Routledge.

Hartman, Geoffrey. 1980. *Criticism in the Wilderness*. New Haven: Yale University Press.

Harvey, David. 1990. *The Condition of Postmodernity*. Cambridge, MA: Blackwell.

Hayes, Carleton J. H. 1941. *A Generation of Materialism: 1871–1900*. New York: Harper Torchbooks.

Hayles, Katherine. 1984. *The Cosmic Web: Scientific Field Models and Literary Strategies in the Twentieth Century*. Ithaca: Cornell University Press.

1995. "Boundary Disputes: Homeostasis, Reflexivity, and the Foundations of Cybernetics," *Configurations*: 2, 441–67.

Heidegger, Martin. 1962. *Being and Time*, trans. John Macquarrie and Edward Robinson. Oxford: Blackwell.

1967. *What is a Thing?*, trans. W. B. Barton and Vera Deutsch. Chicago: Henry Regnery Co.

1972. *On Time and Being*, trans. Joan Stambaugh. New York: Harper and Row.

1984. *Nietzsche. Volume 2: The Eternal Recurrence of the Same*, trans. David Krell. New York: Harper Collins.

1991. *Nietzsche: Volume 4: Nihilism*, trans. Frank Capuzzi. New York: Harper Collins.

Heilbroner, Robert. 1953. *The Worldly Philosophers*. New York: Simon and Schuster.

Heisenberg, Werner. 1952. *Philosophic Problems of Nuclear Science*, trans. F. C. Hayes. New York: Fawcett World Library.

1958. *Physics and Philosophy: The Revolution in Modern Physics*. New York: Harper Torchbooks.

1983. *Encounters with Einstein*. New York: Harper Books.

Hjelmslev, Louis. 1961. *Prolegomena to a Theory of Language*, trans. Francis Whitfield. Madison: University of Wisconsin Press.

Hobsbawm, Eric. 1987. *The Age of Empire 1875–1914*. New York: Pantheon Books.

　1990. *Nations and Nationalism Since 1780: Programme, Myth, Reality*. Cambridge: Cambridge University Press.

Hoffman, Piotar. 1986. *Doubt, Time, Violence*. Chicago: University of Chicago Press.

Hoffmann, Banesh. 1973. "Relativity." In *Dictionary of the History of Ideas*, Philip Weiner, editor in chief. New York: Charles Scribner's Son's, vol. IV, 74–92.

Holenstein, Elmar. 1976. *Roman Jakobson's Approach to Language*, trans. Catherine Schelbert and Tarcisius Schelbert. Bloomington: Indiana University Press.

Horkheimer, Max and Theodor Adorno. 1972. *Dialectic of Enlightenment*, trans. John Cumming. New York: Seabury Press.

Hudson, Kenneth. 1983. *The Archaeology of the Consumer Society: The Second Industrial Revolution in Britain*. Cranbury, NJ: Fairleight Dickinson University Press.

Hynes, Samuel. 1968. *The Edwardian Turn of Mind*. Princeton: Princeton University Press.

Jakobson, Roman. 1956. *Fundamentals of Language*. The Hague: Mouton.

　1971. Untitled speech on "Structuralism" in *Selected Writings: Volume II, Word and Language*. 'S-Gravenhage: Mouton & Company, pp. 711–12.

　1977. "A Few Remarks on Peirce, Pathfinder in the Science of Language," *MLN*: 92, 1026–32.

　1987. *Language and Literature*, ed. Krystyna Pomorska and Stephen Rudy. Cambridge MA: Harvard University Press.

Jameson, Fredric. 1979. *Fables of Aggression: Wyndham Lewis, the Modernist as Fascist*. Berkeley: University of California Press.

　1981. *The Political Unconscious*. Ithaca: Cornell University Press.

　1991. *Postmodernism; or The Cultural Logic of Late Capitalism*. Durham: Duke University Press.

Johnson, Samuel. 1958. *Rasselas, Poems and Selected Prose*, ed. Bertrand Bronson. New York: Holt, Rinehart and Wiston.

Joyce, James. 1961. *Ulysses*. New York: Viking Books.

　1967. *Dubliners*. New York: Penguin.

Kafka, Franz. 1974. *The Castle*, trans. Willa Muir and Edwin Muir. New York: Schocken Books.

Kenner, Hugh. 1968. *The Counterfeiters*. New York: Anchor Books.

　1973. *A Reader's Guide to Samuel Beckett*. New York: Farrar, Straus and Giroux.

　1978. *Joyce's Voices*. Berkeley: University of California Press.

　1988. "Self-Similarity, Fractals, Cantos." *ELH*: 44, 724–30.

Kermode, Frank. 1968. "Lawrence and Apocalyptic Types." *Critical Quarterly*: 10.

Kern, Stephen. 1983. *The Culture of Time and Space: 1880–1918.* Cambridge MA: Harvard University Press.

Keynes, John Maynard. 1931. *Essays in Persuasion.* London: Macmillan and Company.

Kierkegaard, Sören. 1960. *The Diary of Sören Kierkegaard,* ed. Peter Rohde. New York: Philosophical Library.

Kroker, Arthur and David Cook. 1986. *The Postmodern Scene: Excremental Culture and Hyper Aesthetics.* New York: St. Martin's.

Kuhn, Thomas. 1977. *The Essential Tension.* Chicago: University of Chicago Press.

Kundera, Milan. 1984. *The Unbearable Lightness of Being,* trans. Michael Henry Heim. New York: Harper and Row.

Lacan, Jacques. 1989. "Seminar on 'The Purloined Letter,'" trans. Jeffrey Mehlman. In Robert Con Davis and Ronald Schleifer, *Contemporary Literary Criticism,* 2nd edition. New York: Longman, pp. 301–20.

   1977. *The Four Fundamental Concepts of Psycho-Analysis,* trans. Alan Sheridan. Penguin: Harmondsworth.

Latour, Bruno. 1987. *Science in Action.* Cambridge MA: Harvard University Press.

   1988. "A Relativistic Account of Einstein's Relativity." *Social Studies of Science*: 18, 3–44.

   1993. *We Have Never Been Modern,* trans. Catherine Porter. Cambridge MA: Harvard University Press.

Latour, Bruno and Steve Woolgar. 1986. *Laboratory Life: The Construction of Scientific Facts.* Princeton: Princeton University Press.

Lawrence, D. H. 1915. *The Rainbow.* New York: Modern Library.

   1966. *Selected Literary Criticism,* ed. Antony Beal, New York: Viking Press.

Lears, Jackson. 1994. *Fables of Abundance.* New York: Basic Books.

Leibniz, G. W. 1902. *Discourse on Metaphysics, Correspondence with Arnauld, Monadology,* trans. George Montgomery. La Salle, IL: Open Court Press.

Levenson, Michael. 1984. *A Genealogy of Modernism.* Cambridge: Cambridge University Press.

Levinas, Emmanuel. 1986. *Face to Face with Levinas,* ed. R. A. Cohen. Albany: State University of New York Press.

   1989. "Time and the Other," trans. Richard Cohen. In *The Levinas Reader,* ed. Sean Hand. Oxford: Blackwell, pp. 37–58.

Lévi-Strauss, Claude. 1975. *The Raw and the Cooked,* trans. John and Doreen Weightman. New York: Harper Torchbook.

   1984. "Structure and Form: Reflections on a Work by Vladimir Propp," trans. Monique Layton, rev. Anatoly Liberman. In Vladimir Propp, *Theory and History of Folklore.* Minneapolis: University of Minnesota Press, pp. 167–89.

Lloyd, Genevieve. 1993. *Being in Time: Selves and Narrators in Philosophy and Literature.* London and New York: Routledge.

Lowe, Donald M. 1982. *History of Bourgeois Perception*. Chicago: University of Chicago Press.

Lyons, John. 1968. *Introduction to Theoretical Linguistics*. Cambridge: Cambridge University Press.

Lyotard, Jean-François. 1993. "Defining the Postmodern." In *The Cultural Studies Reader*, ed. Simon During. New York: Routledge, pp. 170–73.

MacCabe, Colin. 1979. *James Joyce and the Revolution of the Word*. New York: Barnes and Noble Books.

Markley, Robert. 1993. *Fallen Languages: Crises of Representation in Newtonian England 1660–1740*. Ithaca: Cornell University Press.

Marvin, Carolyn. 1988. *When Old Technologies Were New: Thinking About Electric Communication in the Late Nineteenth Century*. New York: Oxford University Press.

Matheson, Iain. 1995. "The End of Time: A Biblical Theme in Messiaen's *Quatuor*," in *The Messiaen Companion*, ed. Peter Hill. Portland, Oregon: Amadeus Press, pp. 234–48.

Marx, Karl. 1967. *Capital, Vol. 1, The Process of Capitalist Production*, trans. Samuel Moore and Edward Aveling. New York: International Publishers.

Mayer, Arno. 1975. "The Lower Middle Class as Historical Problem." *Journal of Modern History*: 47, 409–36.

1981. *The Persistence of the Old Regime*. New York: Pantheon Books.

McCracken, Grant. 1988. *Culture and Consumption*. Bloomington: Indiana University Press.

McDonald, Henry. "Philosophical Confrontations," unpub. ms.

McLeod, Hugh. 1977. "White Collar Values and the Role of Religion." In *The Lower Middle Class in Britain 1870–1914*. New York: St. Martin's Press, pp. 61–88.

Miller, J. Hillis. 1991. "The Two Rhetorics: George Eliot's Bestiary." In *Victorian Subjects*. Durham: Duke University Press, pp. 289–302.

1982. *Fiction and Repetition*. Cambridge MA: Harvard University Press.

1992. *Illustration*. Cambridge MA: Harvard University Press.

Mink, Louis O. 1970. "History and Fiction as Modes of Comprehension." *New Literary History*: 1, 541–58.

Moore, A. W. 1990. *The Infinite*. London and New York: Routledge.

Morson, Gary Saul and Caryl Emerson. 1990. *Mikhail Bakhtin: Creation of a Prosaics*. Stanford: Stanford University Press.

Moses, Stéphane. 1989. "Walter Benjamin and Franz Rosenzweig." In *Benjamin: Philosophy, Aesthetics, History*, ed. Gary Smith. Chicago: University of Chicago Press, pp. 228–45.

Myers, Greg. 1990. *Writing Biology: Texts in the Social Construction of Scientific Knowledge*. Madison: University of Wisconsin Press.

Nagel, Thomas. 1986. *The View from Nowhere*. New York: Oxford University Press.

Newton, Isaac. 1964. *The Mathematical Principles of Natural Philosophy.* New York: The Citadel Press.

Nietzsche, Friedrich. 1954. *Thus Spoke Zarathustra,* trans. Walter Kaufman. In *The Portable Nietzsche,* ed. Walter Kaufman. New York: Viking, pp. 103–439.

1968. *The Will to Power,* trans. Walter Kaufmann and R. J. Hollingdale. London: Weidenfeld and Nicolson.

1969. *On the Genealogy of Morals,* trans. Walter Kauffmann and R. J. Hollingdale. New York: Vintage Books.

1974. *The Gay Science,* trans. Walter Kaufman. New York: Vintage Books.

1983. *Untimely Meditations,* trans. R. J. Hollingdale. Cambridge: Cambridge University Press.

O'Hara, Daniel. 1987. "Yeats in Theory." In *Post-Structuralist Readings of English Poetry,* ed. Richard Machin and Christopher Norris. Cambridge: Cambridge University Press, pp. 349–68.

Penrose, Roger. 1989. *The Emperor's New Mind: Concerning Computers, Minds, and the Laws of Physics.* New York: Penguin Books.

Plotnitsky, Arkady. 1993. *Reconfigurations: Critical Theory and General Economy.* Gainsville: University Press of Florida.

1994. *Complementarity: Anti-Epistemology after Bohr and Derrida.* Durham: Duke University Press.

Proust, Marcel. 1934. *Remembrance of Things Past,* Vol. 1, trans. C. K. Scott Moncrieff. New York: Random House.

Readings, Bill. 1991. *Introducing Lyotard.* New York: Routledge.

Richards, Thomas. 1990. *The Commodity Culture of Victorian England: Advertising and Spectacle, 1851–1914.* Stanford: Stanford University Press.

Ricoeur, Paul. 1984. *Time and Narrative.* Vol. 1, trans. Kathleen McLaughlin and David Pellauer. Chicago: University of Chicago Press.

1985. *Time and Narrative.* Vol. 2, trans. Kathleen McLaughlin and David Pellauer. Chicago: University of Chicago Press.

1988. *Time and Narrative.* Vol. 3, trans. Kathleen Blamey and David Pellauer. Chicago: University of Chicago Press.

Rorty, Richard. 1979. *Philosophy and the Mirror of Nature,* Princeton: Princeton University Press.

Ruggiero, Guido de. 1959. *The History of European Liberalism.* Boston: Beacon Press.

Russell, Bertrand. 1917. *Mysticism and Logic.* New York: Doubleday Anchor.

1919. *Introduction to Mathematical Philosophy.* Rpt. London: Routledge 1993.

1923. *The ABC of Atoms.* London: Kegan Paul, Trench, Trubner & Co.

1925. *The ABC of Relativity.* New York: Harper & Brother.

1956. "The Philosophy of Logical Atomism." In *Logic and Knowledge, Essays 1901–1950,* ed. R. Marsh. London: Allen and Unwin, pp. 175–282.

Said, Edward. 1993. *Culture and Imperialism.* New York: Knopf.

1994. "The Politics of Knowledge," in *Contemporary Literary Criticism,* 3rd edition, ed. Robert Con Davis and Ronald Schleifer. New York: Longman, pp. 144–53.

Sampson, Geoffrey. 1980. *Schools of Linguistics*. Stanford: Stanford University Press.

Sassover, Raphael. 1990. "Scarcity and Setting the Boundaries of Political Economy," *Social Epistemology*: 4, 75–91.

Saussure, Ferdinand de. 1959. *Course in General Linguistics*, trans. Wade Baskin. New York: McGraw Hill.

Sayer, Derek. 1991. *Capitalism and Modernity*. New York: Routledge.

Schivelbusch, Wolfgang. 1986. *The Railway Journey: The Industrialization of Time and Space in the Nineteenth Century*. Berkeley: University of California Press.

1988. *Disenchanted Night: The Industrialization of Light in the Nineteenth Century*, trans. Angela Davies. Berkeley and Los Angeles: University of California Press.

Schleifer, Ronald. 1984. "Irony and the Literary Past: On *The Concept of Irony* and *The Mill on the Floss*." In *Kierkegaard and Literature*, ed. Ronald Schleifer and Robert Markley. Norman: University of Oklahoma Press, pp. 183–216.

1987. *A. J. Greimas and the Nature of Meaning*. Lincoln: University of Nebraska Press.

1990. *Rhetoric and Death: The Language of Modernism and Postmodern Discourse Theory*. Urbana: University of Illinois Press.

1999. "'What is this Thing Called Love?': Cole Porter and the Rhythms of Desire." *Criticism*: 41, 7–23.

2000 *Analogical Thinking: Post-Enlightenment Understanding in Language, Collaboration, and Interpretation*. Ann Arbor: University of Michigan Press.

Schleifer, Ronald, Robert Con Davis, and Nancy Mergler. 1992. *Culture and Cognition: The Boundaries of Literary and Scientific Inquiry*. Ithaca: Cornell University Press.

Sennett, Richard. 1977. *The Fall of Public Man*. New York: Vintage Books.

Shaviro, Steven. 1990. *Passion and Excess: Blanchot, Bataille, and Literary Theory*. Tallahassee: Florida State University Press.

Smith, Adam. 1937. *The Wealth of Nations*. New York: Modern Library.

Smith, Gary. 1989. "Thinking Through Benjamin: An Introductory Essay." In *Benjamin: Philosophy, Aesthetics, History*, ed. Gary Smith. Chicago: University of Chicago Press, pp. vii–xlii.

Spurr, David. 1994. "Myths of Anthropology: Eliot, Joyce, Lévy-Bruhl." *PMLA*: 109, 266–80.

Stambaugh, Joan. 1972. *Nietzsche's Thought of Eternal Return*. Baltimore: Johns Hopkins University Press.

Steiner, George. 1975. *After Babel*. New York: Oxford University Press.

1977. "Introduction." In Walter Benjamin, *The Origin of German Tragic Drama*. London: Verso, pp. 7–24.

Stevens, Wallace. 1972. *The Palm at the End of the Mind: Selected Poems and a Play*, ed. Holly Stevens. New York: Vintage.

Stoekl, Alan. 1985. "Introduction." In George Bataille, *Visions of Excess: Selected Writings, 1927–1939*. Minneapolis: University of Minnesota Press, pp. ix-xxv.

Stravinsky, Igor. 1982. *Themes and Conclusions*. Berkeley: University of California Press.

Swift, Jonathan. 1960. *Gulliver's Travels*. New York: Signet Books.

Taylor, Charles. 1964. *The Experience of Behaviour*. New York: The Humanities Press.

1991. "Discussion: Ricoeur on Narrative." In *On Paul Ricoeur: Narrative and Interpretation*, ed. David Wood. London: Routledge, pp. 174–79.

Terdiman, Richard. 1993. *Present Past: Modernity and the Memory Crisis*. Ithaca: Cornell University Press.

Tichi, Cecelia. 1987. *Shifting Gears: Technology, Literature, Culture in Modernist America*. Chapel Hill: University of North Carolina Press.

Tiedemann, Rolf. 1989. "Historical Materialism or Political Messianism? An Interpretation of the Theses 'On the Concept of History.'" In *Benjamin: Philosophy, Aesthetics, History*, ed. Gary Smith. Chicago: University of Chicago Press, pp. 175–209.

Tipton, Frank B. and Robert Aldrich. 1987. *An Economic and Social History of Europe, 1890–1939*. Baltimore: Johns Hopkins University Press.

Toulmin, Stephen. 1992. *Cosmopolis: The Hidden Agenda of Modernity*. Chicago: University of Chicago Press.

Tuchman, Barbara. 1967. *The Proud Tower: A Portrait of the World Before the War, 1890–1914*. New York: Bantam Books.

Vattimo, Gianni. 1988. *The End of Modernity*, trans. Jon R. Snyder. Baltimore: Johns Hopkins University Press.

West, Cornel. 1993. "The New Cultural Politics of Difference." In *The Cultural Studies Reader*, ed. Simon During. New York: Routledge, pp. 203–17.

Wiener, Norbert. 1961. *Cybernetics*. Cambridge MA: MIT Press.

1967. *The Human Use of Human Beings*. New York: Avon Books.

Williams, Raymond. 1961. *The Long Revolution*. Harmondsworth: Penguin Books.

1977. *Marxism and Literature*. New York: Oxford University Press.

1989. *The Politics of Modernism*. London: Verso Press.

Wittgenstein, Ludwig. 1958. *Philosophical Investigations*, 3rd ed., trans. G. E. M. Anscombe. New York: Macmillan.

1965. *The Blue and Brown Books*, [no trans.]. New York: Harper Torchbooks.

1990. *Tractatus Logico-Philosophicus*, trans. C. K. Ogden. London: Routledge.

Wolf, Fred Alan. 1989. *Taking the Quantum Leap: The New Physics for Non-Scientists*. New York: Harper and Row.

Wolin, Richard. 1989. "Experience and Materialism in Benjamin's Passagenwerk." In *Benjamin: Philosophy, Aesthetics, History*, ed. Gary Smith. Chicago: University of Chicago Press, pp. 210–27.

Wood, David. 1991. *The Deconstruction of Time.* Atlantic Highlands, NJ: Humanities Press.

Woolf, Virginia. 1953. *Mrs. Dalloway.* New York: Harvest Books.

   1954. *A Writer's Diary*, ed. Leonard Woolf. New York: Harvest Books.

   1985. *A Sketch from the Past*, in *Moments of Being*, ed. Jeanne Schulkind. New York: Harvest/HBJ Books.

Yeats, W. B. 1965. *A Vision.* New York: Collier Books.

   1969. *Collected Poems.* New York: Macmillan.

Xenos, Nicholas. 1989. *Scarcity and Modernity.* New York: Routledge.

# Index

abundance, x, xv, 4, 5, 18, 28–29, 46, 47, 48, 52, 60, 66, 84, 129, 215, 222, 223; and abstraction, 175–183; and aesthetics, 146; and analogical figures, 95–103; and arrangement, 177; articulations of, 96; and J. L. Austin, 198; and Niels Bohr, 198; as central concern of post-Enlightenment Modernism, 107; and constellations, 177; crisis of, xi, 11, 35–36, 109, 123, 222; culture of, 173; definition of, 201–202; and desire, 132, 136; and discontinuity, 173; and electricity, 133; and experience of time, 48–52, 1–7, 109–110; and finance capital, 136; and Werner Heisenberg, 198; and history, 62; of knowledge, 208; and Bruno Latour, 198; and linguistics, 146, 198; logic of, 1–2, 13–14, 17–18, 23, 37, 95–103, 112, 139, 146, 150, 151, 183, 232, 243n1; and lower middle class, 109, 129, 131; and mathematics, 146; and non-transcendental disembodiment, 112, 122; and panic, 57; and physics, 146; post-Enlightenment literary responses to, 52–60; and post-Enlightenment understanding, 60, 63; post-Enlightenment world of, 28–29; and poverty, 22–29, 55; and problem of representation, xii; and professionalization of work, 136; and quotation, 96, 98; and telephones, 134–135; and time, 8, 232; and transformation of Enlightenment inheritance, 109; and understanding, 5, 8, 187; *see also* dearth; post-Enlightenment; second Industrial Revolution; subject; understanding

Adorno, Theodor, 4, 27, 28, 86, 87, 88, 91, 93, 96, 238n10; *Dialectic of Enlightenment*, 238n10

aesthetics, 3, 9, 16, 17, 19, 20, 21–22, 23, 29, 55, 146, 15, 151; and answerability, 19, 21–22; and Modernism, 190; of the moment, 17, 21, 22, 23, 139, 145; of poverty,

28–29; and time, 6–7; *see also* Bakhtin, M. M.

Albright, Daniel, 7, 23, 24, 25, 26, 53, 251n1

allegory, 8; and Walter Benjamin, 92–94; of meaning, 75; Modernist definition of, 226; and nomological science, 85; and time, 67–107

analogy/analogical thinking, xiv, xv, 7, 11, 13–15, 18, 20, 21, 23–24, 25, 27, 50, 60, 89, 165, 184–207; and allegory, 92–93; and arrangement, 14; and articulation of non-transcendental disembodiment, 243n1, 243n3; and M. M. Bakhtin, 13–14; and Eve Tavor Bannet, 11; and Walter Benjamin, 13, 142, 173, 182; and collision, 14; and comparison, 69; and constellations, 14, 69, 91–92; and correspondence, 182; and dialectics, 102; and discontinuity, 173; and Albert Einstein, 14, 164, 182; and example, 200–203; and formalism, 149; and Werner Heisenberg, 13, 142, 208; and image, 99–103; and D. H. Lawrence, 142, 173; and logic of abundance, 13–15, 95–103, 133–134; and operational definition, 14; and paraphrase, 164; and quotation, 95–96, 99, 102–103; and Paul Ricoeur, 173; and Bertrand Russell, 13, 164, 178, 182, 185; and second mode of interpretation, 159; and semantic formalism, 172, 243n1, 250n10; and Wallace Stevens, 20; and Igor Stravinsky, 20, 169; and time, 14, 93, 164; and transformation, 164; and Ludwig Wittgenstein, 11, 185; *see also* understanding; post-Enlightenment

Anderson, Perry, 119–120, 121; on poststructuralism, 185

Anselm, St., 204

anthropology, 36, 118

Aristotle, 41, 131

Augustine, St., 152, 153, 154, 159, 246n1